RELIGION SAVES

Re:Lit Books

RELIGION SAVES

+ NINE other MISCONCEPTIONS

MARK DRISCOLL

CROSSWAY BOOKS
WHEATON, ILLINOIS

To all those who are kind enough to listen to my sermons on the Internet. It means a great deal to me that you would give me your time and invite me into your life as you exercise, clean your house, commute, and work your job. I love what I do, and I love the people who appreciate it, so thank you. With all sincerity, you are a source of enormous encouragement. One day in Jesus' kingdom it will be fun to finally meet everyone who tunes in and I look forward to that day.

CONTENTS

RELIGION
SAVES

INTRODUCTION

While preaching through 1 Corinthians some time ago, I was struck by the fact that the letter was a series of answers to various questions that the people in the Corinthian church had asked. My guess was that there were more questions than Paul answered, but that somehow those he did answer were deemed to be of the greatest interest and importance. I thought it might be interesting to do something similar by preaching a series answering the big questions and issues in our own day, which could subsequently be addressed in an even more thorough fashion as a book.

Then, while preaching through 1 Corinthians 9:22–23, I was again struck by Paul's strong call for cultural relevance: "I have become all things to all people, that by all means I might save some. I do it all for the sake of the gospel, that I may share with them in its blessings." So we tried an experiment, opening up a section of our church's Web site for people to post any question, make comments about posted questions, and vote up to ten times a day for their favorite question. We deleted the votes of those people who violated the rules. And in the end, 893 questions were asked, 5,524 comments were made, and 343,203 votes were cast. I answered the top nine questions in a sermon devoted to each.[1] Here in the book we'll start with the ninth most popular question and work our way to the most popular question.

During the "Religion Saves" sermon series, we experimented with live questions from people in our late Sunday evening service, which is attended predominantly by urban students and singles, and it offers no child care because the hour is late and young children are not present. Those in attendance text-messaged questions related to the sermon subject, and I answered them live on the stage, which led to a number of helpful, clarifying questions and some tough questions. The questions included whether a young woman in the church who had performed oral sex on her boyfriend was still a virgin, whether masturbation is okay, and if another woman in the church who was pregnant following a rape could have an abortion. To say the least, it was an intense way to finish more than six hours of preaching.

My off-the-cuff, on-the-spot answers to these text-message questions are available on our Web site and can also be found on Youtube. com. As a warning, some of the content is frank and for mature audiences, so if you are a minor, please get your parents' permission before tuning in.

Before we proceed, the title "Religion Saves" merits a bit of explanation. The one thread that weaves this book together is religion; many of the questions that made the top nine are highly religious in nature. Religious people are prone to go beyond the teaching of the Bible to argue for positions that are not clearly taught in Scripture. They are further prone to go beyond the biblical principles on these issues and seek to impose their method on others, as if they alone are truly biblical. Religious people tend to have very strong and vocal opinions about the issues we will examine. In fact, religious people were often the most devoted voters for the questions that comprised the "Religion Saves" sermon series and this book.

Religious people are prone to draw firm lines on these issues, thereby making them points of debate, distinction, and even division among Christians. The issues fall into some curious categories. Questions 9, 5, and 3 are all related to issues of sex and dating, as sex is the most popular religion in the world. Questions 8 and 2 deal with missional aspects of the emerging church and how Christians should relate to mainstream culture and lost people. Question 7 is the endless debating point between Calvinists and Arminians. Question 4 is the perennial debating point between Catholics and Protestants. And Question 1 is a point of concern between old school and new school Calvinists.

Thus, each chapter of this book will debunk the junk promulgated by religion on everything—how we become Christians, why we do good works, how we have sex, what birth control we use, who we date, what we laugh at, which church we attend, and how we worship God.

Religious people mistakenly think that they are saving people from such things as a fruitless life, sinful sex, bad relationships, unholy humor, wayward churches, evil birth control, and what they call "strange fire." However, religion never saved anyone, and religious answers to complex questions are simply misconceptions, which is why I have titled this book, "Religion Saves: And Nine Other Misconceptions."

I had a tremendous time preaching this series and writing this book. I pray it is of help to you as you consider some of the big issues in our day.

QUESTION 9: **BIRTH CONTROL**

There's no doubt the Bible says children are a blessing, but the Bible doesn't seem to address the specific topic of birth control. Is this a black-and-white topic, or does it fall under liberties?

I was standing in line at the grocery store with my five young children when a typical Seattleite in line behind us made a point of rebuking me for having so many children and thereby ruining the planet and contributing to overpopulation and global warming. Trying to make light of a tense moment, I said I knew the world had a lot of people, and I did not like most of them, so I was just trying to create some people I did like. Further, I was hoping global warming would hit Seattle so we would see the sun more than once every presidential election.

Not dissuaded, my critic continued her illogic. I patiently tried to educate her and told her that theoretically everyone on the earth could live in the state of Texas, each with roughly seventeen hundred square feet of space; further, problems such as starvation are the result of wars, disasters, and distribution more than overpopulation. I also explained to her that we are a faithful recycling family that has only one garbage can, which is never full, but two recycling cans and a glass bin, which are full every pick-up day.

Nonetheless, she continued to decry the existence of my children while my children looked at me with furrowed brows, wondering why someone they did not know hated them so much. The woman then asked me, "Don't you know what causes this problem?"

At that point, my middle son, the not-yet-kindergarten-age

"buddy" Calvin, rolled his eyes and looked at me, in essence begging me to defend his existence. Hoping to shut her up, I said, "Yes, a beautiful wife with a pleasant disposition has caused this, but don't fret, you won't ever have to worry about it."

She grew more agitated and reiterated that there were too many people on the planet. In a moment that was admittedly not very pastoral, I told her that maybe she should find another planet for herself, thereby freeing up space on mine.

Eventually, we concluded our purchases and left the store. Once in the car, my oldest daughter, Ashley, asked me why so many people hate children. Since then she has also told me that she gets embarrassed when people stare at our family and whisper when we are out, as if we are freaks that escaped from an Amish compound. My wife has even been yelled at for driving a Suburban, despite the fact that we intentionally drive very little, roughly one-third as many miles as the average American, thereby using less fuel than the average hybrid car driver.

In short, there is a great cultural debate about sex, marriage, children, and birth control, with heated opinions on all sides. This question is intriguing for me, personally, on a number of levels. I was raised as the oldest of five children in a working-class, Irish-Catholic family. That branch of Christianity considers nearly all forms of birth control sinful and emphasizes the sanctity of all human life. My Catholic mother stayed home to raise five children out of her convictions that children are a blessing and that motherhood is a high calling. Today, I am the blessed father of five children (we would have six had we not suffered a miscarriage) and my wife, Grace, stays home to work a more than full-time job as a mom. We are raising our children in the city of Seattle, which is among the least likely places in our nation to see a child, since there are more dogs than children.[1] Our city is also among the least churched and most overpriced cities in the nation, which make having a big Christian family unusual, complicated, and expensive.[2]

A BIBLICAL WORLDVIEW

By God's grace, our church has seen thousands of mainly young people come to know Jesus or come back into a transforming relationship with Jesus after years of rebellion. As a result, we see a lot of couples in our premarital counseling classes, and we answer questions constantly about sex, children, and birth control. Nowhere in the Bible do we find terms such as *contraception*, *birth control*, or *family planning*. Still, the Bible does speak to those issues in principle. Therefore, to best answer these and other questions, we have to begin with a Christian worldview and then explore how the Bible principally establishes ethical guidelines by which contemporary birth control questions can be answered. The biblical worldview necessary for answering this question is comprised of sixteen truths.

Truth 1:   God is the Creator and author of human life.[1]

Truth 2:   God made humanity in his image and likeness, which means that human life is unique and sacred.[2]

Truth 3:   God intends for human beings to fill the earth.[3]

Truth 4:   God authored that life begins at conception and declares that an unborn baby is a sacred life.[4]

Truth 5:   God knows us from our mother's womb.[5]

Truth 6:   God declares that when human life is taken without just cause (e.g., capital punishment, just war, self-defense), the sin of murder has been committed.[6]

Truth 7:   God made humanity to exercise dominion by ruling over creation.[7]

Truth 8:   God made humanity to steward creation by exercising wise discernment based upon natural revelation, conscience, the Holy Spirit, counsel, and most authoritatively, Scripture.[8]

Truth 9:   God made humanity male and female.[9]

Truth 10:   God created marriage as a covenant for one man and one woman.[10]

Truth 11:   God created sex as a gift only for a married couple.[11]

Truth 12:   God is sovereign over the womb and can ultimately open and close it as he wills.[12]

Truth 13:   Children are a blessing from God to be provided and cared for by parents and extended family and church, including those who are adopted as Jesus was.[13]

---

[1]Genesis 1–2; Deut. 32:39; Ps. 139:13–16.
[2]Gen. 1:27; James 3:9.
[3]Gen. 1:28; 9:1.
[4]Ex. 1:16–17; 21:22–25; Lev. 18:21; Jer. 7:31–32; Ezek. 16:20–21; Mic. 6:7; Matt. 2:16–18; Acts 7:19.
[5]Jer. 1:5; Job 10:9–12; 31:15; Ps. 119:73; Eccl. 11:5.
[6]Gen. 9:5; Ex. 20:13.
[7]Gen. 1:26.
[8]1 Pet. 4:10.
[9]Gen. 1:27, 31.
[10]Gen. 2:24–25, cf. Matt. 19:5, Mark 10:7–8, Eph. 5:31; Prov. 2:16; Mal. 2:14.
[11]Gen. 2:24–25.
[12]Gen. 20:18; 29:31; 30:22; 1 Sam. 1:5–6; Isa. 66:9; Luke 1:24–25.
[13]Gen. 1:28a; Pss. 127:3–5; 128:3–4; Matt. 18:5–6; Mark 9:36–37, 10:16; 1 Tim. 5:8.

Truth 14:   God desires Christians to raise godly offspring.[14]

Truth 15:   God commands his people to lovingly help care for widows and orphans.[15]

Truth 16:   God expects single nonparents to help parents raise children, as Jesus' own life as a single man exemplifies.[16]

With this Christian worldview in place, we are ready to examine the various options for a Christian couple considering birth control.

THE HISTORY OF BIRTH CONTROL

It is important to note that birth control is not a new issue. Birth control has been around for thousands of years, although not all methods have been safe or effective.[3] Two thousand years ago, Egyptian women soaked their crocodile-dung tampons in honey, onion juice, and mint sap, and then actually inserted them. Other methods included cocoa-butter vaginal suppositories. Ancient Chinese remedies included swallowing a live tadpole and eating the scrapings from inside a deer's antlers. Greek and Roman women soaked their tampons in hemlock and quinine. Saxon women used roasted horse manure. Japanese prostitutes inserted balls of bamboo tissue paper in the vagina, Islamic and Greek women used balls of wool, and Slavic women used linen rags. These were intended to soak up sperm but the attempts were unsuccessful. Italian men would wrap a wet cloth around the erect penis and tie it with a pink ribbon.

One Catholic article claims, "Scrolls found in Egypt, dating to 1900 BC, describe ancient methods of birth control that were later practiced in the Roman Empire during the apostolic age. Wool that absorbed sperm, poisons that fumigated the uterus, potions, and other methods were used to prevent conception. In some centuries, even condoms were used (though made out of animal skin rather than latex)."[4]

Egyptian physicians offered prescriptions for the prevention of pregnancy, according to Egyptian papyri dating from 1900 to 1100 BC.[5] In the Greco-Roman world, birth control potions were recorded in fifth-century BC writings from the Hippocratic school of medicine.[6] In

---

[14]Mal. 2:15; Jer. 29:4–9.
[15]James 1:27.
[16]Matt. 19:13–14; Mark 10:13–16.

early medieval European history, the Celtic and Germanic peoples used various medicines to control birth.[7] The Arabian philosopher and doctor Avicenna wrote *The Canon of Medicine* during the eleventh century, and the work discussed spermicides, vaginal suppositories, potions, and abortifacients. The work was the standard medical textbook for the next five hundred years.[8]

In 1873 the United States passed the Comstock Law, named after the Christian who proposed it, which made it illegal to mail or import contraceptives, and most states outlawed the sale and advertisement of contraceptives.[9] In 1880 the diaphragm was invented, and by 1935 over two hundred types of artificial contraceptive devices were in use in the Western world.[10] In 1936 the courts overturned the Comstock Law.[11] The first "birth control clinics" in the United States opened during the 1920s, available only for married and engaged women who could prove their status with appropriate paperwork.[12]

As the number of birth control options has increased and continues increasing, so has the need for discernment. Therefore, we will examine various options that fall along a birth control continuum.[13] I will differentiate between no birth control, contraception, which literally means "against (*contra*) conception" (such methods prevent conception, whereby a sperm fertilizes an egg), and abortion, which terminates the life of a fertilized egg.

LEVELS OF BIRTH CONTROL

Level 1: No Birth Control

At the very least, every Christian married couple should cover every aspect of their marriage with prayer, including future children God may bless them with. Through prayer, the Christian couple is demonstrating faith in the goodness and sovereignty of God over all of life, including the womb.

Some Christian couples determine to use only prayer in their family planning. As a result, they simply enjoy normal marital sexual relations and trust that if God desires that they have children, he will provide according to his timing. When a Christian couple chooses this approach, trusting that whatever happens is God's good will, it is acceptable.

A Legalistic Version of No Birth Control

When this form of family planning is dogmatically pushed as the only faithful Christian option, such foolish legalism can lead to both self-righteousness and harm. This kind of narrow thinking is popular in networks such as Quiverfull and often promulgated through some sectarian homeschool networks and promoted in some Christian books, which are not bad on all points but widely miss the mark on the issue of birth control.[14] Vision Forum Ministries, which includes authors such as R. C. Sproul Jr., published the book *Be Fruitful and Multiply* in which Nancy Campbell, who publishes *Above Rubies* magazine, says, "'Contraception, sterilization, and abortion.' . . . Each one is masterminded in hell!"[15] Similarly, in *Lies Women Believe and the Truth That Sets Them Free*, Revive Our Hearts national radio show host and best-selling author Nancy Leigh DeMoss, says:

> So anything that hinders or discourages women from fulfilling their God-given calling to be bearers and nurturers of life furthers Satan's efforts. . . . The Christian world has been unwittingly influenced by this way of thinking [secular feminism], leading to the legitimization and promotion of such practices as contraception, sterilization, and "family planning." As a result, unwittingly, millions of Christian women and couples have helped to further Satan's attempts to limit human reproduction and thereby destroy life.[16]

Ironically, although DeMoss does have some good things to say on other topics in this book, she falls into her own error by doing exactly what her mother Eve did, namely, adding to God's Word by declaring something that God has not said.

Furthermore, she quotes at length from Mary Pride, a homeschooling proponent and overreacting former feminist, who wrote in her book *The Way Home: Beyond Feminism, Back to Reality*, "Family planning is the mother of abortion. . . . Abortion is first of all a heart attitude. 'Me first.' 'My career first.' 'My reputation first.' 'My convenience first.' 'My financial plans first.' And these exact same choices are what family planning, which the churches have endorsed for three decades, is all about."[17]

Obviously, the self-centeredness of pride is something that Christians are to repent of, but the generalized character attacks by some—that women who use any form of birth control are working in concert with Satan and motivated solely by pride—go way too far.

Most certainly there are sinful people who use birth control for a variety of unbiblical reasons, including greed (they want to make as much money as possible without the responsibilities or costs of childbearing); selfishness (they have no desire to undertake the work involved in lovingly raising a child); an unbiblical view of children as a burden instead of a blessing; and an irresponsible lifestyle (they refuse to grow up and assume adult responsibilities). However, there are also a host of valid reasons why some godly people use birth control, such as working on a very troubled marriage in need of attention or dealing with serious health troubles, like a friend of mine who is taking birth control while battling cancer.

There are also many practical reasons why a Christian couple would choose not to use birth control. Sadly, some couples using birth control wait too long to begin their family and, as a result, suffer great complications. Infertility and miscarriage are common complications, especially as a woman gets older. Women are most fertile between the ages of eighteen and twenty-five. Fertility begins a slow decline at age twenty-five and speeds up dramatically at thirty-five.[18]

To compensate for the age factor, in vitro fertilization (IVF) has become increasingly popular. According to one report, "IVF accounts for over 90 percent of late-in-life pregnancies and can cost anywhere from $10,000–$100,000."[19] The average cost of one IVF cycle in the United States is $12,400.[20]

Furthermore, the statistics indicate that the older a woman is when (and if) she becomes pregnant, the greater the odds that she will suffer medical complications, such as high blood pressure, diabetes, miscarriage, and stillbirth,[21] and her child will have increased odds for birth defects and low birth weight. If she does give birth, she will be far more exhausted as a mom because her energy levels drop as she ages.[22]

Therefore, the woman who assumes she can simply postpone her childbearing in an effort to finish her education, establish her career, or pursue her travel goals may in fact be wasting her most fertile years. Instead, it may be wise not to wait to attempt motherhood by using birth control but rather to make it a priority, as God does in Scripture. Nonetheless, to declare that anyone who uses birth control is a selfish feminist working in concert with Satan is ludicrous. To illustrate this folly, I want to dispel the groundless arguments promulgated against any form of birth control.

Arguments against Any and All Birth Control

First, it is commonly argued that modern birth control is evil because it was promoted by racists such as Thomas Malthus and Margaret Sanger (founder of Planned Parenthood). Sanger tried to implement Darwinism practically by encouraging the use of birth control and abortion among those peoples and races deemed less fit. She set up her first clinics in the poorest and most ethnic neighborhoods.[23]

Theologian Wayne House says, "In 1933 the magazine for Planned Parenthood, known in Sangers [sic] day as *Birth Control Review*, actually published 'Eugenic Sterilization: An Urgent Need,' by Ernst Rudin, Hitlers [sic] director of genetic sterilization and founder of the Nazi Society for Racial Hygiene."[24] Furthermore, later that same year the magazine "published an article by E. A. Whitney, entitled 'Selective Sterilization,' which strongly praised and defended Nazi racial programs."[25]

Sanger saw birth control as the most effective way to get rid of people she called "feebleminded," meaning those whose mental ability was less than that of a twelve-year-old.[26] Sanger also once said, "Birth control appeals to the advanced radical because it is calculated to undermine the authority of the Christian churches. I look forward to seeing humanity free someday of the tyranny of Christianity no less than Capitalism."[27]

Sanger was simply a wicked woman, and no Christian should agree with her principles or practices. Nevertheless, to say that all birth control is sinful is fallacious, because it is a classic *ad hominem* attack that seeks to simply dismiss birth control as evil by connecting it with an evil person. Just because something is promulgated by a godless person does not mean it cannot be redeemed by God's people and used in a godly manner. Pornographers, for example, are responsible for many of the gains in media, from inexpensive digital movie cameras to high-speed Internet downloads, but that same technology can also be used to download sermons and Bible studies to edify God's people.

Second, it is argued that Christians never endorsed any form of birth control until 1930. The rhetoric postulates that Resolution 15 of the Anglican Lambeth Conference on August 14, 1930, was the first time in the church's history that birth control in certain forms and for certain purposes was accepted. The conference did not endorse abortion, and furthermore did issue "its strong condemnation of the use of any methods of conception-control from motives of selfishness, luxury, or mere convenience."[28]

Yet theologians such as Wayne House have refuted the erroneous claim that Christian birth control did not exist until 1930:

> Christians in all ages have generally practiced some form of birth control, whether through medical devices or by more natural means, such as restricting intercourse to certain periods of the month or through coitus interruptus [a.k.a. Vatican Roulette]. Though the Roman Catholic church declared birth control a violation of natural law in the papal encyclical *Humanae Vitae* (1965), most Protestants have considered some forms of birth control morally acceptable....
>
> Contraceptive devices were known and used in the pre-Christian Mediterranean world. For example, five different Egyptian papyri, dating between 1900 and 1100 BC, have recipes for contraceptive concoctions to be used in the vulva. Other papyri describe preparations aimed at blocking or killing semen. Legal scholar John Noonan, in his authoritative work on contraception, has provided abundant evidence that such formulas were also used in Christian Europe during the medieval period (AD 450–1450) and the premodern period (AD 1450–1750).[29]

Third, it is argued that God commands his people to have children, yet in Genesis 1:28 we read, "God *blessed* them. And God said to them, 'Be fruitful and multiply and fill the earth.'" Children are a blessing, not a command. Were we commanded to have children, then those who never marry, like Jesus, and those who are barren would be in sin for not obeying God's command. To turn a blessing into a command is a common error of legalism, which twists something we get to do in delight into something we have to do in duty. Christian married couples typically should desire and pursue children, either on their own or through adoption or fostering, and celebrate if or when God blesses them with children. Yet to state that any couple that is not continually doing all it can to have children is sinning is to misrepresent what God communicated to our first parents.

Fourth, it is argued that because children are a blessed gift from the Lord, Christian couples should seek to have as many as possible. The staff at John Piper's Desiring God ministry has issued an insightful refutation to this point:

> It is very important to delight in the reality that "children are a gift of the Lord." But some people go further and argue from this that since children are gifts from God, it is wrong to take steps to regulate the timing and number of children one has.
>
> In response, it can be pointed out that the Scriptures also say that a wife is a gift from the Lord (Proverbs 18:22), but that doesn't mean that it is wrong to stay single (1 Corinthians 7:8). Just because something is a gift from the Lord does not mean that it is wrong to be a steward of when or whether you will come into possession of it. It is wrong to reason that since A is good and a gift from the Lord, then we must pursue as much of A as possible. God has made this a world in which tradeoffs have to be made and we cannot do everything to the fullest extent. For kingdom purposes, it might be wise not to get married. And for kingdom purposes, it might be wise to regulate the size of one's family and to regulate when the new additions to the family will likely arrive. As Wayne Grudem has said, "it is okay to place less emphasis on some good activities in order to focus on other good activities." . . .
>
> In reality, then, although it is true that "blessed is the man whose quiver is full of [children]," we need to realize that God has not given everyone the same size quiver. And so birth control is a gift from God that may be used for the wise regulation of the size of one's family, as well as a means of seeking to have children at the time which seems to be wisest.[30]

Fifth, it is argued that any attempt to regulate if or when a birth occurs effectively negates God's sovereignty. However, because God is sovereign, we cannot negate his sovereignty. God is bigger than our choices and efforts, and he can accomplish his will whenever he wills it. This explains why, in Scripture, we see one virgin and a line of elderly barren women having babies. Furthermore, this line of reasoning becomes plain silly when applied to other areas of life. When I get a haircut, do I not trust the Lord to make it grow to the length he sovereignly chooses?

Sixth, it is argued from history that we should do all we can to reproduce because we don't know what God might have in store for those children in the future. Charles Wesley was the thirteenth child, George Whitefield was the seventh child, and George Washington was the fifth out of ten. While this proves the point that each family must prayerfully consider its family size, it does not necessarily follow that the more children we have, the better, because those children might impact the world. Adolf Hitler was the sixth child born into his Catholic family, which probably opposed birth control, and my guess is that most of us would have preferred that his parents found a box of condoms somewhere and started using them after their fifth child.

Seventh, it is argued by some Protestants and many Catholic theologians that birth control is forbidden based upon Genesis 38:10. The hillbilly redneck soap opera of Jacob's family takes a very daytime-television, trash-talk-show turn in Genesis 38. There, both Abraham and Isaac dreaded the thought of their sons intermarrying with Canaanite women because it would cause them to wander from God.[17] Nevertheless, Judah did just that and had three sons named Er, Onan, and Shelah. Er then married a woman named Tamar and, without fanfare or details, we are told that Er was a wicked man whom God killed. It was customary in that time for a widow to marry her husband's brother, who would care for her, protect her, and give her sons to ensure she had a stake in the family's inheritance and to look after her in her old age.[18] The duty to care for Tamar fell on the next son, Onan. Onan was happy to have sex with Tamar but refused to meet his obligation of impregnating and caring for her. So, he practiced *coitus interruptus*, pulling out of Tamar at the moment of ejaculation, in an effort to not impregnate her, like so many teenagers do in our own day.[31]

Nonetheless, Onan's sin was disobeying God and dishonoring Tamar by having sex without wanting to be obligated in any way or care for her, or, as Genesis 38:8 says, to "perform the duty of a brother-in-law." In short, Onan got whacked for treating Tamar like a booty call and not a bride.

---

[17] Gen. 24:3; 28:1.
[18] Deut. 25:5–6.

The false understanding of Onanism as a condemnation of all forms of birth control is based on the early church father Augustine (AD 354–430), who said of Onan, "Intercourse even with ones [*sic*] legitimate wife is unlawful and wicked where the conception of the offspring is prevented. Onan, the son of Judah, did this and the Lord killed him for it."[32]

Augustine was part of the Manichaean cult prior to his conversion to Jesus at age twenty-nine. That cult favored contraceptive drugs and discouraged procreation.[33] Augustine overreacted to his background and said that to be pure from sin marital sex had to have procreation in view.[34] He went on to say that the use of any contraceptive method turned "the bridal chamber into a brothel."[35]

Eighth, and perhaps most bizarrely, it is argued by some that sex in marriage is solely for the purpose of procreation. Thus, for sex not to be sinful, it needs to be done with the possibility of conception occurring. On this point House writes, "In the postapostolic period marriage was generally viewed as being for procreation. Clement of Alexandria [AD 150–215] expresses this attitude when he says, 'Intercourse performed licitly is an occasion of sin, unless done purely to beget children.'"[36] C. W. Scudder writes, "Such fathers as Clement viewed the sexual union between husband and wife as a sign of moral imperfection. Celibacy and continence within marriage were made the spiritual goal to which Christians should aspire. This self-denial was considered preparation for the life to come (in contrast to the 'worldly' act of sex)."[37]

In addition, Mary Pride says, "The Bible teaches us that sex is only legitimate within marriage. It further teaches, as we have seen, that the natural purpose of marital sex is (1) physical oneness and (2) fruitfulness. Nowhere does the Bible say that the purpose of marital sex is climax, much much [*sic*] less climax at the *expense* of fruitfulness and oneness."[38]

Practically, this would mean that apart from the fertile days a woman experiences each month, sexual intercourse in marriage would be sinful. Furthermore, this would mean that intercourse with an infertile wife or sex with a postmenopausal wife would also be sinful. All of this is incredibly nonsensical and unbiblical for many reasons. A woman's clitoris is a nerve center created by God with only one purpose: pleasure, not reproduction. God also made women multiorgasmic for the joy of sexual pleasure in marriage. Proverbs 5:19 reveals that a wife's breasts are not solely for baby food but also for husband fun: "Let her breasts fill you at all times with delight."

Regarding the unbiblical thinking that undergirds this false view of marital sex, Wayne House says, "History reveals that such notions owed more to Greek Stoicism than to the New Testament,"[39] and he quotes historian John T. Noonan Jr.: "Stoicism was in the air the intellectual converts to Christianity breathed. Half consciously, half unconsciously, they accommodated some Christian beliefs to a Stoic sense."[40] As a result of this Stoicism,

> emotions were downplayed and self-control was exalted. This even became true in marriage, where passion was considered suspect. Marriage must have another purpose namely, the continuance of the human race. In the words of the Stoic philosopher Ocellus Lucanus, "We have intercourse not for pleasure but for the purpose of procreation. . . . The sexual organs are given man not for pleasure, but for the maintenance of the species."[41]

This horrid, pleasureless, godless, unbiblical teaching is repackaged worldly Greek philosophical dualism (in which the body and its pleasures are not holy) instead of truth from God's Word (in which our body and its pleasures are holy gifts from God to be used as God intends). In Scripture we see that marital lovemaking serves the purposes of pleasure (throughout the Song of Solomon married sex is extolled and children are never mentioned), children,[19] oneness,[20] knowledge,[21] protection,[22] and comfort.[23]

Furthermore, the Song of Solomon includes many sexual acts that are given by God for married couples to enjoy; each of them is solely for pleasure, and none are necessary for the sole purpose of procreation. They include kissing,[24] oral sex (*fellatio*) by her initiative,[25] manual stimulation by her invitation,[26] petting by his initiative,[27] oral sex (*cun-*

---

[19]Gen. 1:28.
[20]Gen. 2:24.
[21]Gen. 4:1.
[22]1 Cor. 7:2–5.
[23]2 Sam. 12:24.
[24]Song 1:2.
[25]Song 2:3.
[26]Song 2:6.
[27]Song 4:5.

nilingus) by his initiative,[28] striptease by her,[29] and new places, including the outdoors, and new positions by her initiative.[30] In addition, 1 Corinthians 7:5 clearly states that the normative scenario for Christian marriage is free and frequent sexual intimacy: "Do not deprive one another, except perhaps by agreement for a limited time, that you may devote yourselves to prayer; but then come together again, so that Satan may not tempt you because of your lack of self-control."

Response to the Anti-Birth-Control Arguments

While God has not changed, the world has, and his people need wisdom, not legalism, to live in it. In the days of the Old Testament, most people lived in a rural culture as farmers, which meant that children were assets as both laborers with their parents and caregivers for their parents in old age. Today, with more than half the world's population now living in cities, where culture is made, it is more important than ever that God's people heed the counsel of texts such as Jeremiah 29:5–7: "Build houses and live in them; plant gardens and eat their produce. Take wives and have sons and daughters; take wives for your sons, and give your daughters in marriage, that they may bear sons and daughters; multiply there, and do not decrease. But seek the welfare of the city where I have sent you."

While not every Christian should live in the city, too few do. Statistically, the closer you venture to a major city, from which culture and influence emanate, the less likely you are to find Christians, in general, and Christian families, in particular. This separation of Christian families from cities and culture-making centers is often a failure by parents to understand their role as that of training their children to be the next generation of missionaries, evangelists, and church planters. More than ever, major cities need Christian families who love the city and seek to introduce the people there to Jesus.

In its early days, Christianity spread as a primarily urban phenomenon from city to city, with a particular concern for raising children to love Jesus. In the Roman Empire during the days of the New Testament it was common for children to be severely beaten and even tossed into the garbage or dung heap either to die or to be

---

[28]Song 4:12–5:1.
[29]Song 6:13b–7:9.
[30]Song 7:11–13.

taken by someone and used as a slave, a prostitute, or a gladiator.[42] Infant mortality was so high that only half of children lived to their fifth birthday, and less than 40 percent lived until their twentieth birthday.[43] Consequently, a family would need to birth five children to raise two and usually waited between eight and nine days after the birth to name the child to see if he or she lived through the first week. Poorer families often bred children to help earn income and later care for their aging parents. Infanticide was common, particularly with disabled children and girls. Methods of infanticide included abandonment in the desert, drowning in a river while tied to a rock, and even suffocation at the hand of a parent.

As pastor of an urban church and father of five children, my desire is for missional Christians to live in cities and have children for the sake of the gospel. Nevertheless, I recognize that there are reasons today why a godly Christian couple might want to consider using some form of birth control—reasons that do not constitute sin or selfishness. I want to offer some practical, real-life examples from people I know personally. In them you will see that while writing books and declaring legalisms is easy, living for God's glory amidst a fallen and imperfect world is far more complicated.

• A man married a single mother with rebellious teenage children and chose to postpone having any children with his new wife for a season while he first pursued a deep heart-level relationship with his adoptive children.

• A virgin woman who married for the first time in her forties chose to wait to attempt conception until after their first year of marriage. She and her husband had both been single for so long that they recognized they were a bit selfish and set in their ways and first needed to learn to care for one another selflessly.

• A woman had a difficult pregnancy that resulted in such great tearing of her body that her organs literally started falling out, so she wanted to wait a few years for her body to heal before birthing again.

• A family had a very sickly child who was unlikely to live more than a few years and required constant medical attention, which prompted the couple to wait before having another child, though they did desire more children.

• A husband woke up with a debilitating and painful arthritic condition that kept him bedridden for a few years and unable to work; thus, he and his wife used birth control so that his wife could work to feed their children.

• A missionary couple took an assignment in a war-torn area that was hit with famine; facing the possibility of starvation, they chose to postpone their childbearing efforts by using birth control.

• A mother of small children had been brutally raped and was dealing with such trauma that her husband lovingly agreed to wait to have any more children until she had physically and emotionally recovered.

• My wife, Grace, and I met while in high school and were married four years later, in the summer before our final year of college. We chose to postpone childbearing at that time so that I could finish my degree and start my career as a pastor, whereby I would be able to provide a salary and medical benefits to our now five children, in line with 1 Timothy 5:8, which says, "If anyone does not provide for his relatives, and especially for members of his household, he has denied the faith and is worse than an unbeliever."

It is true that some people sinfully postpone children for reasons motivated by greed and selfishness. It is conversely true that some idealists have children prematurely, before they are truly able to care for them.

In summary, using no birth control of any kind beyond prayer is acceptable for Christian couples. However, it is sinful when it is imposed upon or demanded of all Christian couples. Many years after graduating from college, my wife, Grace, and I were reunited with a family that we had greatly learned from and enjoyed while students. They contacted us and came to visit us and spend a night at our home—with their twelve children! They are a beautiful Christian family in which the parents have a great marriage, the wife has been able to birth all her children without major physical trauma, and the children all love and serve Jesus. As one would expect, they have had to live simply, as with ten daughters it is at times difficult to meet all of the financial needs. But, to be honest, it was an absolute joy to have their family in our home, and in every way but financial they are one of the richest families I have ever known. Their position is very mature: they are both convicted that God has called them not to use any birth control, yet, they do not believe that is God's will for everyone, and they do not judge or look down on Christian families who use birth control.

The Case of Andrea Yates

Conversely, the legalistic opposition to any use of any birth control and its devastating effects was the subject of much media scrutiny when allegedly Christian homeschool mom Andrea Yates murdered her five children by drowning them in the family bathtub. In 2002 *Time* ran a story detailing the life of Rusty and Andrea Yates, who are described as "a well-intentioned husband, strong willed yet seen as lacking empathy" and "a woman who had a vision of violence from the time just after her first child was born but who kept her demons secret to preserve the image of family and motherhood she and her husband treasured."[44] Even at their wedding in 1993 they expressed their plans not to use birth control; they wanted as many children as God would give them. They were pregnant within three months and eventually had their five children in six years.

The Yates family did not attend church but rather had family Bible studies three times a week because Rusty was leery of organized religion and had not found a church he liked. Andrea was on and off various drugs for her bouts of depression and multiple suicide attempts. Her doctor warned that if her illness returned, it could be more severe; but "Rusty and Andrea both believed, Rusty says, that if the depression were to return, Rusty could easily recognize the symptoms and seek early intervention."[45] Andrea became obsessed with the Bible. She finally succumbed to the voices in her head and played out her violent visions on the morning of June 20, 2001.

> The kids were still having breakfast when she began. First was "Perfect Paul," the 3-year-old who had been her most joyful and least trouble. He died in seconds, held violently underwater by the mother whose hands had carefully washed his hair so that the soap would not sting

his eyes. She carried his soaked body to her bed, tucking him beneath a maroon blanket, his head on the pillows. After Paul, she drowned Luke, 2, and moved on to John, 5. Next she killed their baby sister Mary, whom she had distracted with a bottle so she wouldn't scoot away and hurt herself while her brothers were being killed.

Noah, her firstborn, was the last to die. The 7-year-old left his half-eaten cereal on the kitchen table when Andrea summoned him. Walking into the bathroom, Noah saw his sister facedown in the water, her tiny fists clenched. He asked, "What's wrong with Mary?" and then, according to the account Andrea would give police, he tried to run away. His mother chased him down, dragged the wailing boy to the bathroom and forced him facedown into nine inches of cold water in the tub, his sister's body floating lifeless next to him. Noah came up twice as he fought for air. But Andrea held her grip. She then laid Mary in bed with her brothers, wrapping their arms around the baby. She left Noah in the tub....

Later she told jail doctors that nothing could mute the patter that said she was a lousy mother. The death of her children, she said, was her punishment, not theirs. It was, she explained, a mother's final act of mercy. Did not the Bible say it would be better for a person to be flung into the sea with a stone tied to his neck than cause little ones to stumble?[46]

For those most overbearing, legalistic husbands who ignore parts of the Bible that teach about being wise and loving your wife, seeing the faces of the children before their troubled mother killed them might be helpful.[47] Indeed, children are a blessing and so are prudent Spirit-led parents headed by a daddy who looks at his bride and sees a wife, not just a womb, who needs love and not just labor.

A Word to Husbands

Admittedly, I have hammered this nail hard. I have done so because I have met too many idiotic husbands who seem to think that birthing is akin to scoring points in a sporting event, and all they want to do is outscore their buddies, though they neglect to provide the kind of spiritual, emotional, mental, and financial support to enable their wife to be loved as Christ does his church. The result is often a wife who looks like a cash-strapped, exhausted, breastfeeding, homeschooling mom without any help—from a babysitter, housecleaner, decent home, or

dependable car—detached from meaningful church community and
kept under the thumb of her husband, who conveniently overlooks
the fact that even the quintessential Proverbs 31 wife and mother had
a husband who made an income sufficient for her to pay for help and
invest what was left over.

Such folly is often done falsely in the name of headship, which I
actually adhere to in its biblical form, by narrow-minded, impish men
who fail in their duties while having a hard time settling into a church
that meets their legalistic expectations and telling their wives to suffer
in the name of submission until the weaker vessel invariably breaks.
One group of women I know, suffering under this kind of husband,
actually talk openly about their nervous breakdowns, as if such breakdowns are simply part of being a Christian mom. Assuming that the
right hand of fellowship has now found the jaw of my blockheaded
brothers, we will proceed to consider various categories of birth control
for Christians.

Level 2: Natural Birth Control

Natural methods include any kind of contraception through which
pregnancy is prevented by abstaining from vaginal sexual intercourse
on days when the wife is likely to be fertile. The most popular natural
method is the calendar-based rhythm method, which has been replaced
by more effective methods such as the symptothermal method and the
standard-days method. Fertility computers are a new development in
contraceptive technology that make these natural methods easier to
use by telling a couple when sex will or won't result in pregnancy. The
Roman Catholic Church approves the use of natural methods. One
common myth is that a mother cannot become pregnant while nursing,
which, while true for some women, is not true for all women.[48]

Abstaining from sexual intercourse does not necessarily require
abstaining from all sexual activity. Some married couples enjoy such
things as oral sex or a helping hand of manual stimulation from one
another, depending upon what their conscience permits, during the
wife's fertile days.

Natural birth control methods have many benefits, including the
involvement of both husband and wife, as well as the fact that such
methods are free, safe, and reversible. Additionally, these methods

require no surgery, chemicals, devices, or drugs. Natural methods can also be used with other methods, such as a condom, during fertile times. One of the potential difficulties is that natural methods require discipline and planning, which not everyone is equally faithful to ensure. In conclusion, natural birth control is permissible for a Christian couple.

Level 3: Non-abortive Birth Control

Like the natural methods, non-abortive birth control methods also seek to influence the timing of conception but do so by taking either temporary or permanent additional measures. This method of birth control has quite a long history.

Barrier Methods

Temporary non-abortive birth control methods are generally barrier methods. Barrier methods of contraception include all methods that permit intercourse but prevent the sperm and egg from coming together. Perhaps the most common is the male condom, which was invented three thousand years ago by an Egyptian couple using a linen pouch.[49]

As many as five thousand years ago, sea sponges were soaked in diluted lemon juice and then inserted into the vagina to absorb semen.[50] Women also tried soaking sea sponges in olive oil, vinegar, and brandy.[51]

More than three thousand years ago, ancient Egyptians, Greeks, and Romans inserted combinations of herbs, tree resins, and honey oil into their vaginas.[52] Some African women used hollowed-out okra pods as a vaginal pouch that was in some ways like the modern female condom.[53] Roman women used goat bladders in a similar manner.[54]

Male condoms in the seventeenth century were made from animal intestines and were actually somewhat successful.[55] In the second half of the nineteenth century, the rubber condom came into use.[56] Regarding effectiveness, there is a reported 3 to 12 percent pregnancy rate per year with typical use.[57] Using only a condom but doing so correctly means that a couple has a 3 percent chance of becoming pregnant in a one-year period.[58]

Male condoms are the best method for preventing the transmission of sexually transmitted diseases, if the husband or wife is infected. Complaints about male condoms include the unromantic need to stop in the moment of passion to put one on, diminished pleasure sensation for the husband, and the physical barrier between a husband and wife in their moment of greatest intimacy.

Male condoms are the only barrier method available for husbands, with the possible exception of a guy with one eyebrow who refuses to use breath mints because they are not mentioned in the Bible and wears shirts bought only from an auto parts store or a beer company and scratches himself a lot and wants his wife to play "pull my finger" before bedtime. In that instance, he is his own barrier method.

Female barrier methods include the diaphragm, contraceptive sponge, cervical cap, and female condom. Spermicides are also considered barrier methods because they kill sperm before they can reach a waiting egg, thus preventing fertilization. Also effective as a barrier is constant nagging, which keeps a husband far away.

The factors to consider with these methods are many. Sponges can be dangerous if left in too long, even causing infection or toxic shock. Female condoms are less effective than male condoms but can be inserted up to eight hours before intercourse, thereby enabling greater spontaneity than male condoms.[59] Most spermicides (including sponges with spermicides) use nonoxynol-9, which can create infection in some women but is helpful alongside other methods, such as a condom, because it kills sperm. However, the use of spermicides has been linked to a higher-than-normal incidence of severe birth defects—twice the rate of nonusers.[60] The cervical cap has been a favorite contraceptive method in Europe since the mid-1800s and today is considered 60 to 80 percent effective. It can be inserted more than a day before intercourse so as to allow greater spontaneity.[61] The reported failure rate of the diaphragm is anywhere from 2 to 20 percent.[62]

Permanent Methods

Permanent non-abortive birth control methods are often chosen by couples who have decided not to enlarge their family. (For the purposes of this chapter I am referring to voluntary versus involuntary sterilization.) Such preventatives can be achieved by either female sterilization, also called tubal ligation, or by vasectomy for men. Both of these methods require minor surgery and should be considered permanent, although it is theoretically possible, but difficult, to undergo a reversal. One of the elder candidates at our church had a vasectomy when he was a young non-Christian. After meeting Jesus and growing in his understanding of marriage and family, he actually underwent a vasectomy reversal before becoming a pastor in our church in order to set a good example. He reported that the entire process was painful and complicated.

The first vasectomy clinic in the United States opened in 1969.[63] Some men reportedly experience depression after the surgery because they feel they have lost something of their masculinity. Others who become divorced or widowed can later regret their decision when they remarry and desire to have children with their new wife.

The first tubal ligation was performed on women during the nineteenth century.[64] Some women reportedly experience depression after the surgery because they feel they have lost something of their femininity. Others who become divorced or widowed regret doing something so permanent when they remarry and desire to have children with their new husband.

Three things need to be mentioned regarding permanent non-abortive birth control methods. First, the heart needs to be examined regarding motive on this issue; this method should never be used to completely abandon the blessing of children, as Tom Leykis suggests. He is the most popular radio show host for young men in the nation and encourages young men (i.e., in their early twenties) to have a vasectomy so that they will never have to worry about getting their girlfriend pregnant or being stuck with paying child support to their ex-wife, should they ever get married and then divorced.

Second, it is unwise to make this decision too early in life, because it is not uncommon for a couple to later desire more children, or for someone to remarry after being divorced or widowed and desire to have children with their next spouse. I personally know of many couples who underwent just such a surgery after having a few children and later deeply regretted their decision and wished they had not done it.

Third, some Christians are legalistic on this issue and declare that there is essentially never a good reason for such a permanent measure. However, life in a fallen world is complicated and painful. A pastor and his wife, good friends of mine, suffered eighteen miscarriages before he had a vasectomy to stop what had become for them incredible physical and emotional pain. Also, my wife, Grace, had complications with the birth of our first daughter, Ashley, and had to have an emergency C-section. The doctor advised us to continue using C-sections, but after five C-section surgeries and one miscarriage we prayed James 1:5 and fasted and then decided that she would undergo a tubal ligation in conjunction with the birth of our last child. We have remained convinced that we made a wise decision for the sake of her health. Additionally, we are open to adoption or fostering in the future if God calls us to that, since we do consider children a blessing.

To summarize, levels 1 to 3 are options that Christian couples can consider without concern of terminating a fertilized egg, thereby taking a human life.

Level 4: Potentially Abortive Birth Control

At the next birth control level we tread into murkier waters, where it is more difficult to discern what is biblically right. "The pill" is a categorical term for more than forty types of oral contraceptives, which are also referred to as birth control pills and sometimes combination pills because they contain a mixture of estrogen and progestin. These hormonal contraceptives are designed to override the female body's normal cycle and "trick" the woman's brain into believing she's already pregnant, thus preventing the release of an egg from the ovaries.

Birth control pills were introduced to America in the 1950s. In 1965 the U.S. Supreme Court declared unconstitutional the nineteenth-century law prohibiting the use of contraceptives.[65] Today, fifty to sixty million women worldwide take the pill each day, and it is the most widely prescribed drug in the world.[66]

Generally speaking, hormonal birth control methods run the risk of causing an abortion. Because female hormones direct the process of ovulation, synthetic hormones can be used to keep an egg from being released so that sperm are not able to fertilize it. These same synthetic hormones can also prevent a fertilized egg from implanting in a woman's uterus and growing into a baby. Combined pills are generally very effective, as long as they are taken correctly: "With careful use, fewer than 1 woman in every 100 will get pregnant in a year. With less careful use, 3 or more women in every 100 will get pregnant in a year."[67] However, research indicates that those numbers may be considerably higher, up to 4 percent among "generally consistent and conscientious users" and up to 8 percent "among those who use the pill inconsistently and incorrectly."[68]

Hormonal Methods

Hormonal methods of birth control tend to be more effective than others but also pose greater health risks. They include systems with estrogen and progestin such as combination oral contraceptives, the vaginal ring, and the contraceptive patch, as well as estrogen-free methods such as the mini-pill (progestin-only pills), contraceptive injectables, and some intrauterine devices (IUDs). These are the same drugs used in emergency contraceptive pills. There are no hormonal methods available for men.

The Pill Debate

The debate over hormonal birth control, particularly the pill, is whether it results in the taking of a life by destroying a fertilized egg. Author, pastor, and pro-life leader Randy Alcorn has written a great deal on this subject.[69] Alcorn writes, "The Pill is used by about fourteen million American women each year. Across the globe it is used by about sixty million. The question of whether it causes abortions has direct bearing on untold millions of Christians, many of them prolife, who use and recommend it."

Alcorn goes on to point out that there is not one but rather three purposes for birth control pills. First, the pill exists to inhibit ovulation, which is its primary means of birth control. Second, the pill thickens the cervical mucus so that it becomes more difficult for sperm to travel to the egg. Third, the pill thins and shrivels the lining of the uterus so that it is unable or less able to facilitate the implantation of the newly fertilized egg. On this last point, Alcorn says, "Reproductive endocrinologists have demonstrated that Pill-induced changes cause the endometrium to appear 'hostile' or 'poorly receptive' to implantation."[70] Furthermore, "Magnetic Resonance Imaging (MRI) reveals that the endometrial lining of Pill users is consistently thinner than that of nonusers—up to 58 percent thinner."[71]

The bottom line is this: the first two purposes of birth control pills are contraceptive in nature and therefore acceptable for use by a Christian couple. However, the third function of birth control pills is potentially abortive in that it seeks to disrupt the ongoing life of a fertilized egg. That potentiality is incredibly controversial; thus, faithful Christians who are staunchly prolife and believe that life begins at conception are divided over the issue.

To help provide some clarity, Focus on the Family's Physicians Resource Council (PRC), under the leadership of James Dobson, examined the issue for two years. The PRC is comprised of prolife Christian doctors from a wide variety of fields. They sought to thoroughly study the issue of whether combination oral contraceptives (those with both estrogen and progesterone) cause abortion. Ultimately, even they were undecided:

> Pro-life physicians who have carefully and conscientiously studied this issue have come to different conclusions regarding the interpretation and implications of the relevant scientific data. After two years of extended deliberation and prayer, the PRC has not been able to reach a consensus as to the likelihood, or even the possibility, that these medications might contribute to the loss of human life after fertilization. The majority of the experts to which Dr. Dobson has spoken feel that the pill does not have an abortifacient effect. A minority of the experts feel that when conception occurs on the pill, there is enough of a possibility for an abortifacient effect, however remote, to warrant warning women about it.[72]

Similarly, the statement from the Christian Medical and Dental Associations (CMDA) on this issue reads:

> CMDA recognizes that there are differing viewpoints among Christians regarding the broad issue of birth control and the use of contraceptives. The issue at hand, however, is whether or not hormonal birth control methods have post-fertilization effects (i.e., cause abortion). CMDA has consulted many experts in the field of reproduction who have reviewed the scientific literature. While there are data that cause concern, our current scientific knowledge does not establish a definitive causal link between the routine use of hormonal birth control and abortion. However, neither are there data to deny a post-fertilization effect.[73]

Therefore, whether to use birth control pills is a very complicated issue about which faithful prolife Christians and doctors disagree. As a result, it seems legalistic and inappropriate to declare that use of the pill is sinful. Conversely, it seems that Christian couples need to be informed of the potential abortive nature of birth control pills so that they can study the matter further and prayerfully come to an informed decision according to their own conscience and the leading of God the Holy Spirit.

Personally, when Grace and I were first married, she had one semester of college left and I had one year remaining until our degrees were completed. At that time, Grace used the pill to prevent pregnancy until after graduation. She was actively involved in a local prolife group, and we were completely unaware of the potential abortive nature of the pill. Once we uncovered more information on the matter, we prayerfully came to the conclusion together that, in order to err on the side of caution based upon our deep convictions about the sanctity of human life, she would not take the pill. As a pastor who is, admittedly, not medically trained, I do not encourage members of our church to use the pill but also would not discipline a member for sin if they did.

Level 5: Abortive Murder

Abortion is taking a human life by killing a fertilized egg. Biblically, it is also known as the sin of murder. Abortions include medical procedures of various kinds as well as RU-486 and the morning-after pill. Other items that cause abortion are the intrauterine device (IUD) and Norplant, which do not prevent conception but prevent implantation of an already fertilized ovum. The result is an abortion, the killing of a conceived person.[74]

Thomas W. Hilgers of the Mayo Graduate School of Medicine in Rochester, Minnesota, studied over four hundred articles on the subject and concluded, "The primary action of the IUD must be classed as abortifacient."[75] Tragically, some 2.5 to 3 million American women use IUDs.[76]

Focus on the Family also addresses these birth control methods:

Birth control pills which contain only the hormone progesterone do not reliably prevent ovulation (the release of the egg from the ovary).

This is also true of Norplant, a device implanted under the skin which slowly releases progesterone. With these methods, the pregnancies which do occur have a greater chance of being ectopic—that is, outside of the uterus. This may be evidence that these contraceptives act in some cases to disrupt normal implantation of an early pregnancy and not merely to prevent conception. Thus, the use of Norplant and the progesterone-only pill is problematic for those who believe life begins at conception.[77]

It may seem odd that I, as a pastor writing primarily for Christian readers, include this level as a form of birth control. Yet, tragically, many people, including Christians, use abortion as a form of birth control. Undoubtedly, there are very rare cases in which even the most devoutly Bible-believing, pro-life Christians are caught on the horns of an ethical dilemma involving abortion (e.g., when the mother's life is at stake), but for the purposes of this chapter I am speaking of abortion in its majority sense as a murderous form of birth control. Regarding abortion, a division of Focus on the Family says:

> The Alan Guttmacher Institute is a nonprofit corporation for reproductive health research and policy analysis. The Institute is also a public education arm of Planned Parenthood. It reports that one in six women who have had abortions are evangelical Christians. Based on these statistics, 5.6 million women in our churches have chosen abortion as a way out of an unwanted pregnancy. Each year, 1.5 million American women have an abortion. This means 250,000 evangelical Christian women could choose to abort a child this year.
> Women ages 20 to 24 obtain 32 percent of all abortions. Teenagers obtain 20 percent. Forty percent of women ages 15 to 44 have had at least one previous abortion. Fifty percent of women who have abortions use it as their sole means of birth control. Fifty-eight percent of abortion patients say they used birth control during the month of conception.[78]

Christians have always followed the teaching of the Old Testament Jews, that abortion of a preborn child and exposure of a born child are both murderous sins. In the *Didache*, which was an ancient manual for church instruction, we read, "You shall not commit murder. . . . You shall not procure abortion, nor commit infanticide."[79] The Epistle of

Barnabas also says, "Thou shalt not procure abortion, thou shalt not commit infanticide."[80]

Some will argue that there is a difference between a child in a mother's womb and one outside of it, yet the early church saw both as equally living people and the taking of life in either state as equally murderous. Their convictions were based on Scripture, which uses the same word, *brephos*, for Elizabeth's unborn child, John the Baptizer (Luke 1:41, 44), as is used for the unborn baby Jesus in Mary's womb (Luke 2:12) and also for the children brought to Jesus (Luke 18:15).[81] Simply, in the divinely inspired pages of Scripture, God reveals to us that a child in the womb and a child singing and dancing around Jesus in worship are equally human beings, who bear the image of God, and thankfully Mary did not abort the "tissue" in her womb, because he was God.

Prior to being saved from my sins and regenerated by Jesus at the age of nineteen with a new mind, with new understanding, with a new heart, and with new desires, I am sad to say I was vocally pro-abortion to the degree that I was more Malthusian in my outlook. I wrongly believed that less fit people should be sterilized or not permitted to conceive and encouraged, if not required, to abort if impregnated. I argued for this persuasively both in high school classes, as the president of our student body, and later in college classroom debates. I deeply regret my sinful position, and for those who somehow claim to believe simultaneously in Scripture and abortion, my rebuke includes a suggestion of ongoing study as an act of repentance, in order to experience Romans 12:2, which commands, "Do not be conformed to this world, but be transformed by the renewal of your mind, that by testing you may discern what is the will of God, what is good and acceptable and perfect."

Thankfully, Jesus can forgive any sin, even the sin of murder, as he did while hanging on the cross and asking God the Father to forgive those who murdered him. Furthermore, prolife ministries are devoted to extending the love, grace, mercy, compassion, and support needed for men and women who have suffered from abortion to experience healing and new life. In our church this includes a ministry to post-abortive women run by female deacons who were once sexually active and who aborted their own children, only later to meet Jesus, repent, experience new life, and become godly wives, mothers, and church leaders.

SUMMARY

In summary, as a pastor I would support Christian couples practicing levels 1 to 3 of birth control, urge those considering level 4 to prayerfully and carefully reflect on their decision, and oppose any Christian couple considering level 5, unless there are extremely weighty extenuating circumstances. In twelve years as the pastor of Mars Hill Church, which has seen hundreds and hundreds of weddings and pregnancies, I have not yet faced such circumstances, and by God's grace I pray I never do. Should that occasion occur, I will work with the family, aided by prayer from our church, counsel from fellow elders, and outside expert medical counsel, to arrive at a decision based on a careful examination of all the variables involved.[82]

QUESTION 8: **HUMOR**

Why do you make jokes in sermons about Mormon missionaries, homosexuals, trench coat wearers, single men, vegans, and emo kids, and then expect these groups to come to know God through those sermons?

I am on a mission to both put people in heaven and put the "fun" back in "fundamentalism." I believe Christianity should be more fun than a trip to the dentist and that evangelicalism needs a better patron saint than Ned Flanders of *The Simpsons* fame.

As a result, one of the most controversial aspects of my ministry has been my tone, sense of humor, and propensity to make fun of every conceivable group of people. This includes rappers with grills and rims and indie rockers who wear all black, smoking American Spirit cigs and pretending not to care about what other people think; men who can't find their pants and women who work near poles and earn their income in one-dollar bills; gays and straights; publick skewlers and home schoolers where mom wears a denim jumper and dad churns butter in preparation for Armageddon; mullet-wearing, one-tooth NASCAR fans and people who drive hybrid vehicles and promote justification by recycling; and any other groups that come to mind impromptu as I preach and write.

My favorite targets tend to be action-figure–loving single guys who play World of Warcraft at their mom's house while downloading porn and blogging about how the world should be, in between long sessions of sleep in their Star Wars sheets. Vegans are also funny because they get upset every time I promote bacon, and they often tell me that I will die if I eat bacon, to which I reply, "Yes, praise God, I will die and go to heaven . . . full of bacon."

The question on which this chapter is based also mentions Mormons, because in one sermon I referred to two nice, young, clean-shaven men wearing pressed white shirts, riding their bikes to hell. Still, far and away my favorite target (other than myself and my Shrek-sized head) is religious types, particularly those who have their own end-times chart drawn in crayon on an ammo box, anyone who has ever held a praise flag in church, and new Calvinists who get drunk on dead authors and want to tell everyone else what to do while conveniently overlooking the fact that they have never done anything and don't know what they are doing. But the real question is whether it is biblical to be funny.

IS HUMOR BIBLICAL?

The guys with more degrees than Fahrenheit tell us that the Bible does have the occasional funny. They say:

> The Bible is predominantly a serious rather than a funny book. Yet it would distort the Bible to suppress the humor that is present. Arranged on a continuum that ranges from the least intellectual (slapstick comedy) to the most intellectual (irony and wordplay), we can say that the humor of the Bible tends toward the subtle.[1]

They go on to say that the Bible is, in fact, arranged as a comedy:

> A full-fledged comedic plot is a U-shaped story that descends into potential tragedy and then rises to a happy ending as obstacles to fulfillment are gradually overcome. Some comic plots record only the upward movement from bondage to freedom. The progression of a comic plot is from problem to solution, from less than ideal experience to prosperity and wish fulfillment. The comic plot is the story of the happy ending par excellence. The plot consists of a series of obstacles that must be overcome en route to the happy ending. . . . The truth is that comedy is the dominant narrative form in the Bible. There are relatively few full-fledged tragedies in the Bible. The materials for tragedy are everywhere in the stories of sin and disobedience, but the Bible is almost completely an anthology of tragedies averted through

characters' repentance and God's forgiveness. The comic plot is the deep structure of biblical narrative. . . . The overall plot of the Bible is a U-shaped comic plot. The action begins with a perfect world inhabited by perfect people. It descends into the misery of fallen history and ends with a new world of total happiness and the conquest of evil. The book of Revelation is the story of the happy ending par excellence, as a conquering hero defeats evil, marries a bride and lives happily ever after in a palace glittering with jewels.[2]

Comedy and related themes run throughout the Bible. The word *joy* and its derivatives appear roughly two hundred times in our English Bible. The word *laugh* and its derivatives appear roughly forty times.

Sadly, too many coats of varnish have been painted over what is a divinely inspired, earthy book that honestly records the foibles and follies of sinners like us by furrowed-browed, pointy-fingered religious types who forget Ecclesiastes 3:4, which says that there is "a time to laugh." Consequently, very little has been written on the subject of biblical humor. There are a few exceptions, such as *A Serrated Edge: A Brief Defense of Biblical Satire and Trinitarian Skylarking* by Douglas Wilson (Moscow, ID: Canon Press, 2003) and *The Humor of Christ* by Elton Trueblood (New York: Harper & Row, 1964).

However, the Bible includes humor of various kinds, from situational comedy to satire, sarcasm, and irony. Entire books of the Bible, such as Amos, are comedic satire.[3] Perhaps the most humorous line in Amos is where God refers to the female members of the Bashan city council as fat cows: "Hear this word, you cows of Bashan, who are on the mountain of Samaria, who oppress the poor, who crush the needy, who say to your husbands, 'Bring, that we may drink!'"[1]

The names of people in the Bible are also worthy of the occasional chuckle, unless, of course, you named one of your kids by picking a cool name from the concordance without finding out what it meant, such as Achan (trouble), Agrippa (causes pain), Balak (destroyer), Careah or Kareah (baldy), Chesed (a devil), Chilion (dying), Eglon (fat cow), Emmor or Hamor (an ass), Esau (hairy), Gatam or Mordecai (puny), Harumaph (flat nose), Irad (wild ass), Jareb or Midian (contentious), Mahli or Mahlon (sickly), Nabal (fool), Naharis (snorer), Nahash (ser-

---

[1]Amos 4:1.

pent), Og (long neck), Parshandatha (dung), Sanballat (enemy), or Isaac (laughter).[4]

The Bible even uses what the *Dictionary of Biblical Imagery* calls "scatological humor" in both the Old and New Testaments.[5] The story of the godless king Eglon is recorded in Judges 3:15–30. God's holy, divinely inspired word says Eglon was "a very fat man." The Jack Bauer-esque southpaw Ehud "reached with his left hand, took the sword from his right thigh, and thrust it into his [Eglon's] belly. And the hilt also went in after the blade, and the fat closed over the blade, for he did not pull the sword out of his belly; and the dung came out." The story ends by explaining how Eglon's feces came pouring out of his pierced intestine. The stink was so bad that his servants who were waiting outside his chambers, unaware he had been whacked by the Mob, possibly by a guy in a shiny sweat suit complete with gold chains dangling over lots of chest hair, wrongly assumed the stink was a post-chalupa rough go of things on the toilet.

New Testament scatological humor includes Philippians 3:8, where Paul uses a particularly provocative word, *skubalah*, to describe religion. Various translations render it "rubbish," "garbage," "refuse," "filth," "dung," "dog dung," and "turds." Greek scholar and expert Daniel B. Wallace[6] explains the word used in Philippians 3:8:

> If [*skubalah*] is translated "s**t" (or the like), a word picture is effectively made: this is all that the "flesh" can produce—and it is both worthless and revolting. That the apostle is not above using graphic and shocking terms has already been demonstrated in vv. 2–3. The reason for the shocking statement in v. 8, then, may well be to wake up his audience to the real danger of his opponents' views. It is not insignificant that there is precedent for the apostle's white-hot anger over a false gospel being couched in not-so-delicate terms: his letter to the "foolish Galatians" is replete with such evocative language.[7]

Wallace goes on to conclude, "The term conveys both revulsion and worthlessness in this context. In hellenistic Greek it seems to stand somewhere between 'crap' and 's**t.'"[8] Pastor and author Douglas Wilson goes so far as to say that Paul's word for religion is "dog s**t."[9]

We are going to take a look now at some of the more intriguing examples of humor from the Old Testament, the New Testament, and the teachings of Jesus Christ. By doing so, we are not making light of Scripture; rather, we are practicing the teaching of 2 Timothy 3:16–17, which says, "All Scripture is breathed out by God and profitable for teaching, for reproof, for correction, and for training in righteousness, that the man of God may be competent, equipped for every good work." That good work includes knowing when to laugh and when to make fun of others for a prophetic purpose that is deadly serious. As Douglas Wilson summarizes in regard to cutting prophetic humor, "The prophet Jeremiah attacked idolaters, the Lord Jesus attacked self-righteous Pharisees, the apostle Paul attacked Judaizers, Irenaeus attacked Gnostics, and Luther attacked the papists."[10]

Before moving on, it is important to note that the Bible laughs at the expense of sinners upon occasion, but most often at serious religious types who are legalistic, self-righteous, and sinfully judgmental of other people. Though such verbal jabs are painful, they are a demonstration of biblical love. Biblical love, unlike sentimental love, does not merely feel mushy, gooey, and syrupy sweet, but acts for the good of the beloved. These acts include, as needed, confrontation, rebuke, and steady doses of truth delivered in whatever form is most effective, including mockery. Indeed, it is not always the one kissing you who is truly your friend, as Jesus himself experienced with Judas. Proverbs 27:5–6 says, "Better is open rebuke than hidden love. Faithful are the wounds of a friend; profuse are the kisses of an enemy." Therefore, when the Bible laughs at someone, it does so in love, seeking to expose the folly of fools so that they might come to their senses and repent.

HUMOR IN THE OLD TESTAMENT
The Pentateuch

Our study of biblical humor begins, appropriately enough, in the book of Genesis, which is the book of beginnings. There we find one of my favorite funny stories about the "righteous" man Noah. You will remember that he and his family alone were spared God's wrath in the flood. Upon exiting the ark as the father of a new humanity, "Noah began to be a man of the soil, and he planted a vineyard. He drank of the wine and became drunk and lay uncovered in his tent."[2] Every time I read this account I chuckle. Noah is obviously a camping redneck,

---

[2] Gen. 9:20–21.

because only a camping redneck would make his own liquor and pass out naked in his tent wearing nothing but a John Deere ball cap. For all we know, his tent might have been made of blue tarps, and he may have dozed off while singing country songs about the hillbilly trinity of dogs, trucks, and cornbread.

While preaching through Genesis, I was continually amused by Jacob, whose name means "trickster." The previously laid-back, easy-going homebody Jacob[3] rolled in to Haran, where he met the lovely Rachel at the well.[4] He was so excited that to show off his manly strength he removed the stone covering the well, a job so dudely that it normally took a crew of men to get it done. Still flexing his muscles and enjoying his manhood, Jacob kissed Rachel like one of the guys who just won a NASCAR race and locks lips with the trophy girl on the platform. In the ensuing chapters, Jacob the trickster is taken to the woodshed by the Michael Jordan of con artists, Laban. There we read that after working for a full seven years to marry Rachel, Jacob rolled over the morning after his wedding to find lazy-eyed Leah in his bed, not her lovely sister Rachel. Laban had swapped out the girls, thereby forcing the trickster to work another seven years and marry them both! The entire account is dripping with satire.

One of the funniest lines in all of Scripture is found in Exodus 32. While Moses was away with God, his brother Aaron led the people to give their jewelry and wealth to melt down and make a golden calf for idol worship. When confronted by Moses, Aaron's defense was "they gave it to me, and I threw it into the fire, and out came this calf."[5]

The Historical Books

In the history books of the Old Testament, both Gaal[6] and Nabal[7] got drunk and, like drunk guys hopped up on liquid courage often do, popped off about how they could take guys much tougher than them, only to wake up with a hangover, a foreboding sense of dread, and empty colons as they pondered the beating that awaited them. Though it is not said, one wonders if they were frat guys.

---

[3]Gen. 25:27.
[4]Genesis 29.
[5]Ex. 32:24.
[6]Judges 9.
[7]1 Sam. 25:36–37.

Arguably the funniest scene in the entire Old Testament is found in the octagon report of 1 Kings 18:25–29:

> Then Elijah said to the prophets of Baal, "Choose for yourselves one bull and prepare it first, for you are many, and call upon the name of your god, but put no fire to it." And they took the bull that was given them, and they prepared it and called upon the name of Baal from morning until noon, saying, "O Baal, answer us!" But there was no voice, and no one answered. And they limped around the altar that they had made. And at noon Elijah *mocked* them, saying, "Cry aloud, for he is a god. Either he is musing, or he is relieving himself, or he is on a journey, or perhaps he is asleep and must be awakened." And they cried aloud and cut themselves after their custom with swords and lances, until the blood gushed out upon them. And as midday passed, they raved on until the time of the offering of the oblation, but there was no voice. No one answered; no one paid attention.

In this legendary showdown, God shows up and shows off to reveal himself and his servant Elijah. When it came to the prophets of Baal, though, their false god never made it to the ring. So, Elijah mocked them, saying in effect, "Perhaps your god has not yet made it to the octagon because he's sitting on his toilet throne dozing off, so maybe you guys should go bang on the door really loudly and see if you can get your god out here for my God to open a can on." God loved this man so much that he took him straight to heaven in a fiery chariot rather than let him taste death.

The Prophets
The Old Testament prophets are filled with all forms of humor. Amos 6:4–6 sounds like a commentary on MTV's *Cribs*:

> Woe to those who lie on beds of ivory and stretch themselves out on their couches, and eat lambs from the flock and calves from the midst of the stall, who sing idle songs to the sound of the harp and like David invent for themselves instruments of music, who drink wine in bowls and anoint themselves with the finest oils.

Or to put it in our vernacular: there is mad judgment on all vintage-jersey–wearing pimps with phat cribs rolling a fleet of cars decked out in rims with spinners, enjoying the finest strip clubs, sitting in the VIP room sipping Hennessy through crazy straws by the bucket.

Isaiah 3:16–24 says:

> The LORD said: Because the daughters of Zion are haughty and walk with outstretched necks, glancing wantonly with their eyes, mincing along as they go, tinkling with their feet, therefore the Lord will strike with a scab the heads of the daughters of Zion, and the LORD will lay bare their secret parts. In that day the Lord will take away the finery of the anklets, the headbands, and the crescents; the pendants, the bracelets, and the scarves; the headdresses, the armlets, the sashes, the perfume boxes, and the amulets; the signet rings and nose rings; the festal robes, the mantles, the cloaks, and the handbags; the mirrors, the linen garments, the turbans, and the veils. Instead of perfume there will be rottenness; and instead of a belt, a rope; and instead of well-set hair, baldness; and instead of a rich robe, a skirt of sackcloth; and branding instead of beauty.

Or, to put it another way, God promises to clean out the walk-in closet of his daughters just before shaving their heads and putting them over his knee, because they are a trampish bunch who love to strut around the club in push-up bras and clear heels flirting with rich old men, hoping to land a sugar daddy with Viagra in one pocket and a platinum credit card in the other.

Isaiah 44:13–20 mocks Geppetto-esque guys who use their wood-working skills to make a god:

> The carpenter stretches a line; he marks it out with a pencil. He shapes it with planes and marks it with a compass. He shapes it into the figure of a man, with the beauty of a man, to dwell in a house. He cuts down cedars, or he chooses a cypress tree or an oak and lets it grow strong among the trees of the forest. He plants a cedar and the rain nourishes it. Then it becomes fuel for a man. He takes a part of it and warms himself; he kindles a fire and bakes bread. Also he makes a god and worships it; he makes it an idol and falls down before it. Half of it he burns in the fire. Over the half he eats meat; he roasts it and is satisfied. Also he warms himself and says, "Aha, I am warm, I have seen the fire!" And the rest of it he makes into a god, his idol, and falls down to it and worships it. He prays to it and says, "Deliver me, for you are my god!"

Indeed, it is funny that God would take the time to mock a guy who got an *A* in high school woodshop and delights in his ability to discern which end of a log is god and which end is firewood because he studied it in community college.

In addition, Isaiah 64:6 compares religion to a bloody menstrual rag: "We have all become like one who is unclean, and all our righteous deeds are like a polluted garment." This is particularly shocking if you think about it being applied to the sincerely religious, including, for example, a Muslim kneeling on his rug praying to Mecca, or a Mormon wearing his sacred underbritches because some guy in Utah told him that God likes his men to wear onesies with a trap door.

The Wisdom Books

The wisdom literature is likewise filled with humor. In many places we read about God laughing at people, even mocking them. Psalm 37:13 says, "The Lord laughs at the wicked, for he sees that his day is coming." Psalm 2:4 says, "He who sits in the heavens laughs; the Lord holds them in derision." Psalm 59:8 says, "But you, O LORD, laugh at them; you hold all the nations in derision." Also, Proverbs 1:23–27 says:

> If you turn at my reproof,
> behold, I will pour out my spirit to you;
>   I will make my words known to you.
> Because I have called and you refused to listen,
>   have stretched out my hand and no one has heeded,
> because you have ignored all my counsel
>   and would have none of my reproof,
> I also will laugh at your calamity;
>   I will mock when terror strikes you,
> when terror strikes you like a storm
>   and your calamity comes like a whirlwind,
>   when distress and anguish come upon you.

Sarcasm also drips throughout the book of Job. The fact that the Bible college students who kept hounding Job with picky theological criticisms are called his "friends" and "comforters" is an obvious joke. To end the book, God even pokes fun at poor Job in chapter

38, essentially telling him to put a cup on because God planned to kick him in the middle by asking him eighty scientific questions, beginning with, "Where were you when I laid the foundation of the earth?" Getting the sarcasm, Job wisely tapped out and left the ring.

Proverbs makes fun of all kinds of people, especially the sluggard, who, by definition, is someone so lazy that he experiences devolution on his way to becoming a slug. Proverbs 26:14 says, "As a door turns on its hinges, so does a sluggard on his bed." Perhaps quoting what the guy's mom says every morning, Proverbs 6:9 says, "How long will you lie there, O sluggard? When will you arise from your sleep?" Mocking the guy who is too lazy to even exert energy to get the chips from the bowl to his mouth while sitting on the couch devoting his twenties to watching every episode of *Star Trek*, Proverbs 19:24 says, "The sluggard buries his hand in the dish and will not even bring it back to his mouth." Presumably mocking the aspiring musician who freeloads off his girlfriend and crashes at her pad but never goes out to find a job because of one ridiculous excuse after another, like the terror alert being at yellow, Proverbs 22:13 adds this: "The sluggard says, 'There is a lion outside! I shall be killed in the streets!'"

Proverbs also includes more than a few jabs at various kinds of bad women. Speaking of the nagging woman, Proverbs 27:15 says, "A continual dripping on a rainy day and a quarrelsome wife are alike," which is particularly funny if her nagging is about the dripping faucet or leaky gutter. If you ever see a guy camping on the roof, you can assume he is obeying James 1:22: "But be doers of the word, and not hearers only," after reading Proverbs 21:9 and 25:24, which both say it is better for a guy to live on the roof of his house than inside his house with a quarrelsome, nagging wife.

One of the funniest sayings in Proverbs is that a hot gal all dressed up is akin to a pig dolled up with jewelry: "Like a gold ring in a pig's snout is a beautiful woman without discretion."[8] Like I tell the single guys in our church, you can't marry a woman just because she's hot, because so is hell, and if she's a pig you'll be living in hell.

---

[8]Prov. 11:22.

HUMOR IN THE NEW TESTAMENT

Some nice, well-meaning Christians who drink only decaf and listen to music with a soothing acoustic guitar are often quick to quote verses such as Ephesians 4:29, which says, "Let no corrupting talk come out of your mouths, but only such as is good for building up, as fits the occasion, that it may give grace to those who hear," and also Ephesians 5:4, which says, "Let there be no filthiness nor foolish talk nor crude joking, which are out of place, but instead let there be thanksgiving."

However, they tend to be worldly in their definition of what qualifies for these categories. They rarely allow the Scriptures to define appropriate speech but rather import politically correct and/or Victorian worldly definitions of nicety. To do so they often quote verses such as Galatians 5:13–14, which says, "For you were called to freedom, brothers. Only do not use your freedom as an opportunity for the flesh, but through love serve one another. For the whole law is fulfilled in one word: 'You shall love your neighbor as yourself.'" What they conveniently overlook is that this is written by the same guy who said religion is like a steaming pile that the neighbor's dog leaves in your yard. Furthermore, his words that precede this amazing love statement are: "I wish those who unsettle you would emasculate themselves!"[9]

Indeed, we are to be "kind to one another,"[10] which means that Christians should be kind to other Christians, but apparently if someone wants to say that we need Jesus plus something else for our justification (e.g., circumcision for the Judaizers in Galatia) then we should also mock them and ask them to cut their whole pickle off and attend Bobbitt Bible Church as a sign of true varsity religious devotion.

Paul's ability to connect his mocking invitation to self-emasculation with love may be what Peter meant when he said that some of Paul's writings are "hard to understand."[11] Thus, our speech should be not only gracious but also salty, as Colossians 4:6 says: "Let your speech always be gracious, seasoned with salt, so that you may know how you ought to answer each person." We will examine just a few salty sections of the New Testament so we can spend more time studying stand-up Jesus.

In Acts 12:12–17 we read that Peter was locked out of a church prayer

---

[9]Gal. 5:12.
[10]Eph. 4:32.
[11]2 Pet. 3:16.

meeting. Likewise, Revelation 3:20 gives a funny picture of Jesus being locked out of a church potluck and pounding on the door, saying, "Behold, I stand at the door and knock. If anyone hears my voice and opens the door, I will come in to him and eat with him, and he with me."

Also, in Luke 24:18, after Jesus' resurrection, there is a hilarious discussion between Jesus and some guys as they walked together on the road. As if Jesus were stupid and did not watch the news, they asked him about himself, and a guy named Cleopas asked Jesus, "Are you the only visitor to Jerusalem who does not know the things that have happened there in these days?" The subtle irony is worth at least a smirk.

HUMOR AND JESUS

In the closing line of his classic book *Orthodoxy*, G. K. Chesterton speaks of Jesus' lack of humor: "There was some one thing that was too great for God to show us when He walked upon our earth; and I have sometimes fancied that it was His mirth."[11] According to Chesterton, Jesus was probably not funny.

But Jesus was funny. This fact is perhaps the most overlooked aspect of Jesus' entire earthly ministry.

Our inability to see Jesus as funny is not rooted in the pages of Scripture, but rather in the way Jesus has been portrayed in many popular films. In 1927 the legendary director and devout Christian Cecil B. DeMille produced the life of Jesus in the movie *King of Kings*. He was very careful to portray Jesus as very pious with little humanity; he even had a glowing aura around him, which made him appear like something of an icon on the screen. He was without humor and appeared as a very serious holy man.

The Library of Congress holds more books about Jesus (seventeen thousand) than about any other historical figure, roughly twice as many as about Shakespeare, the runner-up.[12] One University of Chicago scholar has estimated that more has been written about Jesus in the last twenty years than in the previous nineteen centuries combined.[13] Yet I have found only one book that examines Jesus' humor, Elton Trueblood's *The Humor of Christ*, published in 1964. Trueblood says:

There are numerous passages . . . which are practically incomprehensible when regarded as sober prose, but which are luminous once we become liberated from the gratuitous assumption that Christ never joked. . . . Once we realize that Christ was not always engaged in pious talk, we have made an enormous step on the road to understanding."[14]

Trueblood goes on to say, "Christ laughed, and . . . He expected others to laugh. . . . A misguided piety has made us fear that acceptance of His obvious wit and humor would somehow be mildly blasphemous or sacrilegious. Religion, we think, is serious business, and serious business is incompatible with banter."[15] Other scholars say, "If there is a single person within the pages of the Bible that we can consider to be a humorist, it is without a doubt Jesus. . . . Jesus was a master of wordplay, irony, and satire, often with an element of humor intermixed."[16] In the appendix of *The Humor of Christ*, Trueblood lists thirty humorous passages of Jesus in the synoptic Gospels alone (Matthew, Mark, and Luke).[17]

There are at least three reasons why modern Bible readers and hearers are remiss in capturing Jesus' sense of humor. First, many people are so familiar with some Bible texts that they wrongly assume they know what the texts mean and are not able to hear them in a fresh manner. Second, because the death of Jesus is the centerpiece of our theology, it has in some ways so dominated our thinking about Jesus that his life prior to his death is seen as little more than one of avoiding sin and being an acceptable sacrifice, which means that his humor and fun are overlooked. But the fact that Jesus was often invited to parties because people liked him, crowds thronged around him, and his fiercest critics falsely accused him of being nothing but a party animal suggests he was fun to hang with.[12] After all, how many people who are as lost as Dick Cheney in the woods keep asking your pastor over to their Texas hold 'em tournaments?

Third, being removed from Jesus by two thousand years means that some of those ancient cultural clues and euphemisms are lost on us. The cultural framework required for humor was made obvious to me while in India, because every time I turned on the television and watched an Indian show I could not figure out for the life of me what

---

[12]Luke 5:33; 7:31–35.

the jokes meant. Nonetheless, it is important to note some of Jesus' ancient funnies.

Jesus said that Christians who don't evangelize are as helpful as a house fire: "Is a lamp brought in to be put under a basket, or under a bed, and not on a stand?"[13] Perhaps his most hilarious funny is Matthew 19:24: "It is easier for a camel to go through the eye of a needle than for a rich person to enter the kingdom of God." In trying to figure out what Jesus was talking about, more than a few Bible commentators have done origami to that section of Scripture. Possibly the most common explanation is that there was some hole in some wall in some town that a camel could pass through only by lying on its gut and shimmying through like a Marine crawling in boot-camp training, and some people called that place "the eye of the needle." Or Jesus was telling a joke, and the guys in suits missed the punch line.

Scholars in the area of humor say, "The most characteristic form of Jesus' humor was the preposterous exaggeration."[18] The whole idea of a camel being threaded through a needle like a line of thread was an ancient funny where he exaggerated to make a point. Likewise, the guy who says he's so hungry he could eat a horse does not intend to masticate an entire horse—hooves, tail, and all.

Another example of Jesus using preposterous exaggeration is found in Matthew 7:3, which says, "Why do you see the speck that is in your brother's eye, but do not notice the log that is in your own eye?" This Hebrew funny probably got the most laughs on the job site with the framing crew who knew the difference between a two-by-four and a speck of sawdust that blows off a table saw.

For yet another example of Jesus' preposterous exaggeration, we can consider his encounter with Peter in Matthew 16:13–20. There, Jesus nicknamed Cephas after the WWE wrestler, calling him Peter, which means "the rock," just before Peter proved he was merely a pebble by rebuking Jesus, and Jesus calling him Satan, or at least Satan's wingman.[14] While calling Peter "the rock" is funny, not funny is the fact that the Catholic Church, in which I was raised and served as an altar boy, missed the punch line, and rather than having a good laugh, ended up with the papacy and a guy with a really big hat.

[13]Mark 4:21.
[14]Matt. 16:21–23.

Jesus and the Pharisees

Jesus' most stinging humor, however, was reserved for the religious types, especially the Pharisees. Jesus called them a bag of snakes[15] and said that their moms had shagged the Devil.[16] While those who suffered under the judgmentalism of these religious types likely had more than a few good laughs when Jesus lampooned them, the Pharisees, of course, did not think it was funny, because apart from repentance sinners are no fun at all.

Despite the fact that the Pharisees were a devoutly religious group, like many cults and religions in our day, Jesus actually made fun of how they did religion. While it will likely shock our sensibilities, which have been refined by postmodern pluralism, Jesus made fun of how they prayed, saying, "And when you pray, you must not be like the hypocrites. For they love to stand and pray in the synagogues and at the street corners, that they may be seen by others."[17]

He also made fun of how they fasted: "And when you fast, do not look gloomy like the hypocrites, for they disfigure their faces that their fasting may be seen by others."[18] Jesus made fun of how they tithed, declaring, "Woe to you, scribes and Pharisees, hypocrites! For you tithe mint and dill and cumin, and have neglected the weightier matters of the law: justice and mercy and faithfulness. These you ought to have done, without neglecting the others."[19] To summarize, Jesus made fun of decent Republican, church-going, tax-paying heterosexual guys for praying wrong, sucking in their faces when they fasted as if they were supermodels, tithing out of their spice racks, and being blind tour guides to hell.

The Pharisees failed to see that they were a joke (and often so do their religious offspring and self-righteous folks in general). Rather than repenting, they fought to defend themselves against Jesus' stinging comedic barbs. In one ironic encounter, they neglect the fact that he is God who has come into their midst, and rather than humbly learning from him, they take the opportunity to rebuke Jesus for not washing his

---

[15]Matt. 23:33.
[16]John 8:44.
[17]Matt. 6:5.
[18]Matt. 6:16.
[19]Matt. 23:23.

hands before dinner, like Miss Manners requires.[20] Sure they are going to hell, but at least it's with clean hands.

Lastly, in Matthew 15:10–14 we read:

> And he called the people to him and said to them, "Hear and understand: it is not what goes into the mouth that defiles a person, but what comes out of the mouth; this defiles a person." Then the disciples came and said to him, "Do you know that the Pharisees were *offended* when they heard this saying?" He answered, "Every plant that my heavenly Father has not planted will be rooted up. Let them alone; they are blind guides. And if the blind lead the blind, both will fall into a pit."

Jesus and Offense

Indeed, not only does the Bible say that we are to love people, but that love is not rude. In our postmodern age of nicety, the only real sin anymore seems to be hurting people's feelings. Never mind if they are homosexual bishops or emergent pastors who finger-paint their doctrinal statements and deny penal substitutionary atonement because some Buddhist deacon, who can put his ankle behind his head for prayer, is an avowed pacifist, as if love is defined by movies made for junior-high girls and greeting cards rather than by Jesus. When the disciples came to Jesus and said, "Do you know that the Pharisees were *offended*?" how did Jesus respond? Knowing their hardened, stubborn, rebellious, religious hearts of unrepentance, Jesus was not ready to schedule a meeting, apologize profusely, blog about his error, or spend the next decade listening to Elton John records alone in the dark, weeping bitterly because he could not shake the horror of hurting someone's feelings.

In the end, Jesus was murdered. This was because he offended a lot of people. Many of them were most offended because they were the butt of his jokes. However, as Jesus says, "Blessed is the one who is not offended by me."[21] Since we are all goofy sinners whose self-righteousness is a joke, the only way not to be offended by Jesus and to laugh at ourselves is to live a life of continual repentance.

---

[20]Luke 11:37–41.
[21]Matt. 11:6.

The best place for this kind of loving prophetic humor is the pulpit. Regarding humor's place in church services, John Frame has said:

> Some may think that humor necessarily trivializes worship. But that is not true, for there is humor in Scripture, for example in Genesis 18:13–15; 21:6–7; Proverbs 26:15; Isaiah 44:12–20; Matthew 19:24; 23:24; and Acts 12:1–19. God laughs at the wicked in Psalm 2:7. Humor has a positive theological purpose: it enables us to see ourselves from God's perspective; it knocks us down a peg or two. It shows the ridiculous discrepancy between God's greatness and our pretensions. As such, the emotion arising from humor can pass very quickly into a deep sorrow for sin and a craving for God's grace. Humor can also express joy in the Lord and the "hilarious" cheer (2 Cor. 9:7 in the Greek) by which God's Spirit frees us from selfishness to serve our brothers and sisters. Humor can also establish a bond between leader and people, reassuring them that he is one of them. Thus, it can strengthen the horizontal side of worship, the unity of the body of Christ.[19]

Therefore, humor is, in fact, biblical, but is it helpful? This is necessary to address, because some people argue that while humor is permissible, it is not helpful.

TEN WAYS HUMOR IS HELPFUL

Humor is incredibly helpful to the gospel, in general, and to my ministry, in particular. Historically, humor has been a great gospel weapon. One of my heroes, the renowned Reformed Baptist preacher Charles Haddon Spurgeon, said:

> I do not know why ridicule is to be given up to Satan as a weapon to be used against us, and not to be employed by us as a weapon against him. I will venture to affirm that the Reformation owed almost as much to the sense of the ridiculous in human nature as to anything else, and that those humorous squibs and caricatures, that were issued by the friends of Luther, did more to open the eyes of Germany to the abominations of the priesthood than the more solid and ponderous arguments against Romanism.... "It [humor] is a dangerous weapon," it will be said, "and many men will cut their fingers with it." Well, that is their own look-out; but I do not know why we should be so particular about their cutting their fingers if they can, at the

same time, cut the throat of sin, and do serious damage to the great adversary of souls.[20]

After pondering the benefits of humor for the cause of the gospel of Jesus Christ, I have uncovered ten reasons why I believe it is beneficial.

1) Jesus Christ laughed, and Christians are supposed to be like Jesus and thus laugh. Trueblood wrote:

> The widespread failure to recognize and to appreciate the humor of Christ is one of the most amazing aspects of the era named for Him. Anyone who reads the Synoptic Gospels [Matthew, Mark, and Luke] with a relative freedom from presuppositions might be expected to see that Christ laughed, and that He expected others to laugh, but our capacity to miss this aspect of His life is phenomenal.[21]

2) Religion is the great enemy of the gospel because it seeks to replace the gifted righteousness of Jesus Christ with some other human work. Therefore, poking fun at the silliness of religious people and their sources of sinful self-righteousness serves both them and others who are prone to follow in their example. Such humor is arresting and difficult to ignore.

3) Too many people take themselves too seriously and God too lightly. Subsequently, like those who rebuked Jesus for not washing his hands but had no problem murdering him, and the homosexual pastors who are more offended by rock worship music in church than their sodomy, the far too serious among us need to be made fun of as a prophetic gift of being awakened from slumber.

4) Nearly everyone makes fun of other people, though not often in public as preachers do. Instead, they post anonymously on blogs and Web sites, send nasty anonymous letters to their church, and gossip behind people's backs so that they can continue to present a holy face in public. Yet, by suffering the blows of sharp comedic criticism, those who make fun of others are often tenderized, becoming more compassionate toward people they would otherwise speak ill to or of.

5) Some things are a joke, and to treat them seriously would be a sin, but turning them into a joke keeps them from being legitimized. For example, anyone who takes seriously a religion with its roots in Utah (Mormonism) or Pittsburgh (Jehovah's Witness) is doing a disservice and wasting a lot of comedic material. Likewise, anyone who thinks the earth created itself, forni-

cating single people who think that God sees their hearts but not their pants and thereby blesses them, and every pothead who knows only two verses (that every seed-bearing plant the Lord God gave is good and, of course, thou shall not judge) are better served by a punch line than a syllogism.

6) When all else fails, and the feces and fan have interfaced, all you can do is laugh it off. On this point, Proverbs 14:13 says, "Even in laughter the heart may ache, and the end of joy may be grief." Life in a sinfully crooked, fallen, jacked-up world is incredibly painful and filled with overwhelming heartache and pain, especially for pastors, who arguably deal with it more than anyone. Sometimes the only way to keep from putting a gun in your mouth while mumbling Lamentations is to find something funny in it all and laugh through your tears.

7) Nehemiah 8:10 says, "The joy of the LORD is your strength." Too many Christians are spiritually weak and sickly, but their souls would be built strong through regular, deep belly laughs just as much as an athlete sculpts his physical body by pumping iron at the gym. Furthermore, it is cheaper and more fun than antidepressants.

8) Cultivating your sense of humor heightens all your other emotions. The person who can laugh deeply is passionate enough to also weep deeply. Those who bottle up their emotions in a Spock-like existence display little if any of the characteristics of their passionate God, who both laughs and weeps, as Scripture says. Scripture also commands us to "rejoice with those who rejoice, weep with those who weep."[22]

9) Laughter is sometimes an act of faith, in that it enables us to rise above the pain of the present while we await the coming kingdom, where there are no tears.

10) Humor is a missiological ministry tool that is necessary for successful evangelism in our culture. In 1 Corinthians 9:22–23 Paul writes, "To the weak I became weak, that I might win the weak. I have become all things to all people, that by all means I might save some. I do it all for the sake of the gospel, that I may share with them in its blessings." The average person listens to talk radio comedic banter on the way to work, downloads funny YouTube videos during break, listens to more drive-time radio banter on the commute home, watches a sitcom after dinner, possibly tunes in to a stand-up comic on Comedy Central, and watches someone like Jay Leno, Jon Stewart, Stephen Colbert, or David Letterman before dozing off. To

---

[22]Rom. 12:15.

reach people, we need to speak their language, and their language obviously includes comedy.

Humor can be evangelistic. In fact, our church has been named one of the fastest growing in America. We started it in 1996, when it was roughly the same size as a Mormon family, and our little church has grown in one of America's least churched cities by reaching mainly young, hip, urban types from the various groups that I regularly make fun of. I cannot explain this phenomenon other than to say it's like punching a guy, who then goes to get two friends so that you can punch them too.

In conclusion, I will lay down some rules of engagement for aspiring sanctified comedians. With these rules I hope to keep at bay the wing nuts who see comedy in the Bible and assume that it endorses their cruel version.

TEN COMMANDMENTS FOR SANCTIFYING COMEDY

1) Don't mock God. God is great. God is not a sinner. God is not to be judged by us. God is God. Further, God has a long history of getting the last laugh. So don't mock God. However, one exception is to mock the false impressions of God that religious people have, showing that their god is not the God. So, for example, if you mock the false Jesus of Mormonism, who is a created being, polygamist, and the half-brother of Lucifer, you are mocking what Paul calls "another Jesus" and not the real Jesus.[23]

2) Don't mock everyone. If you mock your spouse, children, or your own mom, you are a dolt and not funny no matter how many people laugh. Furthermore, don't mock rape victims, abused children, battered women, and the like, because the point of prophetic irony is to bring sinners to repentance, not to bring victims to tears.

3) Don't mock all the time. Only some of the Bible is funny, which means that most of our speech should be serious and that some of our speech should be humorous. In that vein, the majority of my sermons are not funny but, rather, straightforward Bible teaching. Since my sermons last an hour or more, though, I do throw in a few laughs to keep folks with me and to break up the monotony. I don't remember telling any jokes at all during some sermon series because I did not think the content called for humor. While preaching a twelve-week series called "Christ on the Cross" about the murder

---

[23]2 Cor. 11:4.

of Jesus, I don't remember telling a single joke, and the book I wrote on the same subject[22] contains no humor at all.

4) Don't judge yourself by yourself because Paul says that is foolish, no matter how funny you think you are. If someone in authority over you (e.g., boss, parent, pastor) tells you that you have crossed the line and need to apologize and grow up, then repent before you become the joke.

5) Don't worry about getting tempered as you age. With age comes wisdom, if you are perceptive and humble enough to learn from your experiences. Therefore, as you age, you should do so graciously by becoming tempered, though not neutered.

6) Don't keep picking on the same group of people. It is important to expand your comedic horizons and mock lots of groups of people for their self-righteousness. If you keep picking on the same group, eventually people will call you hateful, but if you pick on lots of groups, they will thankfully downgrade you to cruel or, if you are really blessed, maybe just to mean. For the newbies, it is often easiest to start with vegans, homeschoolers, rednecks, NASCAR fans, and any Christian who thinks *Left Behind* is really going to happen any minute.

7) Don't assume you know where the line is. The problem with comedy is that the line is different for everyone, and the line changes from one culture and subculture to the next. So remain teachable and flexible. I once preached a sermon from Philippians 2 on humility and confessed my sin of pride, but one guy let me know he did not think I was genuine because I was wearing a T-shirt with a picture of deejay Jesus spinning turntables. While pride apparently does not trouble this guy, he has chosen to draw a clear line at kitschy Christian T-shirts from Urban Outfitters. The painful truth is that you generally find the line of propriety only by crossing it, and when you do, make sure to apologize and repent.

8) Don't forget to laugh at yourself—often. The best material is the stuff of your own life. You know better than anyone that you are a nut job, so do not waste such precious comedic fodder. Tell stories about yourself, pointing out your imperfections, folly, stupidity, pettiness, self-righteousness, and the like before you turn your funny guns on anyone. By doing so you will reveal that your humor is not scorn but, rather, the acknowledgment of a common mess we are all in as sinners. In the end, we are all hypocrites and good for a laugh. By laughing together at one another and ourselves, we are experiencing biblical fellowship and celebrating gift-righteousness from Jesus; his gift removes

our pride and vain attempts at self-righteousness, which in the end make us deadly serious defenders of our goodness, as if we had any. In short, we are all Pharisees to varying degrees.

9) Make sure you know whom to mock. Psalm 1 does not look favorably at the unrighteous who mock the righteous. Mockery in and of itself is not a sin, but you have to make sure you know whom to mock and why.

10) Don't overlook the importance of discernment in deciding when, where, and how to use prophetic humor. Proverbs 26:4–5 advises, "Answer not a fool according to his folly, lest you be like him yourself. Answer a fool according to his folly, lest he be wise in his own eyes." What appears at first glance to be a contradiction or a goofy Zen saying from a Kung Fu movie or fortune cookie is actually a call to discernment. When a fool is hardhearted, to engage him is to end up descending to his level and becoming a fool who blurts out folly in angry defense. In this case, the art of ignoring him is the best course of action. However, when a fool keeps boasting that he has conquered you and starts heralding his victory to other fools, the best thing to do is take him down a few notches in Jesus' name.

IN DEFENSE OF HUMOR

To those who have been offended by my comedic banter, I would simply ask why. If it is because I have sinned, then I ask your forgiveness. But if it is because I have hit a nerve of sin or self-righteousness, then I would welcome you to repent and have a good laugh with me.

For my critics, as well as others who make it their job to criticize their preacher, as if we preach from a stage so that you can get better aim, I would ask you if you love your preacher, pray for your preacher, and seek to learn from your preacher. Or are you one of those miserable people who expend their energy criticizing from the pew, like the fans at a sporting event who scream at the athletes from, of course, a safe distance, because being an armchair quarterback is far easier than actually carrying the ball? For you, I close with the words of my dear friend, the now departed and no longer chewed-upon-by-the-critic dogs that encircled him, Charles Haddon Spurgeon. In an obscure little book he wrote defending manly oddball preachers with personality quirks, scathing humor, and unbridled passion over effeminate preachers and preachers as "dry as sawdust," he said:

Many hearers lose much blessing through criticizing too much, and meditating too little; and many more incur great sin by calumniating those who live for the good of others. True pastors have enough of care and travail without being burdened by undeserved and useless fault-finding. We have something better to do than to be for ever answering every malignant or frivolous slander which is set afloat to injure us.... There are tender, loving spirits who feel the trial very keenly, and are sadly hindered in brave service by cruel assaults. The rougher and stronger among us laugh at those who ridicule us, but upon others the effect is very sorrowful....

As ministers we are very far from being perfect, but many of us are doing our best, and we are grieved that the minds of our people should be more directed to our personal imperfections than to our divine message....

Filled with the same spirit of contrariety, the men of this world still depreciate the ministers whom God sends them and profess that they would gladly listen if different preachers could be found. Nothing can please them, their cavils are dealt out with heedless universality. Cephas is too blunt, Apollos is too flowery, Paul is too argumentative, Timothy is too young, James is too severe, John is too gentle....

Well then, let each servant of God tell his message in his own way. To his own Master he shall stand or fall.... Judge the preacher if you like, but do remember that there is something better to be done than that, namely, to get all the good you can out of him, and pray his Master to put more good into him.[23]

QUESTION 7: **PREDESTINATION**

Why does an all-loving, all-knowing, and all-sovereign God will into creation people he foreknows will suffer eternal condemnation—and the Romans 9:20 answer seems like a cop-out!

This question arises from a very practical reality: some people turn from sin to Jesus for eternal salvation while others remain in sin away from Jesus for eternal damnation.

Why?

One clue in Scripture is the frequent use of words that, in their Old Testament context, indicate God chooses some people to be saved, such as *plan*,[1] *purpose*,[2] and *choose*.[3] Likewise, the New Testament uses a constellation of words, such as *predestine*,[4] *elect*,[5] *choose*,[6] and *appointed*,[7] to speak of God's choosing to save some people but not all people.

The question that logically follows is: Why are some people saved by God and not others? Is it because they do not choose God, or because God did not choose them?

This leads to the topic of predestination. By *predestination* we are asking, is a person's eternal destiny chosen by God before their birth? Does God predestine people to heaven? Does God predestine people to hell? Theologian Millard Erickson clarifies the applicable theological terms: "'Predestination' refers to God's choice of individuals for eternal

[1]Jer. 49:20; 50:45; Mic. 4:12.
[2]Isa. 14:24, 26–27; 19:12; 23:9.
[3]Num. 16:5, 7; Deut. 4:37, 10:15; Isa. 41:8; Ezek. 20:5.
[4]Rom. 8:29–30; Eph. 1:5, 11.
[5]Matt. 24:22; Rom. 8:33; Col. 3:12.
[6]1 Cor. 1:27; Eph. 1:4; 2 Thess. 2:13.
[7]Acts 13:48.

life or eternal death. 'Election' is the selection of some for eternal life, the positive side of predestination."[1]

TWO POSITIONS

In studying church history we see that there are, generally speaking, two broad categories into which various answers to these questions fall. *Synergism* is the belief that, in varying degrees depending upon who is advocating this position, God and man work together in the process of justification. Conversely, *monergism* is the belief that God alone works for our justification, and we play no part whatsoever in our salvation.

Isaiah writes about salvation and asks, "To whom has the arm of the LORD been revealed?"[8] Building on this analogy of God's arm, for the purposes of this chapter I will call the synergist position "two-handed," in which the imagery is of God reaching down to a sinner and a sinner reaching up to take God's hand and be saved. I will refer to the monergistic position as "one-handed," in which the imagery is of God reaching down to pluck a sinner from death without that person simultaneously reaching back to join God in his saving efforts.

It is important to note that both teams, generally speaking, believe that God is the one who initiates with sinners. In fact, this is the biblical pattern from the garden of Eden forward, when our first parents hid from God after their first sin, and God took the initiative to pursue them. This same concept of God's initiation is echoed throughout Scripture in places such as 1 John 4:19, which says, "We love because he first loved us," and Philippians 1:6, which says, "And I am sure of this, that he who began a good work in you will bring it to completion at the day of Jesus Christ."

THE HISTORY OF THE TWO POSITIONS

Two-handed Origen (AD 185–254) and John Chrysostom (AD 347–407) said that God does not predestine us, but rather God foreknows who will choose him of their own free will, so in essence God chooses those who choose him.

Pelagius (AD 354–420/440) said that God does not predestine us, but we simply choose God. His position was one-handed, without God's involvement at all; in other words, people basically save them-

---

[8]Isa. 53:1.

selves. He was condemned as a heretic for also saying that people are born sinless and pure like Adam and can simply choose God and a life of holiness.

One-handed Augustine (AD 354–430) was the leading opponent of Pelagius and was originally a synergist until later recanting his position and becoming a monergist. He then went on to teach, with great influence that continues to this day, the doctrine of single predestination. This means that everyone is a sinner by nature and choice and therefore fully deserves nothing more than conscious eternal torment in hell; nevertheless, in pure grace, some wholly undeserving sinners are predestined for heaven and saved by Jesus Christ. Meanwhile, those who are not predestined to salvation experience the natural course of sin, which leads to death and hell. Augustine taught that everyone is going to hell except for the predestined elect and that God does not predestine people to hell, but, rather, only predestines some people to heaven. Augustine's position was in effect a very positive celebration of the saving work of a gracious God who worked through Jesus Christ for the good of the elect as it focused on those who are saved, while not seeking to provide any definitive reason apart from sin for those who are eternally damned.

One-handed Gottschalk (also known as Godescalc) of Orbais (AD 804–869) was a Benedictine monk and one of the most influential proponents of double predestination in the history of Christian theology. Gottschalk was a student of Augustine's writings and went beyond his master's teaching to promote not only the singular predestination of the elect to heaven, but also the double predestination of the non-elect to hell. Practically, his position was that God creates some people for hell and some for heaven. He was condemned as a heretic at the Council of Quierzy in 853 on charges that he declared God was the author of human sin; he died without recanting while imprisoned in a monastery.

One-handed John Calvin (AD 1509–1564) was influenced by the writings of both Augustine and Gottschalk and did teach the concept of double predestination. It deserves mentioning, however, that Calvin did not stress the doctrine of predestination in such writings as *The Institutes* as much as Luther and later Calvinists did. Furthermore, for him the doctrine of predestination was used primarily as a pastoral answer to the question of why some people trust in Jesus for salvation while others do not. Admittedly, his teaching was quite controversial;

some of his opponents even named their dogs "Calvin" in mockery. Nonetheless, Calvin wrote of the doctrine in his will: "I have no other hope or refuge than His predestination upon which my entire salvation is grounded."[2]

Two-handed James Arminius (AD 1560–1609) commended the writings of John Calvin but deviated greatly in his understanding of election and predestination. He taught that election was a corporate, not individual, concept in Scripture, according to the Old Testament precedent that Israel was the elect people of God. Furthermore, he taught that God has not predestined people to salvation but, rather, predestined the conditions of repentance of sin and faith in Jesus as the grounds for joining the elect.

My Dad

Prevenient Grace

Two-handed John Wesley (AD 1703–1791), the founder of Methodism, popularized the teachings of James Arminius. He echoed much of Arminius's teaching, especially the concept of prevenient grace, or first grace. According to Wesley, *prevenient grace* is a grace that God gives to open up the will of a sinner so that everyone has the opportunity to freely choose or not choose to trust in Jesus Christ for salvation.[3] This concept was an attempt to defend human freedom of the will without denying the pervasive effects of sin on the human condition.

Theologian Henry Thiessen defined *prevenient grace* thus: "Since mankind is hopelessly dead in trespasses and sins and can do nothing to obtain salvation, God graciously restores to all men sufficient ability to make a choice in the matter of submission to Him. This is the salvation-bringing grace of God that has appeared to all men."[4] Theologian Sam Storms qualifies the concept of prevenient grace: "This grace, however, is not irresistible. Whereas all are recipients of prevenient grace, many resist it, to their eternal demise. Those who utilize this grace to respond in faith to the gospel are saved."[5] Theologian Bruce Demarest summarizes: "Arminians maintain that 'prevenient grace,' a benefit that flows from Christ's death on the cross, neutralizes human depravity and restores to pre-Christians everywhere the ability to heed God's general call to salvation."[6]

The doctrine of prevenient grace has been very controversial because it has little, and arguably no, biblical basis. Furthermore, it assumes that a person can simply exercise faith, when the Bible says not only is salvation a gift from God, but also even the faith to believe in Jesus is a gift of God's grace.[9] Likewise, repentance is spoken of as a gift of God's grace and not the means by which we access it.[10] For these and other reasons, theologian Millard Erickson has rightly said regarding prevenient grace, "The theory, appealing though it is in many ways, simply is not taught explicitly in the Bible."[7]

Much more could be said about the various theologians who have sought to illuminate the doctrine of predestination. For the sake of brevity, though, I will leave this as a simple introduction to the matter. Before proceeding, however, it is helpful to note that both two-handed synergists and one-handed monergists reject Pelagianism, which I will not waste any time on because it was rightly condemned as heresy in the past despite its popularity in some circles today.

TWO SCHOOLS

There are now, broadly speaking, two general Christian schools of thought regarding salvation in general and predestination in particular. These schools follow the teachings of John Calvin and James Arminius. They are called Reformed, or Calvinist, and Arminian, respectively. Arminians can trace their modern history to a theological council that met in 1610. It was called the Remonstrance, which means "protest." They were protesting the Calvinistic position on such doctrines as predestination with what is known as the Five Points of Arminianism, which stressed the freedom of the human will in salvation.

In response, the Calvinist theologians met some 154 times at the Synod of Dort (1618–1619) to consider the Five Points of Arminianism. They responded with the Five Points of Calvinism, which stressed the sovereign choice of God in human salvation. As an aside, regarding the timing of predestination, the Calvinists differed in that some considered God's election to have occurred after the fall in response to human sin (called *infralapsarianism*), while others saw God's election to have occurred before creation and the fall (called *supralapsarianism*). Nonetheless, all Reformed confessions of faith include election (and the Canons of Dort do so in the greatest detail).

---

[9]Acts 5:31; 11:18; Eph. 2:8–10; Phil. 1:29; 2 Tim. 2:24–26; 2 Pet. 1:1.
[10]Acts 5:31; 11:18; 2 Tim. 2:24–26.

Chart 7.1

Five Points of Arminianism	Five Points of Calvinism
1) Free Will	1) Total Depravity
2) Conditional Election	2) Unconditional Election
3) Universal Atonement	3) Limited Atonement
4) Resistible Grace	4) Irresistible Grace
5) Perseverance of Some Saints	5) Perseverance of All Saints

Admittedly, both the Arminian and the Calvinistic camps are very broad and include many nuanced positions that I am unable to fully explore in one chapter. Furthermore, while there are extremists on both teams, including Absurd Arminians and Cruel Calvinists, generally speaking, the two teams hold much in common, such as belief in the Bible; human sinfulness; the death, burial, and resurrection of Jesus alone for salvation; the need for personal faith in Jesus to be saved; and eternality of both heaven and hell. Godly servants of Jesus have been associated with both teams.

Those in the Arminian camp include John Wesley (the founder of Methodism and a great influence on the Nazarenes), Free Will Baptists, and many Charismatic and Pentecostal Christian networks and denominations, such as Foursquare. Popular modern-day Arminian preachers include Chuck Smith and Greg Laurie of the Calvary Chapel movement, Jack Hayford, and Erwin McManus.

Those in the Calvinistic camp, characterized by Reformed theology, include faithful departed servants of Jesus such as Martin Luther, Jonathan Edwards, and Charles Spurgeon, along with the Puritans. Popular modern-day Calvinistic preachers include John Piper, John MacArthur, R. C. Sproul, and Tim Keller, and networks and denominations such as Acts 29, Sovereign Grace, Presbyterians, Reformed Baptists, and some dispensationalists and progressive dispensationalists.

Every Christian must use both proverbial hands to be a good theologian. In a closed hand we must put nonnegotiable doctrines, over which we must fight to preserve what it means to be a Christian. These truths include the perfection and trustworthiness of the Bible; God as Trinitarian creator and redeemer; human sinfulness; Jesus' sinless life, death, burial, and resurrection in our place for our sins alone; and salvation by grace through faith in Jesus alone.

Conversely, in our open hand we must hold more loosely and graciously those doctrines that are important but secondary, in that godly, Bible-believing, Jesus-loving Christians who have prayed and studied fervently disagree over them. These include such things as mode of baptism, exercise of some spiritual gifts, style of worship music, and mode of church government. The closed-handed issues are important for the *being* of the Christian faith, whereas the open-handed issues are important for the *well-being* of the Christian faith. It is important to determine the hand in which we should put the issue of predestination.

As we examine this controversial issue, it is my hope to do so in a way that is gracious and loving, because the Bible is incredibly clear that we must conduct ourselves graciously and lovingly. Before we begin, in the name of fairness I must declare that I am, generally speaking, a Reformed Augustinian with enough respect for John Calvin and Martin Luther to have named my second son Calvin Martin. Therefore, I do not come to this discussion without opinions, but I do not limit my scope of fellowship to others with my personal beliefs. I enjoy many great friendships with Arminian brothers and sisters from whom I learn a great deal and with whom I partner for the sake of the gospel so that as many people as possible would meet the Jesus whom we love for saving us from our sin. Having now established a historical framework, we will more fully explore the issue biblically, since that is what really matters in the end.

WHAT DOES SCRIPTURE SAY?[8]

The Arminian View

To begin with, I will share some of the classic Scripture texts Arminians use to support their position. Since these texts are found in God's holy Word, they must be considered from all viewpoints. Each shows God's love for lost sinners and his earnest desire that sinners would repent and trust in Jesus Christ.

> Say to them, As I live, declares the Lord GOD, I have no pleasure in the death of the wicked, but that the wicked turn from his way and live; turn back, turn back from your evil ways, for why will you die, O house of Israel?[11]

---

[11]Ezek. 33:11.

This is good, and it is pleasing in the sight of God our Savior, who desires all people to be saved and to come to the knowledge of the truth.[12]

The Lord is not slow to fulfill his promise as some count slowness, but is patient toward you, not wishing that any should perish, but that all should reach repentance.[13]

For God so loved the world, that he gave his only Son, that whoever believes in him should not perish but have eternal life. For God did not send his Son into the world to condemn the world, but in order that the world might be saved through him.[14]

At face value, these Scriptures seem to clearly indicate that God does not delight in the death of unrepentant, hell-bound sinners, does desire that everyone would turn from sin to Jesus, is patient so as to give people ample opportunity to be saved, and loves every sinner. As one would expect, Calvinists interpret these verses in ways that differ from the Arminian interpretation. For example, Calvinists say that "all" refers to all the elect and not to all people, and that "world" does not mean "all people" but rather "people from all nations." However, for the purposes of our discussion I will simply leave the verses on their own and accept the straightforward meaning of a simple reading of the verses, as Arminians do.

Furthermore, the Bible is clear that the good news of Jesus' person and work is to be proclaimed to anyone and everyone with a pleading call for people to turn from sin and trust in Jesus for salvation:

> Come, everyone who thirsts,
>   come to the waters;
> and he who has no money,
>   come, buy and eat!
> Come, buy wine and milk
>   without money and without price.[15]

Come to me [Jesus], all who labor and are heavy laden, and I will give you rest.[16]

---

[12]1 Tim. 2:3–4.
[13]2 Pet. 3:9.
[14]John 3:16–17.
[15]Isa. 55:1.
[16]Matt. 11:28.

[handwritten margin note: ISN'T THAT WHAT MAKES SENSE?]

Believe in the Lord Jesus, and you will be saved.[17]

The times of ignorance God overlooked, but now he commands all people everywhere to repent.[18]

The Spirit and the Bride say, "Come." And let the one who hears say, "Come." And let the one who is thirsty come; let the one who desires take the water of life without price.[19]

Despite God's apparent desire for all to be saved, both Arminians and Calvinists agree that not all people are saved and that some people are going to hell. Admittedly, some people called Universalists teach that somehow every person will end up in heaven; others called Annihilationists teach that people will simply cease to exist. While we cannot deal with those erroneous positions here, a simple reading of Jesus' words on the subject are clarifying. He spoke of hell more than anyone else in Scripture and was clear that some people will experience the conscious, eternal torments of hell. Nonetheless, Bible-believing Arminians and Calvinists agree that the Bible plainly states that some sinners reject Jesus as their Savior and are therefore morally responsible for their own sinful rejection of God:

I spread out my hands all the day to a rebellious people, who walk in a way that is not good, following their own devices.[20]

... yet you refuse to come to me that you may have life.[21]

I have come into the world as light, so that whoever believes in me may not remain in darkness. If anyone hears my words and does not keep them, I do not judge him; for I did not come to judge the world but to save the world. The one who rejects me and does not receive my words has a judge; the word that I have spoken will judge him on the last day.[22]

---

[17]Acts 16:31.
[18]Acts 17:30.
[19]Rev. 22:17.
[20]Isa. 65:2.
[21]John 5:40.
[22]John 12:46–48.

You stiff-necked people, uncircumcised in heart and ears, you always resist the Holy Spirit. As your fathers did, so do you.[23]

Or do you presume on the riches of his kindness and forbearance and patience, not knowing that God's kindness is meant to lead you to repentance? But because of your hard and impenitent heart you are storing up wrath for yourself on the day of wrath when God's righteous judgment will be revealed.[24]

But of Israel he says, "All day long I have held out my hands to a disobedient and contrary people."[25]

For if we go on sinning deliberately after receiving the knowledge of the truth, there no longer remains a sacrifice for sins, but a fearful expectation of judgment, and a fury of fire that will consume the adversaries. Anyone who has set aside the law of Moses dies without mercy on the evidence of two or three witnesses. How much worse punishment, do you think, will be deserved by the one who has spurned the Son of God, and has profaned the blood of the covenant by which he was sanctified, and has outraged the Spirit of grace?[26]

And this is the judgment: the light has come into the world, and people loved the darkness rather than the light because their works were evil.[27]

Total Depravity

Furthermore, the Bible teaches that everyone is in the same condition as those who sinfully reject God's offer of salvation through Jesus Christ. Theologically, this means that people are totally depraved. This does not mean that people are utterly depraved, because we could do evil with greater degree and frequency if we were not made with a conscience as God's image bearers and if the restraining power of the Holy Spirit and the rule of such things as governmental law were lifted. Total depravity does mean, however, that we are totally sin-

---

[23]Acts 7:51.
[24]Rom. 2:4–5.
[25]Rom. 10:21.
[26]Heb. 10:26–29.
[27]John 3:19.

ful—our entire person is marred by sin. This includes the mind,[28] the will,[29] the emotions,[30] and the physical body.[31] Subsequently, everyone is a sinner whose inclination is to live for the glory of anyone and anything other than God[32] and is altogether incapable of doing even "good" things for the purpose of pleasing and glorifying God.[33] As the church father Augustine has said, "Man has options, but those options are all sinful in nature. He is free to choose, but merely to engage in one sin rather than another."[9]

The Bible is emphatically clear that our sin is so pervasive that left to ourselves not one person could or would pursue or choose Jesus Christ:

> The LORD saw that the wickedness of man was great in the earth, and that every intention of the thoughts of his heart was only evil continually.[34]

> The intention of man's heart is evil from his youth.[35]

> For there is no one who does not sin.[36]

> Who can say, "I have made my heart pure;
>   I am clean from my sin"?[37]

> Surely there is not a righteous man on earth who does good and never sins.[38]

> The hearts of the children of man are full of evil, and madness is in their hearts while they live, and after that they go to the dead.[39]

> The wicked are estranged from the womb;
>   they go astray from birth, speaking lies.[40]

---

[28]Eph. 4:18.
[29]Rom. 6:16–17.
[30]Titus 3:3.
[31]Rom. 8:10.
[32]Ps. 29:2; Rom. 3:23; 11:36; 16:27.
[33]Matt. 7:17–18; Rom. 8:7–8.
[34]Gen. 6:5.
[35]Gen. 8:21.
[36]2 Chron. 6:36.
[37]Prov. 20:9.
[38]Eccl. 7:20.
[39]Eccl. 9:3.
[40]Ps. 58:3.

All we like sheep have gone astray;
> we have turned—every one—to his own way.[41]

Jesus answered them, "Truly, truly, I say to you, everyone who commits sin is a slave to sin."[42]

Why do you not understand what I say? It is because you cannot bear to hear my word. You are of your father the devil, and your will is to do your father's desires. He was a murderer from the beginning, and has nothing to do with the truth, because there is no truth in him. When he lies, he speaks out of his own character, for he is a liar and the father of lies.[43]

None is righteous, no, not one;
> no one understands;
> no one seeks for God.
All have turned aside; together they have become worthless;
> no one does good,
> not even one.
Their throat is an open grave;
> they use their tongues to deceive.
The venom of asps is under their lips.
> Their mouth is full of curses and bitterness.
Their feet are swift to shed blood;
> in their paths are ruin and misery,
and the way of peace they have not known.
There is no fear of God before their eyes.[44]

You were slaves of sin.[45]

For the mind that is set on the flesh is hostile to God, for it does not submit to God's law; indeed, it cannot.[46]

The natural person does not accept the things of the Spirit of God, for they are folly to him, and he is not able to understand them because they are spiritually discerned.[47]

---

[41]Isa. 53:6.
[42]John 8:34.
[43]John 8:43–44.
[44]Rom. 3:10–18.
[45]Rom. 6:20.
[46]Rom. 8:7.
[47]1 Cor. 2:14.

And you were dead in the trespasses and sins in which you once walked, following the course of this world, following the prince of the power of the air, the spirit that is now at work in the sons of disobedience—among whom we all once lived in the passions of our flesh, carrying out the desires of the body and the mind, and were by nature children of wrath, like the rest of mankind.[48]

Now this I say and testify in the Lord, that you must no longer walk as the Gentiles do, in the futility of their minds. They are darkened in their understanding, alienated from the life of God because of the ignorance that is in them, due to their hardness of heart. They have become callous and have given themselves up to sensuality, greedy to practice every kind of impurity.[49]

For many, of whom I have often told you and now tell you even with tears, walk as enemies of the cross of Christ.[50]

And you, who were dead in your trespasses and the uncircumcision of your flesh . . . [51]

To the pure, all things are pure, but to the defiled and unbelieving, nothing is pure; but both their minds and their consciences are defiled.[52]

We know that we are from God, and the whole world lies in the power of the evil one.[53]

For we ourselves were once foolish, disobedient, led astray, slaves to various passions and pleasures, passing our days in malice and envy, hated by others and hating one another.[54]

Able to Choose?

Clearly, the Bible says that every person without exception turns his or her back on God and is unrighteous, foolish, lost, at war with God, and spiritually dead. Though physically alive, the Bible says that we are not merely sick from sin but spiritually dead in that we are as inclined

---

[48]Eph. 2:1–3.
[49]Eph. 4:17–19.
[50]Phil. 3:18.
[51]Col. 2:13.
[52]Titus 1:15.
[53]1 John 5:19.
[54]Titus 3:3.

toward and capable of seeking God as a dead corpse is inclined and able to run a marathon. As sinners, we are not prone to properly diagnose the depth of our sin; thus, some sinners speak of our condition in less stark terms, as if there is a vestige of goodness in us that can simply choose God of our own free will.

Such a belief is nonsensical for five reasons. First, human beings do make choices for which we are morally responsible before God. This explains why, when we are out for dinner and are handed a menu, we get to order what sounds best to us. Second, our choices regarding God are merely reflections of our hearts, and if our hearts are not for God, then our choices will not be for God. Jesus spoke of this multiple times:

> You will recognize them by their fruits. Are grapes gathered from thornbushes, or figs from thistles? So, every healthy tree bears good fruit, but the diseased tree bears bad fruit. A healthy tree cannot bear bad fruit, nor can a diseased tree bear good fruit.[55]

> Either make the tree good and its fruit good, or make the tree bad and its fruit bad, for the tree is known by its fruit.[56]

> For from within, out of the heart of man, come evil thoughts, sexual immorality, theft, murder, adultery, coveting, wickedness, deceit, sensuality, envy, slander, pride, foolishness. All these evil things come from within, and they defile a person.[57]

Third, Adam and Eve were the only man and woman ever to have had a truly free will in that before they sinned, they did not have a sin nature and were free to choose God and good. Fourth, we truly do not have free will in that we can choose anything we want in life, because only God is free to do as he wills, and we are limited by the choices that are set before us as created beings. For example, we cannot simply choose to be healthy if we are sick, to fly like Peter Pan, or to never taste death, because our will is not free to make such choices. Fifth, as shown in the previous string of Bible verses, we have each chosen to walk away from God, chosen to be unrighteous, chosen spiritual death, chosen to be hostile toward God, and chosen to be enemies of Jesus Christ.

---

[55]Matt. 7:16–18.
[56]Matt. 12:33.
[57]Mark 7:21–23.

In conclusion, our will is truly not free, and even when allowed to choose, it chooses everything and anything but Jesus. As the church father Augustine said, "God does not choose us because we believe, but that we may believe."[10]

By way of analogy, Paul says in Ephesians 2:1 that unrepentant sinners are "dead in the trespasses and sins" and, as such, sinners are akin to Lazarus who was dead and buried and "stinketh," according to the King James Version.[58] Lazarus was not seeking Jesus, reaching out for Jesus, or doing anything, because he was physically dead in the same way that sinners are spiritually dead apart from a work of God. Yet, Jesus came to Lazarus and called him forth to new life physically in the same way he does for us spiritually, and one day he will do so physically—on the day of our bodily resurrection.

Understanding our desperate condition as sinners, the question is not how can a loving God send anyone to hell but, rather, how can a just and holy God allow anyone into heaven? Indeed, apart from divine intervention and an amazing act of saving grace on God's behalf, everyone is utterly doomed and without any hope. Thankfully, God has made a way for sinners who are hostile to him as enemies to be reconciled to him as friends through Jesus Christ. In Romans 5:10 Paul explains this amazing work of redemption by God: "While we were enemies we were reconciled to God by the death of his Son." Indeed, the reconciliation of any sinner to God the Father through God the Son by the power of God the Spirit occurs not when a sinner turns to God offering a hand of friendship but, rather, when he or she is still an enemy at war with God.

The way in which this occurs is further explained in Romans 8:28–10:1. This section of Scripture, along with Ephesians 1:3–11, is regarded by most theologians from most theological traditions to be the most important section of Scripture on the doctrine of predestination.

Romans 8:28–10:1

Paul begins with a description of God's sovereignty as working out all things, even evil and sin, for the glory of his name and the good of his people: "We know that for those who love God all things work together for good, for those who are called according to his purpose."[59] By saying

---

[58]John 11:39, KJV.
[59]Rom.8:28.

this, Paul is not removing the moral responsibility of people but revealing the gloriously encouraging truth that God is bigger and more powerful than sinners and their sins, and he will, in his ultimate redemptive
good, work all things for good.

Paul then grounds our hope in the fact that the goodness of God
will ultimately rule in the doctrine of predestination, saying, "For those
whom he foreknew he also predestined to be conformed to the image
of his Son, in order that he might be the firstborn among many brothers. And those whom he predestined he also called, and those whom he
called he also justified, and those whom he justified he also glorified."[60]
Some theologians call this section the "golden thread" of salvation. To
fully appreciate each of these enormous truths, we will examine them
briefly in succession.

First, God foreknew us. How one defines *foreknowledge* is incredibly
important because in many ways it determines one's view of predestination. Arminius asserted that God foreknew "from all eternity those individuals who would through his preventing [i.e., prevenient] grace, believe,
and, through his subsequent grace would persevere . . . [and] he likewise
knew who would not believe and persevere."[11] Likewise, John Wesley
speaks of foreknowledge, saying, "Salvation begins with what is usually
termed (and very properly) preventing [i.e., prevenient] grace; including
the first wish to please God, the first dawn of light concerning his will, and
the first slight transient conviction of having sinned against him."[12]

Yet foreknowledge does not mean that God simply looked down
the corridor of history and saw who would choose him, which in turn
compelled him to choose them. God is eternal, and thus the concept of
God gazing into the future as we do is nonsensical. Additionally, by saying that God foreknew us, the Bible is speaking of more than cold, hard
facts; rather, God lovingly longed to pursue us for relationship before
we were even born. Examples of this language regarding relationship
abound throughout Scripture and show that God knew us and loved us
before time began, which is far more personal and intimate than simply
knowing what choices we would make.[61] Replying to the Arminian/
Wesleyan definition of foreknowledge, theologian Paul Jewett says,
"The answer is simply that these texts do not say, 'Whom God fore-

---

[60]Rom. 8:29–30.
[61]Jer. 1:5; Amos 3:2; Matt. 7:23; John 10:14; Gal. 4:9.

knew *would believe,* he predestinated,' nor that we as Christians are 'elect according to the foreknowledge *which God has of our faith.*'"[13]

Second, God predestined the elect to be made like Jesus, who was himself predestined to be the Savior of predestined people. By *predestined* I mean that God chose in advance that some people would be granted eternal life through Jesus. This does not lead to loose, immoral living that tramples upon the grace of God; rather, it results in increasing holiness. Predestined people are chosen to be more and more like Jesus.

Third, God not only predestined people for salvation but also predestined some of these people to labor as evangelists and Bible teachers who call sinners to turn from sin and trust in Jesus. They proclaim the gospel to anyone and everyone as the means by which God regenerates them, causing them to be born again with a new heart to love Jesus. God calls the elect to himself outwardly by the preaching of the gospel and the proclamation of Jesus, and he also calls the elect inwardly by allowing the power of the gospel to transform them spiritually.

Fourth, predestined people who are regenerated through the gospel are then justified in the sight of God. This means that although they are guilty sinners, God declares them just and righteous in his sight because of the sinless life, substitutionary death, and bodily resurrection of Jesus in their place for their sins.

Fifth, those people who are predestined are all brought to saving faith in Jesus Christ at some point in their life. Furthermore, they will persevere with Jesus as Christians until the day of their glorification when, following their death, they will receive their glorified, resurrected bodies to live forever with Jesus in his eternal kingdom, free from the presence and power of sin forever. In this vein, John Calvin, after preaching his last sermon and being carried home to die, wrote in his will, "I have no other hope or refuge than His predestination upon which my entire salvation is grounded."[14]

Thus, the thread of salvation from predestination to glorification creates a seamless garment. This golden thread shows that the entirety of salvation began in eternity past—with God choosing us and being faithful to complete his purposes throughout history—and continues all the way to our perfection in the eternal state. Accordingly, Hebrews 12:2 speaks of Jesus as the "founder [or "author" in the NIV] and perfecter of our faith."

Paul goes on to rightly worship God for his great love as shown in his work of predestination in eternity past, which gives us comfort in the present and assurance for our final salvation in the future. He bursts forth in praise to God for the assurance we have as Christians—that nothing can separate us from the goodness of God whose love for us cannot be thwarted:

> What then shall we say to these things? If God is for us, who can be against us? He who did not spare his own Son but gave him up for us all, how will he not also with him graciously give us all things? Who shall bring any charge against God's elect? It is God who justifies. Who is to condemn? Christ Jesus is the one who died—more than that, who was raised—who is at the right hand of God, who indeed is interceding for us. Who shall separate us from the love of Christ? Shall tribulation, or distress, or persecution, or famine, or nakedness, or danger, or sword? As it is written, "For your sake we are being killed all the day long; we are regarded as sheep to be slaughtered." No, in all these things we are more than conquerors through him who loved us. For I am sure that neither death nor life, nor angels nor rulers, nor things present nor things to come, nor powers, nor height nor depth, nor anything else in all creation, will be able to separate us from the love of God in Christ Jesus our Lord.[62]

Paul thus establishes that God is sovereign over all of history as well as sin, while he is also loving and good to save some ill-deserving sinners.

There is arguably no one more fit to speak with authority on the matter of predestination than Paul. In Acts 6–9 we read the story of Paul's dramatic conversion. He was named Saul, and he was violently opposed to Christianity. He even oversaw the murder of the early church deacon Stephen and the persecution of other Christians. In all of human history, Paul was perhaps the least likely person to become a Christian. Nonetheless, Jesus came to Paul with the result that Paul became a Christian who went on to pen much of the New Testament. Indeed, his life testimony is a powerful illustration of the doctrine of election.

Arguments against Predestination

One common argument against the doctrine of predestination is that it leads to a heartless Christian life that is not motivated to do evan-

---
[62]Rom. 8:31–39.

gelism or love non-Christians. Sadly, in some instances this criticism is deserved. Yet, in Paul's writings and in his own life, which he gave wholeheartedly to evangelism and church planting, we see a man who believes in both predestination and passionate evangelism. He thus echoes the heart of Moses:

> I am speaking the truth in Christ—I am not lying; my conscience bears me witness in the Holy Spirit—that I have great sorrow and unceasing anguish in my heart. For I could wish that I myself were accursed and cut off from Christ for the sake of my brothers, my kinsmen according to the flesh. They are Israelites, and to them belong the adoption, the glory, the covenants, the giving of the law, the worship, and the promises. To them belong the patriarchs, and from their race, according to the flesh, is the Christ who is God over all, blessed forever. Amen.[63]

Here Paul is speaking of Jews who had such blessing and instruction from God yet did not come to know and love Jesus as Paul had. Under the inspiration of God the Holy Spirit, Paul anticipates three questions that people in his day and every day since have asked. The remainder of Romans 9 is Paul's effort to explain each of these questions in succession.

Paul's Answer to Questions about Predestination

Question #1: If many Jews did not love Jesus, did God's Word fail?[64]

> But it is not as though the word of God has failed. For not all who are descended from Israel belong to Israel, and not all are children of Abraham because they are his offspring, but "Through Isaac shall your offspring be named." This means that it is not the children of the flesh who are the children of God, but the children of the promise are counted as offspring. For this is what the promise said: "About this time next year I will return, and Sarah shall have a son." And not only so, but also when Rebekah had conceived children by one man, our forefather Isaac, though they were not yet born and had done nothing either good or bad—in order that God's purpose of election might continue, not because of works but because of him who calls—she was

---

[63]Rom. 9:1–5, cf. Ex. 32:32.
[64]Rom. 9:6–13.

told, "The older will serve the younger." As it is written, "Jacob I loved,
but Esau I hated."

Since the Jewish people had descended from Abraham and enjoyed
God's provision and instruction for so many generations, the fact that
when Jesus came, many Jews, though not all, rejected him raises the
question of whether God's Word ultimately failed. To answer this question, Paul turns to Genesis 25. There we read that Abraham's son Isaac
had two sons, who become the focus of attention in the subsequent
twelve chapters of Genesis.

The conflict between the boys began in the womb as they wres-
tled for preeminence. Curious as to what was occurring in her womb,
Rebekah prayed to God for insight, and he told her that the boys would
struggle throughout their lives. The older would serve the younger,
and each boy would grow into a nation in conflict with the other (Esau
became the nation of Edom and Jacob became the nation of Israel).

The first son born was Esau, which means "hairy," and he was also
called Edom, which means "red." Apparently he was a red and hairy
child, perhaps like Elmo on Sesame Street. The second son born was
Jacob, which means "trickster," and he came out of the womb grasp-
ing his brother's heel. As the boys grew, Esau was the man's man who
hunted, ate wild game, and was favored by his father. Jacob was a
momma's boy who preferred to stay around the house and be doted on
by his mother.

As the firstborn, Esau was entitled to the family birthright, which
would grant him a double portion of his father's estate and leave him
as the head of the family upon his father's death. It also allowed him to
receive a special blessing from his father. One day, Esau came home hungry, and his brother, Jacob the trickster, got Esau to trade his birthright
for a meal. In this account, the younger brother displaced the older, as
had happened previously in Genesis with Cain and Abel, and Isaac and
Ishmael.

At the bottom of Esau's sin was indifference about God's covenant
promise to bless the nations through the descendants of Abraham, a
blessing that would ultimately bring forth Jesus Christ. Esau flippantly
dismissed God's covenant for the sake of a meal. In short, neither son
was particularly holy in their early days, and both lived as most unre-

pentant sinful men do. Amazingly, this struggle between two brothers in the womb continued well into the future. In fact, many years later it reached its climax when King Herod, a descendant of Esau, sought to slaughter Jesus Christ, a descendant of Isaac.[65]

Paul then goes on to argue that before Jacob and Esau were born and before they had done anything good or bad, in pure, predestinating grace God chose to have the younger brother rule over the older and supplant him as the head of the family through which Jesus Christ would be born. Paul quotes Malachi 1:2–3, which is a source of great interpretive controversy. Some commentators claim that Malachi is saying that God, for no reason whatsoever, chose to love Jacob and hate his brother Esau. Admittedly, this makes God appear cruel and capricious, as if he were playing "duck, duck, damn." Other commentators make an argument from the original language, claiming that the word *hate* literally means "to pass over" or "not choose to use," so that God chose to work through Isaac to bring forth Jesus and chose to not work through Esau.

Finally, looking at the context of the verse, still other commentators argue that Paul shifts from speaking of God's election of Jacob over Esau in Genesis to speaking of their descendants in terms of the nations of Israel and Edom, which proceeded from these men, respectively. They further argue that in the days of Malachi, Edom sinfully sought to destroy Israel; thus, God's hate for them was justifiable and not capricious because he was responding to their hatred of his chosen people.

Whatever one's conclusion regarding these interpretive options, one thing is clear: God does choose to bless some people and not others, and God can choose to bless some nations and not others. The one thing that Jacob and Esau and Israel and Edom had in common was the absolute failure to merit God's grace in any way. That God would give grace to anyone speaks of how wonderful he is to some ill-deserving—not just undeserving—people.

Therefore, Paul's answer to the first question is that within physical Israel there is a remnant saved by grace, which is spiritual Israel. While on the surface it appears that God had attempted to redeem Israel and failed, Paul reveals that God and his gospel have not failed. This is because while Israel was predestined by God to be blessed as a nation,

---

[65]Matt. 1:1–2; 2:13.

only some members of that nation—along with some members of other nations—were to receive the blessing of salvation through God's predestined sovereign choice. His examples of Jacob and Esau, who came from the same mother and father, serve as illustrations that although both were physical Israel, they were not necessarily spiritual Israel. Even though both were born in the line of Abraham physically, only one was born again in the line of Abraham spiritually. Paul describes this spiritual Israel found within the physical Israel: "So too at the present time there is a remnant, chosen by grace."[66]

Question #2: Is God unjust to choose some people for salvation and not others?[67]

> What shall we say then? Is there injustice on God's part? By no means! For he says to Moses, "I will have mercy on whom I have mercy, and I will have compassion on whom I have compassion." So then it depends not on human will or exertion, but on God, who has mercy. For the Scripture says to Pharaoh, "For this very purpose I have raised you up, that I might show my power in you, and that my name might be proclaimed in all the earth." So then he has mercy on whomever he wills, and he hardens whomever he wills.

By saying that God chooses to save some people and not others "not because of works,"[68] Paul anticipates the charge that God is unjust for doing so. To answer this objection biblically, he deftly turns to Moses and the book of Exodus. There we discover that the Israelite people, numbering a few million, are enslaved to a cruel tyrant named Pharaoh who ruled as the most powerful man on earth and was worshiped as a god. God called Moses to proclaim to the pharaoh God's demand that his people be released to worship him freely. To authenticate Moses' divine call, God promised to allow him to perform miraculous feats.

This initial demonstration of spiritual power was important for the validation of Moses' ministry. The Egyptians were dualistic; they believed there were two realms, a physical world in which people lived, and a spiritual world that was filled with multitudes of gods

---

[66]Rom. 11:5.
[67]Rom. 9:14–18.
[68]Rom. 9:11.

and spiritual beings. They believed that magic and sorcery were the means by which the spiritual world intersected with the physical world. Therefore, Moses' miraculous wonders would have meant to the pharaoh that Moses worked for a powerful god, or perhaps *the* God.

The Exodus account to which Paul refers introduces the concept of the hardening of Pharaoh's heart, a subject that appears nineteen more times in upcoming chapters.[69] Some of these verses say that it was God who hardened Pharaoh's heart, while others indicate that Pharaoh hardened his own heart. Still, some theologians have said that the wording merely reflects the Hebrew understanding of the world, and that the issue is largely one of semantics because they would have seen every action as ultimately a work of God.

The question that has erupted from these verses is whether God could have overridden Pharaoh's will, hardened his heart, and then punished him for his sin. If God had done that, then God would have been unjust and morally responsible for making Pharaoh sin yet still punishing Pharaoh for doing what he was forced to do. Likewise, any abusive father who throws his child across the dinner table and then spanks him for spilling his milk is unjust.

Paul is emphatic that God did in fact harden Pharaoh's heart, and so we must accept that truth. Still, the question of how God hardened Pharaoh's heart is incredibly important if the justice of God is to be defended. The answer is that God hardened Pharaoh's heart with patience and grace. God did not need to send Moses to Pharaoh on multiple occasions to invite Pharaoh to repent of his sin and free the Israelites. God did not need to perform miracles in front of the pharaoh to prove his power and sovereign rule over even the pharaoh. Furthermore, God knew that Pharaoh's heart was hard and that in asking him to repent and come under the leadership of the real God, Pharaoh would only grow all the more angry and hardhearted. Therefore, it was grace that hardened Pharaoh's heart, similar to heaping burning coals on the head of one's enemies, as Jesus said.

Subsequently, God remains gracious and is not unjust. The responsibility for the hard heart is ultimately the unrepentant, sinful pharaoh who repeatedly rejects God's offer of grace. Thus, the truism of the Puritans rings true that "the same sun that melts the ice hardens the clay."

---

[69]Ex. 7:3, 13, 14, 22; 8:15, 19, 32; 9:7, 12, 34–35; 10:1, 20, 27; 11:10; 13:15; 14:4, 8, 17.

Paul's point is that we are each like Pharaoh—living as little gods, rejecting the grace of God all the time. God would be fully just to send every one of us to hell. However, he chooses to have mercy and compassion on some of us, as he did for Moses. In fact, this is exactly how God describes himself through Moses in Exodus 34:6–7, which is the most frequently quoted verse in the Bible:

> The LORD passed before him and proclaimed, "The LORD, the LORD, a God merciful and gracious, slow to anger, and abounding in steadfast love and faithfulness, keeping steadfast love for thousands, forgiving iniquity and transgression and sin, but who will by no means clear the guilty, visiting the iniquity of the fathers on the children and the children's children, to the third and the fourth generation."

Question #3: Is God unfair to save some people and not others?[70]

> You will say to me then, "Why does he still find fault? For who can resist his will?" But who are you, O man, to answer back to God? Will what is molded say to its molder, "Why have you made me like this?" Has the potter no right over the clay, to make out of the same lump one vessel for honorable use and another for dishonorable use? What if God, desiring to show his wrath and to make known his power, has endured with much patience vessels of wrath prepared for destruction, in order to make known the riches of his glory for vessels of mercy, which he has prepared beforehand for glory—even us whom he has called, not from the Jews only but also from the Gentiles? As indeed he says in Hosea, "Those who were not my people I will call 'my people,' and her who was not beloved I will call 'beloved.' And in the very place where it was said to them, 'You are not my people,' there they will be called 'sons of the living God.'" And Isaiah cries out concerning Israel: "Though the number of the sons of Israel be as the sand of the sea, only a remnant of them will be saved, for the Lord will carry out his sentence upon the earth fully and without delay." And as Isaiah predicted, "If the Lord of hosts had not left us offspring, we would have been like Sodom and become like Gomorrah."

The final question that Paul seeks to answer is, if God chooses to save some people and not others, is he unfair for punishing people who do

---

[70]Rom. 9:19–29.

his will by not believing? Paul then quotes a number of Old Testament verses to show that God is not unfair.

First, Paul says that we must be careful not to stand in the place of Pharaoh and judge God, because that is, in essence, to declare ourselves god. Such folly is akin to a potter making various things out of one lump of clay, and the finished products complaining that they do not like what they have been made to accomplish. Paul is saying that rather than complaining that God is unjust for not saving everyone, we should rejoice that God is gracious and merciful in saving anyone. If you are a Christian, when you see unrepentant, lost sinners destined for hell, you should pursue them with the gospel and thank God that he changed your heart, because apart from his saving you, your condition would be equally pathetic.

As an aside, there is a debate among Bible teachers over whether this metaphor of potter and clay refers to individuals or to nations. The Old Testament uses the analogy in more than one place[71] to refer to both individuals and nations.

Second, Paul quotes Hosea 2:23 and 1:10 to show that God, who is rich in mercy, used election to save some Gentiles who were not pursuing God in any way; apart from God's predestination and pursuit they were without any hope. In this we see the love and mercy of God greatly displayed to ill-deserving sinners.

Third, Paul quotes Isaiah 10:22–23 to show that God had always promised only some of the Jews would be saved. Therefore, God had not failed by saving only some Jewish people; rather, his Word was perfectly implemented in history.

Fourth, Paul closes by quoting Isaiah 1:9 to show that without God's mercy and election, no one would be saved from his wrath. Practically, this means that everyone is a sinner who deserves wrath and hell, and anyone who is saved has received an ill-deserved gift from a loving God who is rich in mercy.

Paul concludes his answer to this question by saying exactly that, illustrating the beauty of God's grace to pursue some people who have not pursued him so that they will not stumble over Jesus but rather trust in him:

---

[71]Isa. 29:16; 45:9–11; Jer. 18:1–6.

What shall we say, then? That Gentiles who did not pursue righteousness have attained it, that is, a righteousness that is by faith; but that Israel who pursued a law that would lead to righteousness did not succeed in reaching that law. Why? Because they did not pursue it by faith, but as if it were based on works. They have stumbled over the stumbling stone, as it is written, "Behold, I am laying in Zion a stone of stumbling, and a rock of offense; and whoever believes in him will not be put to shame."[72]

In a fitting conclusion for a man so zealously committed to evangelism and church planting, the means by which God would work through him to save the elect, Paul says, "Brothers, my heart's desire and prayer to God for them is that they may be saved."[73] Indeed, for Paul, a correct understanding of predestinating election is actually an impetus for fervent evangelistic ministry because no matter how dark and bleak someone's heart may be, there is always the possibility, so long as they are breathing, that God could do a miracle and save them.

ANSWERS TO QUESTIONS AND OBJECTIONS ABOUT PREDESTINATION

What is the order of salvation?

In an effort to simplify much of what has been stated in this chapter, it will be helpful to note the order of salvation, or as the theologians call it, the *ordo salutis*. This order traces the process of a Christian's relationship with God.

1) *Election*. God's sovereign choice in eternity past.
2) *Gospel call*. Proclamation of Jesus' person and work.
3) *Regeneration*. Born again by the Holy Spirit and given a new heart.
4) *Conversion*. Spirit-enabled faith and repentance from the new heart.
5) *Justification*. Legal standing before God.
6) *Adoption*. Membership in God's family, the church.
7) *Sanctification*. Ongoing growth in holiness to be increasingly like Jesus.
8) *Perseverance*. Ongoing loving relationship with Jesus through the Christian life.
9) *Death*. The soul goes to be with Jesus while the body goes into the grave.

---

[72]Rom. 9:30–33.
[73]Rom. 10:1.

10) *Glorification.* Resurrection body like Jesus' reunited with the soul.

It is important to note that salvation biblically entails each of these aspects. Further, their order is incredibly important. A confusion of the order of salvation leads to very differing beliefs about how someone enters into and retains a relationship with God.

Could God have saved everyone?

An analogy might be helpful. In John 5, Jesus healed a man at a pool. He could have healed everyone but chose to heal only that man. He passed over the others who were present and wanted healing. Likewise, in the doctrine of predestination God heals some people spiritually while not doing the same for others. The truth is that God could save everyone, just as Jesus could have healed everyone when he was on the earth. Yet, because God is obligated to no one, the fact that he heals or saves anyone is a gracious gift.

When did God predestine us for salvation?

The Bible repeatedly and emphatically teaches that God sovereignly chose the elect he would save in eternity past, as the following verses reveal:

He chose us in him before the foundation of the world.[74]

Do not be ashamed of the testimony about our Lord ... but share in suffering for the gospel by the power of God, who saved us and called us to a holy calling, not because of our works but because of his own purpose and grace, which he gave us in Christ Jesus before the ages began.[75]

All who dwell on earth will worship it, everyone whose name has not been written before the foundation of the world in the book of life of the Lamb who was slain.[76]

The beast that you saw was, and is not, and is about to rise from the bottomless pit and go to destruction. And the dwellers on earth whose names

---

[74] Eph. 1:4–5.
[75] 2 Tim. 1:8–9.
[76] Rev. 13:8.

have not been written in the book of life from the foundation of the world will marvel to see the beast, because it was and is not and is to come.[77]

Why does God choose some people and not others?

The Bible says that we know and see in part[78] and that God has secrets.[79] Specifically regarding predestination, the Bible speaks of the mystery of his will.[80] Thus, there are some questions, such as this one, that we simply will not know the answers to in this life. Furthermore, Paul asks, "For who has known the mind of the Lord, or who has been his counselor?"[81] What we do know is that his choice is based on his will for his glory, as Ephesians 1:11–12 says: "In him we have obtained an inheritance, having been predestined according to the purpose of him who works all things according to the counsel of his will, so that we who were the first to hope in Christ might be to the praise of his glory." So we who have been chosen by God know that we have been chosen to the praise of his glory, but beyond that God does not reveal the mystery of his will in great detail.

Why should we evangelize if people are predestined?

Romans 9–11 is the great section of Scripture on predestination. It opens in Romans 9:1–5 with Paul's desire for people to be saved, which is echoed again in 10:1. He goes on to say that God is not only sovereign over the ends of saving people but also over the means; he chooses people to bring the good news of Jesus to lost sinners.[82] Paul's own example of evangelistic and church planting zeal must be the context in which his words are understood. Anyone who merely reads his words and does not follow his example is not truly Pauline.

Furthermore, by believing that God elects people, we are relieved of the burden to manipulate and guilt people into becoming Christians and can work more honestly, lovingly, patiently, truthfully, compassionately, and sincerely. Thus, belief in predestination should not quench evangelistic zeal but rather fuel it. After all, no matter how dark people's hearts might be, knowing that there are elect people and that God the

---

[77]Rev. 17:8.
[78]1 Cor. 13:9, 12.
[79]Deut. 29:29.
[80]Eph. 1:9.
[81]Rom. 11:34.
[82]Rom. 10:14–17.

Holy Spirit has chosen to work through the proclamation of the gospel, we can evangelize in hope, eagerly expecting that some will be saved, and not feel guilty when others reject Jesus.

We should evangelize the lost because God has chosen to work through our ministry efforts to save people. He does this so that we would share in his joy and get to know the heart of our Father better. Similarly, when I was a little boy, my dad was a union construction worker who hung sheetrock. I still remember the times when I dressed up like my pop, donning overalls, a white T-shirt, steel-toed boots, and a miniature hard hat, and packed up my lunch box and thermos to go to work with my dad. He would give me a few tasks throughout the day, and by working with my dad I got to know him better and spend time in his world. God is a Father like that. He needs people like me to evangelize the world no more than my dad needed a little boy to build an apartment complex, but he takes his kids to work because he loves them and wants them to be with him doing what he loves.

Does predestination make God unjust?

Some will protest that the doctrine of predestination makes God unjust because not everyone is predestined. However, the existence of hell reveals the fact that God is just, whereas the doctrine of predestination reveals that God is also merciful. After all, because God warned our first parents that sin would result in physical and spiritual death, he is fully just to allow us to die and spend eternity in hell. Therefore, hell is the most just place in all creation.

Nevertheless, by predestinating some people to salvation, God is also unequally merciful. On this point, Paul says, "Isaiah is so bold as to say, 'I have been found by those who did not seek me; I have shown myself to those who did not ask for me.'"[83]

By way of analogy, if a group of people committed themselves to a mass suicide pact and then gathered in a home and set it on fire, no one would claim that their neighbors were unjust if some of them died in the fire. However, if one of the neighbors ran into the blazing inferno to try to rescue them, only to be met with resistance as he threw them one at a time over his shoulder, kicking and screaming, and ran out of the house, and he did this over and over until he saved some people before

---

[83]Rom. 10:20.

he himself died of smoke inhalation, he would be lauded as a hero and not criticized as a villain. No one would accuse him of being unjust because he did not get every suicidal person out of the home. Rather, he was obligated to save no one and gave his own life to save some.

Likewise, we sinned and lit the proverbial house on fire, and it was Jesus who came to lay down his life to save those who were not seeking to be saved or crying out for help. This is why John Stott insightfully says, "If therefore anybody is lost, the blame is theirs, but if anybody is saved, the credit is God's."[15] In response, we should not accuse God of being unjust but rather thank him for such great sacrificial mercy.

Does predestination make God unloving?

Contrary to the erroneous thinking of some people, predestination reveals how loving God is, for three reasons.

1) God predestines some of the most unlovely people. God did not choose only the beautiful, smart, funny, or successful people. In fact, he often chooses the exact kinds of people that no one else would ever choose to love. Scripture says precisely this:

> But God chose what is foolish in the world to shame the wise; God chose what is weak in the world to shame the strong; God chose what is low and despised in the world, even things that are not, to bring to nothing things that are, so that no human being might boast in the presence of God.[84]

2) Because God saves through election, there is hope for those who have never heard about Jesus, for the unborn, for those who died young, and for the mentally challenged. I am in no way encouraging universalism—hell *will* be filled with unrepentant sinners. But if God chooses who goes to heaven, then I know the result will be more loving than if Satan or sinners made the choice, because God is good.

3) The Bible declares that God predestines us not because of anything merit-worthy in us but solely because of the love in himself: "In love he predestined us."[85]

---

[84] 1 Cor. 1:27–29.
[85] Eph. 1:4–5.

Does not predestination make Christians unloving toward non-Christians?

Predestination, when rightly understood, should make Christians more loving toward non-Christians. After all, if we know that we are no better, smarter, holier, or more deserving of salvation than anyone else, then we should be compassionate toward non-Christians. It is precisely the sovereign and free nature of God's predestinating grace that should cause us to lay an ax to the root of any religious pride, smugness, and condemnation. When we understand that people are lost because they are sinners, we are compelled to love them because their condition reminds us of the terrible fate that would be ours had God not freely saved us. We are also compelled to love them in hope that through our love they would begin to see something of God's grace in their lives.

Again, the Scriptures are clear on this point. Paul was so aware of his sin that throughout his letters he repeatedly says that he is the worst of sinners and that by saving him God demonstrates the fullness of his merciful love. Rather than being smugly religious and unloving toward lost people, the man who more passionately argued for predestination in all of Scripture also labored tirelessly to lovingly evangelize lost people and plant churches despite his own poverty, shame, beatings, and imprisonment. Furthermore, in the midst of his great treatise on election in Romans 9–11, his loving heart pours forth:

> I am speaking the truth in Christ—I am not lying; my conscience bears me witness in the Holy Spirit—that I have great sorrow and unceasing anguish in my heart. For I could wish that I myself were accursed and cut off from Christ for the sake of my brothers, my kinsmen according to the flesh. They are Israelites, and to them belong the adoption, the glory, the covenants, the giving of the law, the worship, and the promises. To them belong the patriarchs, and from their race, according to the flesh, is the Christ who is God over all, blessed forever. Amen.[86]

> Brothers, my heart's desire and prayer to God for them is that they may be saved.[87]

---

[86]Rom. 9:1–5.
[87]Rom. 10:1.

Does belief in predestination lead to sinfully loose living?

Some people will protest that if people are taught that their salvation is a predestined gift of grace they cannot merit or unmerit, then they will live sinful lives and abuse that grace. Yet such criticism overlooks the fact that we are predestined to Jesus and to new life with, like, for, through, and to him! Any idea that predestination is anything less could in fact lead to sinfully loose living, as if predestination simply assigns Jesus to follow me around with a shovel, picking up the messes I make instead of changing my life completely.

When Paul speaks of predestination, he stresses not only how we are saved (predestination) but also to whom we are saved (Jesus) and to what we are saved (holy living), as the following verses illustrate.

> For those whom he foreknew he also predestined to be conformed to the image of his Son, in order that he might be the firstborn among many brothers.[88]

> For we know, brothers loved by God, that he has chosen you, because our gospel came to you not only in word, but also in power and in the Holy Spirit and with full conviction.[89]

> Paul, a servant of God and an apostle of Jesus Christ, for the sake of the faith of God's elect and their knowledge of the truth, which accords with godliness . . .[90]

Once we understand that we have been predestined to a new life with Jesus because of Jesus for Jesus and to Jesus, we are free to stop obsessing about whether we are truly saved. Instead of being continually and morbidly obsessed with our own salvation, we are free to live our new life to the glory of God and to the help of others by resting in the fact that God, who began the good work, will be faithful to see it through to completion.

---

[88]Rom. 8:29.
[89]1 Thess. 1:4–5.
[90]Titus 1:1.

Am I elect?

As a pastor, I am asked this question frequently. Most often it is asked by people who love God and have a very tender conscience that takes sin seriously. I often tell them that if someone asks this question, the odds are that he or she is elect. After all, non-elect people tend not to care. If you hate sin and love Jesus, you are elect—the Spirit of God has regenerated your heart to even care about whether you belong to Jesus.

CONCLUSION

It seems fitting to close this chapter with a story from my own life that I hope will help take all of this complicated theology and make it more concretely practical. Sadly, the doctrine of predestination too often devolves into Reformed and Arminian Christians quoting from their favorite pile of verses until they cease to be loving to one another, and winning the never-ending argument takes precedence over glorifying God and helping people. I myself have been guilty of just such actions and would be deeply grieved if this chapter were simply yet another pile of rocks for Christians to throw at each other.

Furthermore, I am a pastor, which means that not only do I love the study of theology, but also I love to help people with the truth. My personal journey with God regarding the doctrine of predestination has been incredibly insightful to my understanding of God as Father and has deepened my worship of him in response to his predestinating me. So, in an effort to show how the doctrine of predestination is inextricably connected to the fatherhood of God, I want to share with you how I see and savor the doctrine of predestination.

I am the happy father of five beautiful children who have been entrusted to the care of my wife, Grace (a.k.a. "Beauty"), and me. We would have six children, but we suffered a miscarriage. I take great comfort in knowing that while my child was never born to hear and respond to the gospel, God knew and loved my child and could have simply saved that child by electing grace, thereby enabling me to perhaps meet him or her one day in God's kingdom.

Concerning our other five children, we have been blessed with three boys and two girls. Our oldest child is Ashley Marisa. I adore her with all my heart and love seeing her blossom into a beautiful, smart, creative, and godly young woman. I shudder to remember the day she nearly died when she was roughly two years old.

At that time we lived off a busy street next to the football stadium of the University of Washington. Beyond our front porch there were perhaps twenty feet of property followed by a sidewalk and then four lanes of nearly constant heavy traffic. One day, when we opened the front door to walk to our parked car, Ashley started running toward the street, so we chased her, grabbed her, and carefully explained to her that she was never to run away from us again toward the traffic. She did not fully understand what we were saying; she just thought it was fun that we would chase her. To her, the whole thing was basically a playtime game. For some weeks she stayed near us as we went to put her in the car . . . until one nearly fateful day.

As we were loading her newborn brother, Zachariah Blaise, into the car, she turned from my side and ran as fast as she could toward the busy street. She was exercising her free will and made her own decision for her life. In panic, I cried out to her, essentially preaching repentance to her, pleading with her to turn around and return to her daddy. She foolishly did not respond, and I will never forget the smile on her face and the look in her eye as she ran toward the street, thinking we were playing a game and not seeing the death that awaited her.

Ashley ran in front of a vehicle parked on the side of the road. As I sprinted toward her, I looked to my left at the oncoming traffic and saw a large delivery truck rumbling down the road, right in the lane where Ashley was about to step. To make matters even worse, she was so short that the truck driver would never see her if she came out from behind the parked car, and I was certain that my daughter was going to die in front of my eyes. I closed in on her just as she stepped into the lane of the oncoming delivery truck. She was a few steps into the street when I grabbed her by the back of her vest and literally pulled her out of the way of the truck. Everything happened so fast that the truck driver did not have time to hit the horn or the brakes. My daughter's life was spared by just inches.

With one arm, I reached out and overrode the free-will decision of my daughter and saved her. I did this because my love for her is more important than her free will.

Tragically, I have heard a well-known Christian radio show host explain the Reformed view of predestination as God being a rapist rather than a lover because God overrides the free will of some people. My heart breaks every time I hear that kind of statement, because rapists are not the only people who impose their will on others; sometimes so do loving daddies who want their kids to live. They reach out their hand to ensure they are saved from death.

Being a daddy myself, the predestinating hand of God the Father reaching down to me through Jesus makes me worship him for being such an amazing Dad.

QUESTION 6: **GRACE**

Of all the things you teach, what parts of Christianity do you still wrestle with? What's hardest for you to believe?

God saved me at the age of nineteen while I was a freshman in college. At that time I had many questions, concerns, and struggles about the Christian faith. In an effort to grow in my understanding, I began reading voraciously. I read the Bible and other Christian books.

My thirty-eighth birthday this year will mark the halfway point of my life in multiple ways. First, if I live to be the same age as the average American male, then the band is about to take the field because I am approaching the halftime of my existence. Second, this year marks the halfway point of my Christian walk; the first nineteen years were spent as a non-Christian, and the ensuing nineteen were spent as a Christian.

The questions I had as a new Christian have long since been answered. As my knowledge of the Bible and Christian theology has increased, though, they have been replaced by new questions. Thankfully, God is gracious and permits us to remain believers in the Jesus of the Bible while we still have questions or doubts that do not rise to the level of unbelief but do compel us to prayerful study in faith that God "rewards those who seek him," as Hebrews 11:6 promises. The great Christian thinker Anselm of Canterbury (AD 1033–1109) was famous for explaining this kind of relationship with God that trusts, yet pursues questions and doubts earnestly with God as "faith seeking understanding."

For me, the Christian truth that I wrestle with and consider the hardest to believe in is the sovereign, pure, free, and efficacious grace of God. I do believe in the gracious grace of God but confess to not remembering it sometimes as passionately and completely as I should. As I read the New Testament, it appears that I am not alone. I have found roughly one dozen instances of various writers "reminding" Christians of the grace of God.

When deeply considered, the grace of God seems to me nearly too good to be true. It reveals that God is unlike any person who has ever lived and unlike any false god invented by any religion. Perhaps this is what the Scriptures mean when they refer to God's attribute of holiness (which means he is both different and good) more frequently than any other. Therefore, this chapter is my effort to remind myself of the grace of God. I invite others who need to be reminded of his grace to listen in.

GRACE IN MY LIFE

To start with, I am a sinner. For many years I struggled to see myself as a sinner. This was because I was prone, as many sinners are, to compare myself to other sinners rather than to Jesus Christ. Furthermore, I was prone to focus on my "good" qualities and dismiss my sins as mistakes, errors, lapses, and the like. Of course, I was prone not to afford that same kind of license to those who sinned against me. As a result, I was far more aware of the speck in the eyes of other people than the lumberyard full of planks in my own.

I can still remember being a senior in high school, when a fellow student who was a Christian attempted to share the gospel with me. He began by telling me that I was a sinner, to which I chuckled. I asked him if he had done any drugs or drunk any alcohol, and I said that I was not really much of a sinner because I had not done those things. I then went on to list all my good deeds, including being the student-body president, editor of the school newspaper, volunteer for a political candidate, advocate for the remodel of our school with the school board, captain of the baseball team, four-year letterman, and student counselor to at-risk students, and I was voted most likely to succeed and man of the year.

I thought it funny that someone who was, in my eyes, more sinful than I sought to convince me that I was a wretched sinner who needed God's grace. To me, all religions were much like hospitals for sick and dying people, and as long as people were not sick or dying, they had no need for any religion. Since I was doing just fine and excelling in life, according to my own flawed understanding, the thought of needing God and religion made as much sense as a healthy person needing a surgeon and a hospital.

In relation to the story of the prodigal son, I was like the older brother. I was the "good guy" who did not go out partying, drinking, and sinning. I was self-disciplined, responsible, and, by all outward appearances, a decent, upright, moral person. Not knowing much Scripture, I basically lived by the pithy statements that are bantered about and that repudiate grace, such as "God helps those who help themselves," "No pain, no gain," and "You get what you deserve." Yet, in my heart I was filled with self-righteousness, pride, condemnation of others, and no real love for God.

Awareness of my own sinfulness hit me in college during a state university philosophy class, of all places. There, God broke through and revealed to me the depth of my sin. We had to read some writings by the church father Augustine, who said that the root of all sin is pride, and that pride is the greatest sin of all and, in effect, the mother sin that births all other sins. Furthermore, he argued biblically that sin is not just what we do but is, in fact, a far deeper problem of who we are by nature. As I read Augustine's words and the fact that Satan was the proudest person who ever lived[1] and that Jesus was the humblest person who has ever lived,[2] it was as if my entire world turned upside down.

I was shaken to my core when I heard that pride was the root of my corruption and not the source of my righteousness. I had not sought to merit my salvation but simply assumed that the "good" life I was living was adequate enough for God to be pleased with me and take me to heaven when my "good" life was concluded.

It was around this time that I moved out of the fraternity I had lived in for a week or two without touching one girl or drinking one beer, as demonstrations of my self-control and superiority over the drunken naked guys, and started reading my Bible while sitting in a dorm room.

---

[1] Isa. 14:11–22.
[2] Phil. 2:1–11.

One of the first books of the Bible I really enjoyed was Proverbs. Yet, as I read it, the theme of pride kept appearing. God hates proud people. Proverbs 6:16–17 says, "There are six things that the LORD hates, seven that are an abomination to him," and at the top of the list is "haughty eyes." Likewise, in Proverbs 8:13 God says, "Pride and arrogance and the way of evil and perverted speech I hate." Worse still, I read that God humiliates proud people. Proverbs 16:5 says, "Everyone who is arrogant in heart is an abomination to the LORD; be assured, he will not go unpunished." Likewise, Proverbs 16:18 promises, "Pride goes before destruction, and a haughty spirit before a fall."

God gave me a great gift of understanding when I accepted the truth that I was a proud sinner. I began reading the Bible with great fervor, attending church, and joining multiple Bible studies to learn more about sin and Jesus.

I discovered that God created this world in a perfect state, and upon the creation of the man and woman God declared his entire creation "very good."[3] The Old Testament describes this intended state of perfect beauty in all things as "shalom."[4] Yet as I looked at my life and the world in which it is lived, it was—and is—readily apparent that something had gone terribly wrong.

The Bible calls this sin. I realized that my sin includes both sins of omission, where I refuse to obey God or do good, and sins of commission, where I do what God has forbidden, which is evil. I realized that my sin also includes my thoughts, words, deeds, and motives.

The Bible told me the unvarnished truth—I am totally depraved. Sin has corrupted my mind, so that I do not think God's thoughts;[5] sin has corrupted my will, so that I do not desire God's desires;[6] it has corrupted my emotions, so that I do not feel what God feels;[7] it has corrupted my body, so that I do not experience the health that God originally intended for me;[8] it has corrupted my relationships with God and people, so that I am separated by sin;[9] and sin has corrupted my behavior, which includes pagan worship of created things rather

---

[3]Gen. 1:31.
[4]Isa. 2:2–4; 11:1–9; 32:14–20; 43:1–12; 60:1–22; 65:17–25; Joel 2:24–29; 3:17–18.
[5]Eph. 4:18.
[6]Rom. 6:16–17.
[7]Titus 3:3.
[8]Rom. 8:10.
[9]Col. 1:21.

than right worship of my creator, God.[10] To make matters worse, my sinful condition is thoroughly my own doing and in no way the fault of God. This is because God does not take any delight in sin[11] but hates and detests sin[12] and hides his face from sinful people.[13] Subsequently, all of my sin comes from the very core of my being, or what the Bible calls my "heart."[14]

I realized that the consequences of my sin are, not surprisingly, put forth in the starkest of terms. As a sinner by nature, I am "evil continually";[15] impure;[16] "full of evil and madness";[17] "wicked" and "estranged";[18] going my "own way";[19] "rebellious";[20] among those who have "loved the darkness";[21] a "slave to sin";[22] a child of the devil;[23] unrighteous; not understanding; not seeking God; a "stiff-necked" resister of the Holy Spirit;[24] turned aside, worthless, not doing good, having a "hard and impenitent heart";[25] without fear of God;[26] "hostile to God";[27] spiritually foolish;[28] spiritually dead and among the "children of wrath";[29] darkened; alienated; marked by ignorance and hardness of heart; "callous" and given up to perversion, greed, and impurity of every sort;[30] among the "enemies of the cross of Christ";[31] "dead";[32] "defiled and unbelieving";[33] under the "power of the evil one";[34] "foolish, disobedient, led astray" and among the "slaves to various passions

[10]Rom. 1:18–31.
[11]Ps. 5:4.
[12]Prov. 6:16; Zech. 8:17.
[13]Isa. 59:2; 64:7.
[14]Prov. 4:23; 20:9; 27:19; Jer. 17:9; Matt. 12:33–34; Mark 7:21–23; Luke 6:45.
[15]Gen. 6:5.
[16]Prov. 20:9.
[17]Eccl. 9:3.
[18]Ps. 58:3.
[19]Isa. 53:6.
[20]Isa. 65:2.
[21]John 3:19.
[22]John 8:34; Rom. 6:20.
[23]John 8:43–44.
[24]Acts 7:51.
[25]Rom. 2:4–6.
[26]Rom. 3:10–18.
[27]Rom. 8:7.
[28]1 Cor. 2:14.
[29]Eph. 2:1–3.
[30]Eph. 4:17–19.
[31]Phil. 3:18.
[32]Col. 2:13.
[33]Titus 1:15.
[34]1 John 5:19.

and pleasures, passing our days in malice and envy, hated by others and hating one another."[35]

Today, the fact of my own sinfulness is one Christian truth that I do not struggle to believe. Only Christianity can explain both the sin that is in me and the sin that surrounds me, despite all the time, money, and energy the world exerts to remedy it, from soldiers fighting wars to counselors prescribing medications.

Therefore, my sin is not the hardest aspect of Christian truth to believe. What I sometimes find hard to believe is that God responds to me with pure grace. I receive grace not despite being undeserving—as one who has not merited grace—but actually as one who is ill-deserving because I am a sinful rebel at war with God. God would be gracious in doing good for strangers, but God goes even further and is gracious to his enemies.

GRACE IN SCRIPTURE

In many ways, the entire concept of God's grace is the defining and unique characteristic of Christianity. It is the canvas upon which all other Christian doctrines are painted. There are more than four hundred occurrences of various words for *grace* in the Old Testament.[1] In the New Testament that number nears two hundred occurrences.[2] Thus, I want to briefly define *grace* as best I can: *grace is God the Father in love doing good for ill-deserving sinners through God the Son by God the Spirit*. It is important to note that all grace, common and saving alike, is from God. First Peter 5:10 simply calls God "the God of all grace."

Common Grace

When the Bible declares that God is love[36] and that God loves the world,[37] it is declaring that, unlike the gods of other religions, the God of the Bible who made us and the rest of creation is entirely good. Furthermore, God's love is manifest to every human being—Christians and non-Christians alike.

Theologically, this grace is called *common grace*, based on the termi-

---

[35]Titus 3:3.
[36]1 John 4:16.
[37]John 3:16.

nology of Augustine, because it is for everyone and therefore common to all human beings. Positively, it reveals something of the goodness of God to all people; honors the image and likeness of God, which we bear by virtue of him creating us; improves the quality of life people experience; and precedes saving grace for the elect. Negatively, common grace does not save people from the wrath of God and the conscious, eternal torments of hell. Therefore, it is only helpful in this life and of no benefit in the life to come unless it is accompanied by God's saving grace. Basically, since everyone deserves hell, anything we receive in addition to that is the grace of God.

To illustrate common grace, the following Scripture passages are helpful:

> From the time that he [the unsaved Pharaoh who thought he was god] made him [Joseph] overseer in his house and over all that he had the LORD blessed the Egyptian's house for Joseph's sake; the blessing of the LORD was on all that he [Pharaoh] had, in house and field.[38]

> The earth is full of the steadfast love of the LORD.[39]

> You visit the earth and water it;
>   you greatly enrich it;
> the river of God is full of water,
>   you provide their grain,
>   for so you have prepared it.[40]

> You cause the grass to grow for the livestock
>   and plants for man to cultivate,
> that he may bring forth food from the earth.[41]

> The earth, O LORD, is full of your steadfast love.[42]

> The LORD is good to all,
>   and his mercy is over all that he has made.[43]

---

[38]Gen. 39:5.
[39]Ps. 33:5.
[40]Ps. 65:9.
[41]Ps. 104:14.
[42]Ps. 119:64.
[43]Ps. 145:9.

He makes his sun rise on the evil and on the good, and sends rain on the just and on the unjust.[44]

He is kind to the ungrateful and the evil.[45]

He did not leave himself without witness, for he did good by giving you rains from heaven and fruitful seasons, satisfying your hearts with food and gladness.[46]

He himself gives to all mankind life and breath and everything.[47]

The effects of God's common grace are innumerable. God's common grace allows even those who despise him to learn and to make gains in areas such as science, philosophy, technology, education, and medicine. God's common grace also fuels the creative process and permits the arts and creativity of all kinds.

The first time I remember this point hitting me was as a new Christian in college. I was sitting in a philosophy class where the atheistic professor was using his brilliant mind and winsome personality given to him from God to argue against the existence of God. Furthermore, God's common grace allows societies to flourish, families to exist, cities to rise up, and nations to prosper.[48] Common grace also allows people who are not connected to God through Jesus Christ to live seemingly decent moral lives of compassion and service, though their deeds are not in any way done to God's glory as acts of worship by the Holy Spirit.

In addition, God's common grace is seen in the restraining of evil by God the Holy Spirit,[49] in the effects of the conscience that God has placed within people,[50] and in the threat of reprisal from governments and laws that God has allowed to exist in the face of human sinfulness.[51] The result of God's common grace is that life as we experience it is far better than would otherwise be possible if sinners were simply left to themselves. Everyone experiences the grace of God to varying degrees, no matter how sinful they are, simply because God is loving and good

---

[44]Matt. 5:45.
[45]Luke 6:35.
[46]Acts 14:17.
[47]Acts 17:25.
[48]E.g., Ex. 31:2–11; 35:30–35.
[49]Gen. 6:3; 2 Thess. 2:6–7.
[50]Rom. 2:15.
[51]Rom. 13:1–4.

and is determined to do good in love. God has withheld his judgment, and at this very moment people are not immediately receiving what their sins deserve.

In responding to God's common grace as a Christian, I am free to enjoy the fullness of the effects of God's grace. On the day that I am writing this, God's grace accounts for the restful sleep and hearty breakfast that I enjoyed this morning before going on a walk to relish a sunny, crisp winter day while thanking God for good health and fresh air, then sitting down in a comfortable chair likely made by someone who does not know Jesus to type on a laptop likely made by someone else who does not love Jesus to write about the love of Jesus.

John Calvin described this common grace of God (which he also called the "general grace of God") saying, "All the notable endowments that manifest themselves among unbelievers are the gifts of God."[3]

Saving Grace

In addition to common grace, which everyone receives, the elect also receive *saving grace*. Unlike common grace, saving grace is ultimately irresistible because it is efficacious, meaning that it accomplishes the salvation that God intends without fail. The entire Trinity is involved in this saving grace, as Demarest points out: "Special grace [or saving grace] originates with God the Father (1 Cor 1:3; Eph 1:3, 6; Tit 2:11), is mediated through the saving work of Jesus Christ (Rom 5:15; 1 Cor 1:4; Tit 3:6–7), and is made experientially real through the ministry of the Holy Spirit (Zech 12:10; Heb 10:29)."[4]

Together common grace and saving grace coalesce into what John 1:16 refers to as "grace upon grace." Like common grace, saving grace has innumerable benefits in this life. However, unlike common grace, it also continues to provide infinite benefits beyond this life. Thus, we will examine in further detail how God's grace has been poured out upon all Christians, as Ephesians 1:7–8 says, "according to the riches of his grace, which he lavished upon us."

Saving grace comes to ill-deserving sinners through Jesus Christ alone. That is why Acts 20:24 speaks of the "gospel of the grace of God." The gospel of Jesus Christ is the same as the gospel of God's grace, because saving grace comes through Jesus Christ alone, as Scripture elsewhere declares:

> And the Word became flesh and dwelt among us . . . full of grace.[52]

> And from his fullness we have all received, grace upon grace. For the law was given through Moses; grace and truth came through Jesus Christ.[53]

> Blessed be the God and Father of our Lord Jesus Christ, who has blessed us in Christ with every spiritual blessing.[54]

> The grace of our Lord overflowed for me with the faith and love that are in Christ Jesus.[55]

> Be strengthened by the grace that is in Christ Jesus.[56]

Demarest notes that Paul speaks of grace more than any other biblical writer, some one hundred times.[5] A reading of the New Testament reveals another curious feature about the writings of Paul. In every single one of his letters, Paul opens and closes with the grace of God. He is thus repeatedly and emphatically illustrating the truth that nothing that is Christian is possible in any way or to any degree apart from the grace of God. He is also following the storyline of the Bible itself, which opens in Genesis 1:1 by revealing the hero of Scripture and history, saying, "In the beginning, God . . . " and ends with the final line of Scripture in Revelation 22:21 revealing that Jesus Christ is the God of grace, "The grace of the Lord Jesus be with all. Amen."

Simply, nothing in all of Christianity makes any sense apart from a proper understanding of the grace of God. Indeed, the Bible is a sword, and the soldier who fails to understand grace will wield it to his own destruction and the death of their hearers, as is sadly done by so many false teachers and cult leaders. They are prone to either legalism or libertinism (also called antinomianism).

---

[52]John 1:14.
[53]John 1:16–17.
[54]Eph. 1:3.
[55]1 Tim. 1:14.
[56]2 Tim. 2:1.

Grace and Legalism

Legalists see only the demands and commands of Scripture and make long lists of rules by which to judge people and enslave them to the law of duty that kills delight. They also overlook all that Jesus has done to fulfill the demands of the law in our place, so that our hope and trust is in our own efforts and not Jesus' finished work, which is a disgrace to grace. Rebuking such erroneous teaching, Paul condemns legalists, saying, "You have fallen away from grace" to people who basically thought that they were saved by grace but kept by their own works and law-keeping so that God would love them.[57] They wrongly believed that if they obeyed, God would love them, rather than believe the truth of grace, which is that God loves us so that we will obey. That is why Paul says that the entire domain in which true Christians live is no longer works but grace, "this grace in which we stand."[58]

The self-efforts of works that dominate every religion but Christianity focus legalistically on what we must do so that God will accept us, forgive us, embrace us, or, in a word, love us. Conversely, Christianity alone says that human works are antithetical to God's grace. Romans 11:6 declares that "if [salvation] is by grace, it is no longer on the basis of works; otherwise grace would no longer be grace." Indeed, we are saved by God's saving grace and are saved to good works. Nonetheless, those good works are also by God's grace through us:

> For by grace you have been saved through faith. And this is not your own doing; it is the gift of God, not a result of works, so that no one may boast. For we are his workmanship, created in Christ Jesus for good works, which God prepared beforehand, that we should walk in them.[59]

The issue is not whether Christians should do good works, such as loving their city, feeding the poor, caring for single mothers and their children, loving their enemies, or telling the truth, but rather how and why. The answer is not that we do good works so that God will love us or because we have to do them. Rather, we do good works because by grace in Jesus Christ, God does love us. Furthermore, God's saving grace

---

[57]Gal. 5:4.
[58]Rom. 5:2.
[59]Eph. 2:8–10.

has so utterly transformed us that we no longer have to do good works, but rather we get to do good works by the empowering grace of God the Holy Spirit, who is at work in our regenerated hearts.

Grace and Liberty

Contrary to legalists, libertines fail to understand that Jesus' death for sin and God's saving grace enable our death to sin. They are prone to simply see God's grace as having no effect until after we have sinned. To them, grace merely forgives the evil we do without transforming us. Anticipating just such an abuse of grace, Paul argues, "What shall we say then? Are we to continue in sin that grace may abound? By no means! How can we who died to sin still live in it?"[60] In context, Paul is not declaring that anyone will achieve sinless perfection in this life. Rather, he is declaring that anyone who has experienced the saving grace of God knows that Jesus can and will forgive sin, and in addition he transforms us with new hearts empowered by the Holy Spirit to pursue new desires for holiness and service for the glory of God and the good of others by the grace of God. Subsequently, those who want to keep sinning and simply expect Jesus to forgive them without experiencing any real repentance or life change have no true saving relationship with God and are abusing the grace of God.

Perhaps the most pathetic man I have ever argued with about this point was an adulterer. He had been divorced a few times, on each occasion for committing adultery on his Christian wife while claiming to be a Christian and then running off with the other women. When I confronted him on his repeated violation of the seventh commandment, he espoused the most pathetic view of grace I have ever heard. He said that as far as he was concerned, God's grace meant that he could do whatever he wanted and that Jesus was obligated to forgive him and give him grace. In his mind, he was an elephant and Jesus was the poor guy with the shovel who follows the elephant around the circus that was his life.

I told him that, by definition, God is not obligated to give him grace, because grace is a gift to the ill-deserving, and that God's grace not only forgives our sin but also transforms our lives so that we put sin to death because Jesus died for sin. He disagreed and said that he could not lose his salvation so he was not worried. I replied that Christians

---

[60]Rom. 6:1–2.

cannot lose their salvation, but by all I could surmise, he was not a Christian; indeed, he would not lose his salvation because he never possessed saving faith.

THIRTEEN EXPERIENCES OF GRACE

God's grace is among the most important truths in all of Christian belief. Therefore, it is not surprising to see that God's grace is among the most dominant themes of Scripture from beginning to end. First Peter 5:10 speaks of "the God of all grace"; following are thirteen ways in which saving grace is experienced in the life of a Christian.

1) Electing grace
2) Preached grace
3) Regenerating grace
4) Converting grace
5) Justifying grace
6) Adopting grace
7) Ministry grace
8) Sanctifying grace
9) Empowering grace
10) Provisional grace
11) Miraculous grace
12) Persevering grace
13) Glorifying grace

Electing Grace

Electing grace is God's sovereign choice in eternity past to love some ill-deserving sinners and save them by his grace alone. Second Timothy 1:8–9 describes this as "the power of God, who saved us and called us to a holy calling, not because of our works but because of his own purpose and grace, which he gave us in Christ Jesus before the ages began." Electing grace transforms the entire motive of spiritual living and everything from prayer to worship and charity to others. One of the wonderful benefits of electing grace is that unlike pagans and their silly religions that seek to manipulate God through everything from good works to self-denial and praying mantras, we do not need to do anything to make God be or do good. Why? Because God is good and

God delights in doing good, to the degree that he is gracious to us by his own initiative, loves us first, pursues us first, and cares for us first. This means that we do not pray, worship, or obey God so that he will love us, but, rather, because in grace he already has.

Preached Grace

Preached grace is the preaching of the gospel, which, when accompanied by the ministry of the Holy Spirit, releases the power of the gospel to transform sinners into saints by saving grace. Colossians 1:5–6 explains, "You have heard before in the word of the truth, the gospel, which has come to you, as indeed in the whole world it is bearing fruit and growing—as it also does among you, since the day you heard it and understood the grace of God in truth." Preached grace liberates us from treating evangelism as yet another sales technique whereby we have to manipulate or pressure people into making a decision for Jesus. The result is that we can freely, passionately, and simply share the love and truth of Jesus with people, knowing that God's grace accompanies the gospel, and if someone is elect, God will open his or her understanding by grace.

Regenerating Grace

Regenerating grace is the powerful work of God in ill-deserving sinners that causes them to be born again with new hearts as new people with new desires that are God's desires, thereby enabling a passionate life of holiness without legalism. In Jeremiah 32:38–41 God speaks of the regenerating gift of grace as the essence of the new covenant:

> And they shall be my people, and I will be their God. I will give them one heart and one way, that they may fear me forever, for their own good and the good of their children after them. I will make with them an everlasting covenant, that I will not turn away from doing good to them. And I will put the fear of me in their hearts, that they may not turn from me. I will rejoice in doing them good, and I will plant them in this land in faithfulness, with all my heart and all my soul.

In the New Testament this regenerating grace of God is referred to in terms of being born again, meaning that in addition to the common grace gift of birth, we also need the special grace gift of new birth to be saved. For example, 1 Peter 1:3 says, "Blessed be the God and Father of our Lord Jesus Christ! According to his great mercy, he has caused us to be born again to a living hope through the resurrection of Jesus Christ from the dead."

Regenerating grace is the source of all that it means to live as a Christian. As new creations with new hearts we have new passions, new desires, and new purposes, which culminate in a passionate life of joy and good works. This is because, as we follow the desires of our new heart, we are also following the desires of God's heart. At its deepest level, the new heart longs for the desires of God and rejoices in the freedom that comes in replacing old sinful longings with new holy longings that give God glory and us joy. As Psalm 40:8 declares, "I delight to do your will, O my God; your law is within my heart."

Converting Grace

Converting grace consists of the gifts of faith in Jesus and repentance of sin, which proceed from the new heart God gives us by his regenerating grace. Luke speaks of faith as a gift from God, of "those who through grace had believed."[61] Paul also speaks of faith as a gift of God's grace so that we would believe in Jesus: "For by grace you have been saved through faith. And this is not your own doing; it is the gift of God."[62] He desires that "God may perhaps grant [sinners] repentance."[63] Converting grace lays an ax to the root of religious pride. Religious pride causes us to boast in who we are, what we do, and how we have chosen God, and it is insidious to God and others. On the contrary, the Scriptures declare that even the faith to believe in Jesus is a gift and all of our salvation is all of grace, which means rather than boasting that we chose Jesus, we can boast in the grace of Jesus that chose to grant us the gifts of faith and repentance.

Justifying Grace

Justifying grace permits us, though legally condemned as sinners, to stand before our holy and righteous God and be justly declared righ-

---

[61]Acts 18:27.
[62]Eph. 2:8.
[63]2 Tim. 2:25.

teous as sinners saved by the death and resurrection of the sinless Jesus in our place for our sins. Romans 3:23–24 describes this justifying grace: "For all have sinned and fall short of the glory of God, and are justified by his grace as a gift, through the redemption that is in Christ Jesus." Justifying grace frees us from the performance trap of treadmill religion. In treadmill religion, we have to work hard and perform at a high level for God to take notice of us.

To make matters even more complicated, the list of rules by which merits and demerits are measured varies by one's religious team. On some teams you are holy if you drink alcohol whereas on others you are unholy if you drink alcohol. And this is only one of innumerable works that religious people squabble over. The problem with treadmill performance religion is that it leads to either pride or despair. If you keep the rules of your religious team, you become arrogant. Conversely, if you fail to keep the rules of your religious team, you despair. Justifying grace gives us full assurance that God will love us no more if we perform well and love us no less if we perform poorly. By justifying grace, our acceptance before God and the grounds for our righteousness are solely Jesus' works of sinless living, substitutionary death, and bodily resurrection and therefore are not in any way contingent upon what we do or do not do.

Adopting Grace

Adopting grace results in God becoming our spiritual Father and including us as members of his family, the church. As Ephesians 1:4–6 says, "In love he predestined us for adoption as sons through Jesus Christ, according to the purpose of his will, to the praise of his glorious grace, with which he has blessed us in the Beloved." Adopting grace completely transforms our motive for holy living. With God as our loving and perfect Father and the church as our helpful brothers and sisters, we seek to live good lives and do good works because that is what our family does; we don't do them in order to be part of the family. This means that rather than adopting grace serving as a license for sin, it makes us part of a people who are so loved and served by their Father that the last thing they would want to do is bring disrepute to his name.

Ministry Grace

Ministry grace is the spiritual gift or gifts that God gives to Christians, enabling them to have fruitful and fulfilling kingdom service. First Peter 4:10 connects spiritual gifts to God's grace: "As each has received a gift, use it to serve one another, as good stewards of God's varied grace." Ministry grace transforms our entire life so that everything we do is seen through the lens of ministry to God by the gracious spiritual gifts and natural talents he has given us. God gifts every Christian for meaningful and rewarding kingdom service to be done at work, home, church, and wherever else they find themselves. The results of using our gifts are glory to God, help to others, and joy for us. The Christian who serves according to the grace of their spiritual gift is able to live a purposeful and passionate life of humble service, which is itself a gift of God.

Sanctifying Grace

Sanctifying grace is the ongoing grace that God gives us in abundance and without limit to say no to sin and yes to God so that we can continually grow to be more and more holy like Jesus. Romans 6:14 speaks of sanctifying grace: "For sin will have no dominion over you, since you are not under law but under grace." Sanctifying grace utterly destroys legalism. Legalism is the human proclivity to pursue holiness by rule keeping and self-effort. Legalistic people tend to be the most miserable of all and often find their joy only in criticizing others and making fun of people who fall into sin. Legalistic people are also the ones who murdered Jesus, though today's legalists tend not to see that when they read their Bibles looking for more rules to add to their list.

Conversely, sanctifying grace allows us to mature increasingly as Christians and to be transformed more and more to the perfect character of Jesus by God's power. The result is that we do obey God, but our motive is that he already loves us, not that he would love us because we make ourselves more lovely and loveable. Jesus is emphatic that he has loved us first, and in return the desire of our regenerated hearts will be to obey him from love.[64] His love transforms us.

---

[64] John 14:15, 21, 23.

Empowering Grace

Empowering grace is God enabling us to do the good works that he has appointed for us to do with great power and humility. Speaking of the effects of empowering grace in his life, Paul says, "But by the grace of God I am what I am, and his grace toward me was not in vain. On the contrary, I worked harder than any of them, though it was not I, but the grace of God that is with me."[65] Empowering grace is nothing less than the power of God the Holy Spirit, "the Spirit of grace," enabling the Christian to live a life patterned after Jesus' life by the same power that empowered him.[66] Empowering grace enables Christians to live lives that are more fruitful and productive than they would have ever dreamed possible. The Christian can live not only on the mountaintop of blessing and victory, but also in the valley of pain and sorrow. In 2 Corinthians 12:9–10 Paul speaks of weakness, pain, and hardship in his own life and reveals how God spoke to him about empowering grace:

> But he said to me, "My grace is sufficient for you, for my power is made perfect in weakness." Therefore I will boast all the more gladly of my weaknesses, so that the power of Christ may rest upon me. For the sake of Christ, then, I am content with weaknesses, insults, hardships, persecutions, and calamities. For when I am weak, then I am strong.

Empowering grace means that, as promised, Jesus has not left or forsaken us, and we are not saved by grace but then expected to live by our own power until we see him face-to-face. No, God works in and through us by the empowering grace of the Holy Spirit so that we are able to live as more than conquerors, even in defeat, and to echo Isaiah 26:12: "You have indeed done for us all our works."

Provisional Grace

Provisional grace accounts for any and every good thing in our lives, from people who love us, to good health and material possessions. James 1:17 describes provisional grace: "Every good gift and every perfect gift is from above, coming down from the Father of lights." Provisional grace transforms our understanding of material possessions so that we

---

[65]1 Cor. 15:10.
[66]Heb. 10:29.

see ourselves as stewards of things God has given us. Too many people believe that everything they have is of their own earning, and as a result they tend to not thank God in sincerity for his provision. Yet the Bible is clear that everything belongs to God and that anything we have is his allowing us to borrow and steward his possessions. Furthermore, provisional grace should utterly condemn in us the propensity to covet. After all, if God has given us gifts we do not deserve, we should in no way lament that he gave other gifts to someone else. Instead, we should rejoice in the way that God has been gracious to us all.

One of the ways provisional grace comes to us is in the form of finances and wealth. Paul commends Christians who lived in Macedonia, saying, "We want you to know, brothers, about the grace of God that has been given among the churches of Macedonia," and he goes on to commend their generous financial giving to their church as an act of grace: "But as you excel in everything—in faith, in speech, in knowledge, in all earnestness, and in our love for you—see that you excel in this act of grace also."[67]

Financial provision is one of the more tangible ways in which we experience God's grace. Simply, every dollar we have is a gracious gift from God. As 2 Corinthians 8–9 illustrates, understanding financial grace transforms our concept of giving. Once we understand financial grace, we see that God is a giver, and that all things we have received come from God, including our wealth. We are thus graced to be generous and cheerful givers, which means that those who are stingy, greedy, and do not give generously to their church and to other needs have much to learn about provisional grace.

Miraculous Grace

Miraculous grace is poured out when God enables signs, wonders, and miracles to accompany his people. For example, "Stephen, full of grace and power, was doing great wonders and signs among the people."[68] Miraculous grace compels us to pray for sinners to repent, for the sick to be healed, and for the hand of God to show up in power as he wills. Because miracles happen by the grace of God, they are not contingent upon the presence of a guru, nor are they assured to those with enough faith or those who manipulate God through some spiritual ritual.

---

[67] 2 Cor. 8:1, 7.
[68] Acts 6:8.

Rather, because God is miraculous and gracious, Christians are given opportunities to see his miraculous hand and are encouraged to pray so that others might also experience his miraculous grace and worship him as the God of all power and grace.

Persevering Grace

Persevering grace enables every true Christian to have an ongoing loving relationship with Jesus that includes repenting of sin and returning to him if and when they stray.[69]

Persevering grace does not mean we will not sin, doubt, wander, or stray. But it does mean that Jesus pursues us and that our new heart eventually longs to return home, much like the prodigal son who eventually came to his senses and returned to his father.

In some ways, living by faith is living in the faith that persevering grace will be awaiting us tomorrow. Many people believe that God's grace saved them in the past, but they worry about God's persevering grace being available for them in the future; as a result, they experience doubt, distress, and even despair. Yet, much like the manna that fed God's people for forty years in the wilderness, God's grace is new every day and will sustain us—even tomorrow.

The result of trusting in God's persevering grace is the ability to echo the words of Paul, who said to his friends, "I am sure of this, that he who began a good work in you will bring it to completion at the day of Jesus Christ."[70] It is worthwhile to note that sleep is a gift that God gives to those who trust in his persevering grace, because they know that God did not begin a work in their life only to fail in its completion.

Glorifying Grace

Finally, glorifying grace is what awaits all who have been saved by grace, when one day their soul (which upon death dwells with Jesus until the day of resurrection) is reunited with their glorified body. They will live forever with Jesus and all his people from all the nations of the earth and generations of history in the eternal and perfect kingdom of God, free from the presence and power of sin. Speaking of this glorifying grace that awaits us, Romans 8:30–32 says:

---

[69]Phil. 1:6–7.
[70]Phil. 1:6.

Those whom he predestined he also called, and those whom he called he also justified, and those whom he justified he also glorified. What then shall we say to these things? If God is for us, who can be against us? He who did not spare his own Son but gave him up for us all, how will he not also with him graciously give us all things?

FOR SINNER AND SAINT

Indeed, grace is not only for the sinner but also for the saint. Glorifying grace will be the hallmark of our eternal state when the work of God's grace is revealed in full glory, seated upon what Hebrews 4:16 calls his "throne of grace." On that day when glorifying grace has completed its powerful transformation of all creation, including our bodies, the blind will see the glory of God, the lame will run to the throne of God, the deaf will hear the voice of God, the weeping will have every tear wiped from their eyes by the hand of God, and all things will be made new by the pure, free, sovereign, unending, inexhaustible, irresistible, efficacious, powerful, glorious, unparalleled, awe-inspiring, praise-evoking, life-changing, earth-shaking, mind-bending, heart-melting grace of God!

Indeed, I do believe in the grace of God. But I must confess that sometimes I easily forget and wander from it. Why? Because it all seems too good to be true. God's grace is true and found only in, by, through, and for Jesus Christ. Therefore, I keep reminding myself of the grace of God and its sufficiency for every aspect of every day of my existence.

To this end, God in his grace has seen fit to give me my wife, Grace, who is gracious with me as a constant reminder of his grace. I find that people are often gifts of God's grace to us. This is true of my wife, in whom the Spirit of grace resides and through whom the grace of God is extended to me. Together Grace and I are finding 2 Peter 3:18 to be a fitting summary of our life, and conclusion to this chapter, as we "grow in the grace and knowledge of our Lord and Savior Jesus Christ. To him be the glory both now and to the day of eternity. Amen."

QUESTION 5: **SEXUAL SIN**

How should Christian men and women go about breaking free from the bondage of sexual sin?

"Naughty coffee" is the new marketing craze in the highly competitive drive-through coffee stands in my hometown of Seattle. The marketing for the naughty coffee stands guarantees that attractive young women will lean over the counter to take your order and turn around to make your order while wearing such things as thong underwear and a push-up bra, a dirty nurse outfit, or a bikini and cowboy boots, depending upon which chain of naughty coffee shops you visit. The line of pickup trucks for these shops is usually very long, and occasionally you will see teenage boys on their bicycles ordering naughty coffee and getting an eyeful of nearly naked women.

How did this happen? How did stripping and coffee coalesce into a whole new meaning for "steaming hot"?

SEXUAL SIN IN SCRIPTURE

The trouble all began in Genesis, which is the book of beginnings. There, we see that our Trinitarian God made everything "good." The only thing that is called "not good" is that our first father, Adam, was alone. He had creation below him and God above him but no one alongside him to walk as an equal. In this way, Adam was unable to show forth the Trinitarian community of God; Adam was alone on the earth and not in community. For this reason, among others, God said it was "not good" for the man to be alone. So, God made a woman, our first mother, Eve, to be Adam's helper and bride. God then essentially walked her down the aisle and officiated the first wedding between the first man and the first woman. Thus, God set the precedent that, though different, men and women are equal as his image bearers and that marriage is a gift for one man and one woman to enjoy, and as a result he called all of this "very good."

Furthermore, God created their bodies for sexual pleasure to be enjoyed in marriage without shame saying, "Therefore a man shall leave his father and his mother and hold fast to his wife, and they shall become one flesh. And the man and his wife were both naked and were not ashamed."[1] Therefore, God's intent is that men and women would marry and enjoy sexual pleasure without shame.

When they do so, a husband and wife become "one" in a way that is analogous to our Trinitarian God being "one" although he is the three persons of Father, Son, and Spirit. Subsequently, a loving marriage is God's best, albeit imperfect, analogy for the Trinity. Using the same word for *one*, the Jews spoke the words of Deuteronomy 6:4 three times a day: "Hear, O Israel: The LORD our God, the LORD is one."

Simply, according to God, marriage and sex are related, connected, and exclusive. Sex as God intends it is for one man and one woman in marriage with the overarching purpose of oneness. Subsequently, by definition anything that contradicts God's intent is sinful. I do not mean to be graphic, but because there is such widespread sexual confusion, I will plainly state what constitutes sexual sin (though this is not meant to be exhaustive). Some acts are always sinful, such as homosexuality, bestiality, fornication, adultery, swinging, friends with benefits, bisexuality, rape, polygamy (including both polyandry and polygyny), pornography, prostitution, pedophilia, sinful lust, and incest. Some acts are sinful outside of marriage, including sex, masturbating another person, phone sex, sexual online chatting, heavy petting, oral sex, anal sex, and dry humping.

Tragically, when sin entered the world, human beings were separated from God and from one another. In Genesis 3 we see our first parents hiding from God and one another in shame that included confusion over their nakedness and sexuality. In the rest of Genesis, sexual sin of every sort and kind springs forth because when sin entered the world, everything was marred by sin, including sexuality.

---

[1] Gen. 2:24–25.

Sexual sin in Genesis includes the disaster of polygamy;[2] tragic love triangles;[3] disobedient marriages between believers and unbelievers;[4] homosexuality;[5] incest;[6] grievous mismatched marriages;[7] a loveless marriage;[8] divorce that includes a child;[9] rape;[10] a son sleeping with his stepmother;[11] attempted adultery;[12] and a false rape accusation.[13]

Sexual sin continues throughout the Old Testament, including a few very graphic references to it in Ezekiel[14] and repeated warnings against it in Proverbs. Unlike so many preachers today who lack the spine to talk about it, the prophets of the Old Testament had no such timidity.

In the New Testament, *porneia* (from which we get the word *pornography*) is translated as "sexual immorality" and encompasses all sorts of sexual sins; it is frequently used as a junk drawer in which every sort of perversion is thrown. This is because God in his wisdom knew that if he only listed certain sexual sins as off-limits, someone would find a loophole by which to keep the letter of the law while denying the spirit and write yet another book explaining how to sin against God in a way that is "biblical."

SEXUAL SIN TODAY

Today, sexual sin shows no signs of slowing down and has only accelerated, thanks in large part to the indoctrination of young people in their schools. Sexual education as we know it began in 1964 with the Sexuality Information and Education Council of the United States (SIECUS). SIECUS was launched at the Kinsey Institute named after Alfred Kinsey, who conducted a famously flawed sexual survey and was himself a homosexual who supported child/adult sex and died of a pelvic infection that resulted from his own sexual perversion. The cofounder and first president of SIECUS was Mary Calderone; she was

[2]Gen. 4:18–24; 28:6–9; 29:14–29.
[3]Gen. 16:1–16; 29:31–30:24.
[4]Gen. 6:1–2.
[5]Gen. 19:1–29.
[6]Gen. 19:30–38; 38.
[7]Gen. 26:34–35.
[8]Gen. 29:31.
[9]Gen. 21:8–14.
[10]Gen. 34:1–2.
[11]Gen. 35:22.
[12]Gen. 39:1–23.
[13]Gen. 39:1–23.
[14]Ezek. 16:25–27; 23:18–21.

also the former medical director for Planned Parenthood. The first gift given to the council was from Hugh Hefner of *Playboy* fame, and today it remains the most influential resource for sex education in American public schools. Calderone wrote of sex education:

> A new stage of evolution is breaking across the horizon and the task of educators is to prepare children to step into that new world. To do this, they must pry children away from old views and values, especially from biblical and other traditional forms of sexual morality—for religious laws or rules about sex were made on the basis of ignorance.[1]

It appears that the advocates of sexual sin have won. The sexual revolution of the 1960s and 1970s radically altered the sexual landscape of our nation so that today sex before marriage and viewing pornography are the culturally accepted norm.

When it comes to sexual sin, there is nothing new under the sun, and the problem is as old as Eden. The problem of sexual sin continues unabated, as the following cultural statistics[2] on premarital sex,[3] pornography, rape, and sex slavery reveal. We can see that, as Scripture predicts, sin leads to sadness, suffering, and ultimately death.

Premarital Sex

When talking with a number of young teens in their junior high years, it has become painfully obvious that the sexual landscape of our culture has rapidly changed even in one generation. Girls, some of whom even claim to be Christian, sign pledges to their parents vowing to remain virgins until their marriage yet engage in oral and anal sex with boys because, for them, those acts do not count as sinful acts that violate their virginity. I have met more than a few young teenage boys who have naked photos of their girlfriends on their phones, because it is now widely expected that if, say, a thirteen-year-old couple is dating, naked photos of their boyfriend or girlfriend will be made available.

Anyone who is surprised to hear of these things would be well served to spend some time surfing online social networking sites for teens and twenty-somethings, such as Facebook and MySpace. You will see that those sites are the new confession booths where young people share their deepest secrets and post pictures of themselves that would have been considered porn when their grandparents were the same age.

Many parents, in general, and Christian parents, in particular, have had their children commit to sexual abstinence. However, the *Journal of Adolescent Health* reports that, of course, adolescents who commit to abstinence do not always honor that commitment. Research shows that "most teenagers who take a pledge to abstain from sex before marriage ultimately go on to have sex before marriage, and they are somewhat less likely to use contraception at first intercourse than adolescents who did not pledge."[4]

There is some benefit to abstinence pledges, however, according to the *Center for Data Analysis Report*, which says that "because they typically experience first sex 18 months later than teens who do not pledge, teenage girls who pledge are less likely to become pregnant as teenagers."[5]

Indeed, most adolescents and adults end up having sex before marriage. The mean age of first intercourse in the United States is now 16.4.[6] The implications of premarital sex by adolescents and adults alike are enormous. The *National Vital Statistics Reports* reveal that from 1960 to 1998, birth rates more than doubled for unmarried teens ages fifteen to nineteen (from 15.3 to 41.5 percent), as well as for unmarried women aged fifteen to forty-four (from 21.6 to 44.3 percent).[7]

Simply put, many children are conceived by teenage girls and unmarried women every year, with many being aborted and others being born into the world. The National Center for Health Statistics reports that in 2005, 420,000 girls under the age of twenty in the United States gave birth—83 percent out of wedlock.[8] Therefore, with increasing numbers of adolescents and adults engaging in premarital sex, "millions of children are being born every year into family contexts that do not bode well for their future financial, emotional, and social welfare."[9]

A number of social scientific studies also find that adolescent premarital sex, particularly casual sex (where there is no romantic relationship), is linked to psychological pathologies such as depression, suicidal thoughts, and suicide attempts.[10] The evidence for this correlation is so overwhelming that anyone who loves adolescents has to take it seriously.

This association between adolescent sex and psychological problems is also markedly stronger for girls than it is for boys. One study found that the association between sex and depression was almost twice as powerful among teenage girls.[11] A study of twelve- through sixteen-year-old students found that sexually active girls were 6.3 times more likely to report having attempted suicide than were virgin girls.[12]

Adolescents who abstain from sex are less likely to be involved in antisocial or risky behaviors such as drinking, drug use, and delinquency.[13] A study of 1,052 urban adolescents found that abstinence was associated with significantly lower levels of tobacco, alcohol, marijuana, and other illegal drug use.[14] A study of 3,054 Massachusetts high school students found that students "with more [sexual] partners are more likely to have greater frequency and severity of lifetime and recent drug use."[15]

Studies indicate that the academic consequences of teenage sex are strongest for boys.[16] A longitudinal study of 1,120 Florida adolescents found that boys who experienced sex between waves of the study were significantly more likely to suffer a decline in their academic performance relative to peers who remained virgins. The authors concluded: "To the extent that adolescent premarital coitus has long-term effects on academic performance, and to the extent that school performance is a good indicator of success in later life, premarital coitus may have far-reaching negative consequences for a white male's future well-being."[17]

Pornography

I remember when, as a new Christian in college, I had a conversation with another young Christian who frequently viewed pornography. He told me that was okay because he had examined the Bible thoroughly and never saw the word *pornography*. But he had conveniently missed the mountain of verses that speak about lust. This is typical among people who, as Paul says, want to suppress the truth so they can keep on sinning sexually.[15]

The purpose of pornography is clearly lust. Lust for anyone but your spouse is condemned by God as a grievous evil repeatedly throughout both the Old and New Testaments.[16] The act of lusting after the unclothed body of a person is not a sin. The issue is *which* person's

---

[15]Rom. 1:18–24.
[16]Prov. 6:25; Job 31:1; Matt. 5:28; Col. 3:5; 1 Thess. 4:5; 1 Pet. 4:3.

unclothed body you are lusting after. If he or she is your spouse, then you are simply making the Song of Solomon sing again to God's glory and your joy. If he or she is not your spouse, then you are sinning.

It was God who clothed our first parents after their sin, and only sinners undress themselves for purposes that do not glorify God. While both men and women get entangled in pornography, it is particularly enticing for men, because there is a biological connection between a man's eyes and his genitals that causes him to be easily stimulated visually. Pornography has the sad effect of objectifying people, thereby divorcing them from their body and consequently diminishing their dignity as God's image bearers.

Defining pornography is terribly difficult, as evidenced by the inability of our nation's Supreme Court to clearly articulate exactly what it is. For the purposes of our study, by *pornography* I am referring to graphic, sexually explicit material involving adults engaged in sexual acts. I do not necessarily include as pornographic such things as nude works of art or a romantic scene in a movie, but I acknowledge that sinners can lust at almost anything. I do include such things as porno movies, magazines, Web sites, online filthy sexual chat, trashy romance novels, phone sex with paid operators, explicit movies, lingerie catalogs, and even the swimsuit issues of sports magazines, the increasingly base men's and women's magazines that show more skin than pornographic magazines did just a few generations ago, and anything else I have forgotten that some son of Adam or daughter of Eve finds titillating.

My inclusion of mainstream magazines may seem extreme in light of our crass culture. Still, we must remember that in the early 1950s no stores carried soft pornography; in the 1960s *Playboy* was made available out of sight behind the counter; in the 1970s *Penthouse* made it next to *Playboy* on the shelf; and today's decline has soft and hard pornography available on the magazine rack for perusal by children and adults who pick it up. In our increasingly brazen and desensitized culture, we have to be careful not to define pornography in terms of only harder forms while neglecting the softer forms. As an example, on an international flight I once took, movies with full nudity and sex scenes played on the headrest televisions around me while bored young children looked on.

Most experts agree there are four basic aspects to virtually all heterosexual pornography, which constitutes the majority of porn:

1) The message is consistent that all women want sex from all men all the time in all kinds of bizarre ways and are essentially nymphomaniacs.
2) Women really enjoy whatever any man does to them sexually.
3) Any woman who does not meet the stereotype of (1) and (2), above, can quickly be changed through a bit of force or intimidation.
4) The woman is dominated and degraded by the man in a way that exploits her as essentially a tool for the pleasure of the man; she is not really a person but mere parts.

That final point is a direct attack on the fact that God made every human being in his image and likeness with dignity, value, and worth. Men who seek to objectify and degrade women do so with a handful of particularly base terms. One example is Tom Leykis, America's most popular talk radio show host for young men. His show exists to teach men how to get "more tail for less money" and often refers to women's bodies as "toilets" where men go to drop their fluids. As recently as 1991, police in a southern California community closed all rape reports made by prostitutes and addicts, placing them in a file stamped "NHI," which stands for "No Human Involved."[18]

My point? Our culture is becoming less and less biblical in its thinking and more sexualized in its practice, and it has taken forty years to go from one dirty magazine under the counter at the local convenience store to today, where the following statistics are staggering.

Annual pornography revenues are over $90 billion worldwide.[19] The U.S. spent $13 billion on pornography in 2006, more than the combined revenues of all professional football, baseball, and basketball franchises[20] or the combined revenues of ABC, CBS, and NBC ($6.2 billion).[21] Of the $13 billion, $2.84 was spent on Internet porn.[22] In each of the last ten years, America has spent at least $10 billion—the same amount it spends on foreign aid.[23] In 2005, more than 13,000 new hardcore movie titles were released in the U.S.[24] Every forty minutes a new pornographic video is being created in the United States alone; every second $3,075.64 is being spent on pornography; 28,258 Internet users are viewing pornography; and 372 Internet users are typing adult search terms into search engines.[25]

Porn on the Internet

On the Internet, the top word searched for is *sex*, with *porn, nude, Playboy*, and *erotic stories* also in the top twenty.[26] Furthermore, 70 percent of porn traffic occurs between 9 AM and 5 PM, while people are sitting at work.[27]

Porn sites account for 12 percent of all Internet sites.[28] Porn is the content of 25 percent of daily search engine requests.[29] Over 40 percent of Internet users view porn.[30] Fully 20 percent of men admit accessing pornography at work.[31] No less than 13 percent of women admit accessing pornography at work.[32] Additionally, 53 percent of Promise Keepers men viewed pornography during the previous week, according to one study.[33]

In 2004 Steve Kroft reported for *60 Minutes* on the state of sexually explicit material in the U.S.: "Hilton, Marriot, Hyatt, Sheraton and Holiday Inn . . . all offer adult films on in-room pay-per-view television systems. And they are purchased by a whopping 50 percent of their guests, accounting for nearly 70 percent of their in-room profits."[34]

In 2003, the *Des Moines Register* reported:

> A study . . . found searches for child pornography at 230 colleges nationwide. . . . 42% of all searches on file-to-file sharing systems involved child or adult pornography. The study also found that 73% of movie searches were for pornography, 24% percent of image searches were for child pornography, and only 3% of the searches did not involve pornography or copyrighted materials.[35]

Additionally, in 2002 the U.S. Customs Service estimated that there were already more than 100,000 Web sites offering child pornography, which is illegal worldwide.[36]

Frighteningly, porn use is increasingly common among children. A staggering 90 percent of children between the ages of eight and sixteen have viewed pornography on the Internet, in most cases unintentionally.[37] The average age of first Internet exposure to pornography is eleven years old.[38] Youth with significant exposure to sexuality in the media have been shown to be significantly more likely to have had intercourse at ages fourteen to sixteen.[39]

Pornography and Sexual Addiction

Proverbs 27:20 says, "Sheol and Abaddon are never satisfied, and never satisfied are the eyes of man." God in his wisdom likens death and destruction to the increasingly deadly appetites fueled by the lustful eyes of sinners. If we apply this principle to pornographic lust, it becomes apparent that seeing such smut is not going to satisfy someone's lust but, rather, inflame it for more images. Those with lusting eyes may begin with a magazine, Web site, or video and continue to view more magazines, Web sites, or videos until they become bored, and then they descend into strip clubs, prostitutes, and experiences with other enslaved people, which eventually become boring and lead to orgies, voyeurism, exhibitionism, pedophilia, and wherever else a crooked human heart can venture. Don't kid yourself—sin is an on-ramp to death. If you get on it and don't repent, turn around, and exit, you will find the landscape getting darker, grosser, filthier, and deadlier.

The National Online Resource Center on Violence Against Women reports, "As pornography has become more acceptable, both legally and culturally, the level of brutality toward, and degradation of, women has intensified."[40] One pornography director said it this way: "People just want it harder, harder, and harder. . . . what are you gonna do next?"[41] Another director described his task this way:

> One of the things about today's porn and the extreme market, the gonzo market, so many fans want to see so much more extreme stuff that I'm always trying to figure out ways to do something different. . . . It's definitely brought porn somewhere, but I don't know where it's headed from there.[42]

Therefore, not surprisingly, porn addiction is now not only more extreme but also more prevalent. While we can only speculate what percentage of porn addicts does not admit its sin, 10 percent of American adults do admit to being addicted to Internet porn.[43] Of these, 28 percent are women.[44] While only 10 percent of Americans admit to addiction, more than 70 percent of men from eighteen to thirty-four visit a pornographic site in a typical month.[45] Porn addiction has also found its way into the lives of Christians, as 57 percent of pastors say that addiction to pornography is the most sexually damaging issue to their congregation.[46]

In the late 1970s, Patrick Carnes, a psychologist and researcher, was instrumental in the initial identification and treatment of sexual addiction as a condition. In addition to conducting the initial research on sexual addiction, Dr. Carnes was the clinical director for sexual disorder services at The Meadows in Wickenburg, Arizona, from 1996 until 2004. Carnes's list of criteria for sexual addiction is helpful for people to consider for their own lives and the lives of those they know who are potentially sexually addicted:[47]

- A pattern of out-of-control behavior
- Severe consequences because of sexual behavior
- Inability to stop despite negative consequences
- Severe mood changes around sexual behavior
- Persistent pursuit of high-risk behaviors
- Ongoing effort to stop and/or limit behaviors
- Inordinate amounts of time spent on sexual matters
- Increasing amounts of sexual experiences
- Sexual obsession and fantasy as a primary coping tool

Clinically speaking, sexual addiction has many different forms: compulsive masturbation, sex with prostitutes, anonymous sex with multiple partners, multiple affairs outside a committed relationship, habitual exhibitionism, habitual voyeurism, inappropriate sexual touching, repeated sexual abuse of children, and episodes of rape. Of all forms of sexual addiction, none is more harmful to both the addict and the victim than childhood sexual abuse. The beginnings of sexual addiction are usually rooted in adolescence or childhood. Over 80 percent of sexual addicts were abused by someone during their childhood.[48]

Sex addicts have no comprehension of the risks they are taking and have completely lost both perspective and control. To deal with the pain, the addict may resort to other addictions such as alcoholism, eating disorders, and abusive drugs. Many times suicide is a constant thought. The addicts might punish themselves by engaging in sexual acts that are degrading, as a sick form of false atonement whereby they seek to pay God back, or at least appease their conscience.

The link between pornography, sexual addiction, and rape is widely known. Robin Morgan's phrase, "Pornography is the theory, rape is the practice," captures the connection between what is seen on a screen and what is subsequently done to a victim. Admittedly, there is an endless debate surrounding whether prolonged exposure to hardcore pornography results in the sex addict being more prone to sexual violence. Still, the question is not whether there is a direct causal link between pornography viewing and rape but, rather, how pornography is part of sexual violence. Pornography encourages sinful lust, feeds sinful desires, blurs the line between reality and fantasy, empowers the sinful flesh, and does nothing to restrain evil and promote virtue.

Regarding the link between pornography and behavior, 80 percent of prostitution survivors at the WHISPER Oral History Project reported that their customers showed them pornography to illustrate the kinds of sexual activities in which they wanted to engage. Also, 52 percent of the women stated that pornography played a significant role in teaching them what was expected of them as prostitutes. Furthermore, 30 percent reported that their pimps regularly exposed them to pornography in order to indoctrinate them into an acceptance of the practices depicted.[49]

Pornography and Ted Bundy

Perhaps most chilling are some excerpts from serial killer Ted Bundy in an interview conducted by James Dobson hours before he was executed:[50]

> DOBSON: For the record, you are guilty of killing many women and girls.
>
> BUNDY: Yes, that's true.
>
> DOBSON: How did it happen? Take me back. What are the antecedents of the behavior that we've seen? You were raised in what you consider to be a healthy home. You were not physically, sexually or emotionally abused.
>
> BUNDY: No. And that's part of the tragedy of this whole situation. I grew up in a wonderful home with two dedicated and loving parents,

as one of 5 brothers and sisters. We, as children, were the focus of my parents' lives. We regularly attended church. My parents did not drink or smoke or gamble. There was no physical abuse or fighting in the home. I'm not saying it was "Leave it to Beaver," but it was a fine, solid Christian home. I hope no one will try to take the easy way out of this and accuse my family of contributing to this. I know, and I'm trying to tell you as honestly as I know how, what happened.

As a young boy of 12 or 13, I encountered, outside the home, in the local grocery and drug stores, softcore pornography. Young boys explore the sideways and byways of their neighborhoods, and in our neighborhood, people would dump the garbage. From time to time, we would come across books of a harder nature—more graphic. This also included detective magazines, etc., and I want to emphasize this. The most damaging kind of pornography—and I'm talking from hard, real, personal experience—is that that involves violence and sexual violence. The wedding of those two forces—as I know only too well—brings about behavior that is too terrible to describe . . .

Basically, I was a normal person. I wasn't some guy hanging out in bars, or a bum. I wasn't a pervert in the sense that people look at somebody and say, "I know there's something wrong with him." I was a normal person. I had good friends. I led a normal life, except for this one, small but very potent and destructive segment that I kept very secret and close to myself. Those of us who have been so influenced by violence in the media, particularly pornographic violence, are not some kind of inherent monsters. We are your sons and husbands. We grew up in regular families. Pornography can reach in and snatch a kid out of any house today. It snatched me out of my home 20 or 30 years ago. As diligent as my parents were, and they were diligent in protecting their children, and as good a Christian home as we had, there is no protection against the kinds of influences that are loose in a society that tolerates. . . .

Prostitution

The vast majority of young women involved in prostitution were sexually abused as children; estimates range from two-thirds to 95 percent.[51] Estimates of the prevalence of incest among prostitutes range from 65 to 90 percent.[52] The Council for Prostitution Alternatives, Portland, Oregon, Annual Report in 1991 stated that 85 percent of prostitutes/clients reported a history of sexual abuse in childhood; 70 percent reported incest.[53] The higher percentages (80 to 90 percent) of reports of incest and childhood sexual assaults of prostitutes come from anecdotal reports and from clinicians working with prostitutes.[54] One woman has said with devastating precision, "Incest is boot camp [for prostitution]."[55]

The average age of entry into prostitution is thirteen years.[56] According to the Trafficking Victims Protection Reauthorization Act of 2005, an estimated 100,000 to 300,000 adolescents are commercially sexually exploited annually in the U.S.[57] Most of these are girls who were recruited or coerced into prostitution. Others were "traditional wives" without job skills who escaped from or were abandoned by abusive husbands and went into prostitution to support themselves and their children.[58]

The life of a prostitute is incredibly dark: 62 percent report having been raped in prostitution; 73 percent report having experienced physical assault in prostitution; 72 percent are currently or were formerly homeless; and 92 percent state that they want to escape prostitution immediately.[59] In one study, 75 percent of women in escort prostitution had attempted suicide; prostituted women comprised 15 percent of all completed suicides reported by hospitals.[60] Describing the trauma of prostitution and its consequences, one fourteen-year-old stated: "You feel like a piece of hamburger meat—all chopped up and barely holding together."[61]

BREAKING FREE

How should Christian men and women go about breaking free from the bondage of sexual sin? Having examined in painful detail the kinds and consequences of sexual sin, we will now consider eleven tips for Christian men and women seeking to break free from the bondage of sexual sin.

1) Understand why your physical body craves sinful desires.

Stephen Arterburn's New Life Ministries says:

> Sexual pleasure is one of the most intense human experiences. Physically speaking, when a man or woman reaches sexual excitement, nerve endings release a chemical into the brain called "opioid." "Opioid" means opium-like and is a good description of the power

of this chemical. Apart from a heroin-induced experience, nothing is more physically pleasurable than sex. This is a wonderful thing in a committed marriage relationship, because it helps to bond two people together and bring joy to living together and building a relationship.

There can be a downside to the pleasure of sex, however. If sexual experiences happen outside of marriage and are constantly repeated, a sex act can move from being a simple pleasure to an addiction. Instead of being bonded with a person, you become bonded to the act itself. If the sexual experiences are pornography, your flesh will instantly recall the images you viewed for "re-lusting" purposes. These images are stamped into your brain with the aid of hormones released during sexual arousal.[62]

In other words, anything associated with sexual pleasure can become addictive. In a faithful marriage, this can mean that being a one-woman man, as Paul commands pastors to exemplify and for everyone in the church to imitate, will result in physical desires and responses being conditioned in such a way that their sexual desires will be for their spouse. Conversely, as a pastor, I have seen men and women so addicted to masturbation that they could not experience any sexual climax except by masturbating, leaving them with no desire or use for marital relations. Practically speaking, it is vital that, through obedience to God, we condition our bodies to enjoy and desire that which is holy rather than that which is sinful.

2) See sex as a potentially false and demonic religion.

In Romans 1:24–25, Paul says that either people worship God our Creator and enjoy his creation—including our bodies—or people worship creation as God, and in sexual sin offer their bodies in worship. Paul goes on to explain that those who worship creation invariably worship the human body, because it is the apex of God's creation. In this upending of rightful worship, sex becomes a religion and the sex act a perverse sacrament.

Christianity today is comprised of three basic denominations: Protestant, Catholic, and Orthodox. Likewise, the religion of Sex also includes three "denominations": Straight, Gay, and Bisexual. Like Christian denominations, the Sex denominations have Web sites (e.g., social networks, chat rooms, classified ads), designated houses of wor-

ship (e.g., bars, clubs, strip joints), and followers who vigorously evangelize and recruit new members.

In sum, the greatest threat to Christianity is Sex. Perversion of
every sort and kind is the worship that defines which denomination
of Sex one is in. Everyone who settles for the worship of Sex is deep
down truly seeking an intimacy, joy, and connection that is found only
through faith in relationship with God. As the famous quote goes, "The
young man who rings the bell at the brothel is unconsciously looking
for God."[63]

3) See sex as an act of worship.

Paul accused people in his day of worshiping their stomachs as god,
and in our day it appears that the god we worship has moved a short
distance south. Paul flatly states in Romans 12:1 that worship is offering our bodies.[17] Therefore, in a very real sense all sexual sin is idolatry.
(Idolatry is the worship of someone or something other than the one
true God.) Paul makes this connection between sexual sin and idolatry
in 1 Corinthians 10:7–8: "Do not be idolaters as some of them were; as
it is written, 'The people sat down to eat and drink and rose up to play.'
We must not indulge in sexual immorality as some of them did, and
twenty-three thousand fell in a single day."

Be honest—is there anything sexual in your life that is sinful or has
possibly even risen to the level of an addiction?

Is there sexual sin in your life that you have simply learned to tolerate
and live with rather than putting it to death because Jesus died for it?

Do you have a secret side to your life, such as surfing the net, renting
movies, buying magazines, frequenting strip clubs or seedy massage
parlors, lurking on naughty chat rooms, flirting with people, having
sinful sex, or privately masturbating?

Do you feel guilty, ashamed, and embarrassed after a sexual sin and
want to stop but find that over time you become desensitized and do it
again?

Has your sexual sin become depersonalized for you so that it has
disconnected you from other people?

Do you see a cycle behind your sexual sin? Perhaps it happens at

---

[17]Rom. 12:1, NIV.

fairly predictable intervals. Maybe you sin sexually as a reward for doing well or as a way to find relief from life's pressures.

Do you undergo withdrawal symptoms when you do not satisfy an urge for sexual sin?

Are you deceiving yourself by trying to convince yourself that your sexual sin is not a big deal or that you can manage it and keep it from getting out of control?

Has your sexual sin become so strong and you so weak that you have lost your willpower to fight sinful temptation and have either just accepted it or considered yourself a victim of it and powerless to stop it?

Has your sexual sin become so pervasive that you have a loss of focus in your life? Has your sexual sin taken so much of your time, energy, and money that it has started to dominate a large portion of your life?

If you are guilty of sexual sin, who are your victims? Who is suffering because of you, and how? Does your spouse suffer because you are distant in shame? Do your children suffer because you are distracted and therefore unattentive to them? Does your job suffer because your sin is now affecting your work? Does your church suffer because your sin has caused you to distance yourself from other Christians?

Are you closer to or further from God because of your sexual practice?

In the end, it must be accepted that sexual sin is idolatry and the worship of someone or something other than God as a god. Since the first two commandments tell us that there is only one God and that we are to worship him alone, nothing could be bigger than this issue. Sexual sin is ultimately a worship disorder.

4) Take your sexual sin as seriously as God does.

In 1 Peter 4:3 we read, "For the time that is past suffices for doing what the Gentiles want to do, living in sensuality, passions, drunkenness, orgies, drinking parties, and lawless idolatry." Christians are commanded not to return to their pagan patterns of reckless living and sexual perversion. In 1 John 2:15–17 we are urged:

> Do not love the world or the things in the world. If anyone loves the world, the love of the Father is not in him. For all that is in the world—the desires of the flesh and the desires of the eyes and pride

in possessions—is not from the Father but is from the world. And the
world is passing away along with its desires, but whoever does the will
of God abides forever.

John's dire warning is that the lust of our eyes is continually enticed
by the images and perversions of the world in which we live, and we
must remain vigilant not to love the tempting sins of the world. John's
warning rings even more true in a culture where, because of technology,
it is now easier to see someone naked than to get something out of the
fridge—to get to the fridge you at least need to stand up and walk.

First John 3:9 teaches that "no one born of God makes a practice of
sinning, for God's seed abides in him, and he cannot keep on sinning
because he has been born of God." Clearly, while none of us can become
perfect in this life,[18] God does promise that Christians can put their sin
(including sexual sin) to death, because Jesus died for it.

In 1 Corinthians 5:9–11, Paul says that those who claim to be
Christians but live in habitual, unrepentant sexual immorality are not
fit for Christian friendship and community unless they repent, because
they are defiling their friends and their church with their perversion.
The cold hard truth is that most people's struggles are known only by
their fellow Christian friends, and unless Christians spend their energies holding one another accountable to get dominion over their pants,
then Christian friendship is nothing more than Christian fakery.

In 1 Corinthians 10:8, Paul says, "We must not indulge in sexual
immorality as some of them did, and twenty-three thousand fell in a
single day." Speaking of God's people in Exodus, Paul warns us that
throughout history God was so sickened by sexual sin that he killed
perverted multitudes in the desert, as well as in places like Sodom and
Gomorrah. Yes, God does justly kill some people. Sometimes it's all at
once, and sometimes it's a bit at a time, say, with a sexually transmitted
disease. Worse still, some victims of sexual sin experience sickness, like
my buddy who got herpes from his wife, and even death, like guys who
give their wives AIDS.

In 1 Corinthians 6:9–10, Paul says, "Or do you not know that the
unrighteous will not inherit the kingdom of God? Do not be deceived:
neither the sexually immoral, nor idolaters . . . will inherit the kingdom

---

[18] 1 John 1:8.

of God." Clearly, God takes the sexual sins of his people so seriously that those who remain enslaved to sexual sin will die in their sins and wake up in the eternal torments of hell. Sure, the naked people you like looking at are hot . . . but so is hell.

My single point with all of these warnings from Scripture is to implore you to take sexual sins as seriously as your God does. Paul summarizes this thought perfectly in 1 Thessalonians 4:3–8:

> For this is the will of God, your sanctification: that you abstain from sexual immorality; that each one of you know how to control his own body in holiness and honor, not in the passion of lust like the Gentiles who do not know God. . . . For God has not called us for impurity, but in holiness. Therefore whoever disregards this, disregards not man but God, who gives his Holy Spirit to you.

The way out of sexual sin is not more guilt, more shame, more condemnation, or the like. The way out of sexual sin is to be controlled by the Holy Spirit, who is more powerful than sin in the life of a believer. Galatians 5:16–25 says it this way:

> Walk by the Spirit, and you will not gratify the desires of the flesh. For the desires of the flesh are against the Spirit, and the desires of the Spirit are against the flesh, for these are opposed to each other, to keep you from doing the things you want to do. But if you are *led by the Spirit, you are not under the law. Now the works of the flesh are evident: sexual immorality, impurity, sensuality,* idolatry, sorcery, enmity, strife, jealousy, fits of anger, rivalries, dissensions, divisions, envy, drunkenness, orgies, and things like these. I warn you, as I warned you before, that those who do such things will not inherit the kingdom of God. But the fruit of the Spirit is love, joy, peace, patience, kindness, goodness, faithfulness, gentleness, self-control; against such things there is no law. And those who belong to Christ Jesus have crucified the flesh with its passions and desires. If we live by the Spirit, let us also walk by the Spirit.

It is the Holy Spirit who gives us desires that are deeper and stronger than sinful desires. Thus, a holy life is the most passionate life that does not settle for petty things like sexual sin but, rather, passionately pursues the glory of God in all things.

5) Get to the heart of the matter.

Jesus wisely taught that sexual sins are committed not only in what we do but also in what we think in our mind and desire in our heart. In Matthew 5:27–28 he taught, "You have heard that it was said, 'You shall not commit adultery.' But I say to you that everyone who looks at a woman with lustful intent has already committed adultery with her in his heart." Also, in Mark 7:21–23, Jesus said, "For from within, out of the heart of man, come evil thoughts, sexual immorality, theft, murder, adultery, coveting, wickedness, deceit, sensuality, envy, slander, pride, foolishness. All these evil things come from within, and they defile a person."

Thus, sexual sins are not out there in the media or strip club. Truly, the problem is in you. It is from the sinfulness of your heart that lust and sin proceed like sewage from a culvert. This is the painful, unvarnished truth.

Practically, this means that only you and God truly know your heart, and, rather than trying to obey legalistic rules, you must be honest about the lusts in your heart and reduce those triggers that stimulate you. This does not mean you should be a legalist who seeks to impose your unbiblical rules on others, arguing that things such as a computer, Internet access, or television are inherently sinful and that no Christian should use them. However, you must have personal legalisms. Personal legalisms are ways in which you follow the conscience God gave you in order to guard your heart.

I will use myself as an example. One of my personal legalisms is having a male assistant who travels with me so that I can be sure to account for my time away from home and remain "above reproach," as the Scriptures require. It is not a sin for someone to travel alone, but for me, it is a rule I have made so as to operate according to conscience and be considerate of my wife, whom I love.

Romans 13:13–14 says, "Let us walk properly as in the daytime, not in orgies and drunkenness, not in sexual immorality and sensuality, not in quarreling and jealousy. But put on the Lord Jesus Christ, and make no provision for the flesh, to gratify its desires." To do this practically means that some who know their heart should live with a roommate if they are single, should discontinue the cable television package that offers shows they keep watching but should not, or have an Internet accountability partner who gets a regular report of which sites they are visiting to help them "walk in the light," as Scripture says. Still, in the end, rules and precautionary methods work only if we have a change of heart, seeing our sin as sin and growing in our deepest desires to obey God. Outward life changes are good, but without an inward heart change, the bottom line is that we will not be able to obey 1 Peter 2:11 and "abstain from the passions of the flesh, which wage war against your soul."

6) Repent and keep on repenting.

The Protestant Reformation began with Martin Luther nailing his Ninety-five Theses to the Wittenberg church doors; the first line of the theses reads, "Our Lord and Master Jesus Christ . . . willed the entire life of believers to be one of repentance." Luther's point is that repentance is not only the first step, but every step of the Christian life.

Since behavior is based on belief, we must repent of any lies we believe, because behind every sin is a lie.[19] Therefore, any change in our behavior has to start with a change in the thinking of our mind.[20] Repentance is first a change of our mind about who is in charge (God, not us), what is and is not sin, and how we are to worship God in all of life. Any attempt to change behavior without repentance in the mind is simply doomed to fail. The only way to change people's mind in a helpful way is through applying the Scriptures to their life and sin. Changed behavior is the fruit, or result, of repentance that begins in the mind.

This should include considering in detail your history of sexual sin and taking time to repent to God of all you have done. See your sexual sin in its totality as God does. This should also include confessing your past sexual sin to your fiancèe or spouse so that there is nothing hidden in your past that would cause you to think wrongly about your sexuality. This should also include confessing any sexual sin committed against you, such as molestation or rape, and getting biblical counseling so that you can be freed from any lies that you believe about sex and your own worth as God's image bearer. This is what John Piper meant when he once said, "Theology can conquer biology." So the following

---

[19]John 8:44.
[20]Rom. 12:2.

questions are offered to help you uncover any repentance that needs to begin in your mind.

- What lies do you believe about your body?
- Do you believe that the sexual parts are dirty, less holy, or somehow shameful?
- Do you believe that it is okay to strut your sexuality and flaunt your body for attention?
- What lies do you believe about sex?
- Do you view sex as if you were an animal enslaved to your base desires?
- Do you view sex as dirty rather than as something that a Christian should enjoy?
- Do you believe sex is only for functional purposes such as procreation or taking care of your spouse?
- Do you believe that your sexual sin is not a big deal or does not hurt anyone because it is private or just in your mind?
- What lies do you believe about your past?
- Do you not believe that you are really forgiven in Jesus Christ for any and all of your past sexual sin?
- Do you believe that what you have done or what has been done to you means that you are damaged forever and that you simply will never be sexually healthy?
- Do you believe that because you have enjoyed sexual pleasure sinfully in your past that you should deny yourself holy pleasure as a way to pay God back, as if Jesus did not already accomplish that on the cross?

Simply, a repentant mind will allow you to see your body as a temple that houses God the Holy Spirit and your sexuality as either worship or participation with demons.[21] This kind of repentant thinking and renewed mind will help you to "flee from sexual immorality" and literally to run away from sin like Joseph did, no matter what the cost. His words to a woman who sought to seduce him are particularly insightful because they reveal his repentant mind: "How then can I do this great wickedness and sin against God?"[22]

---

[21]1 Cor. 6:18b–20.
[22]Gen. 39:9.

The end goal of repentance is to put sin to death so that we can live in freedom as worshipers of God. This is what Paul meant when he said, "Put to death therefore what is earthly in you: sexual immorality, impurity, passion, evil desire, and covetousness, which is idolatry. On account of these the wrath of God is coming. In these you too once walked, when you were living in them. But now you must put them all away."[23]

A repentant mind is one that wants to put sin to death because sin killed Jesus. Therefore, the goal is never managing our sin, minimizing our sin, hiding our sin, or blaming others for our sin, but rather battling our sin and killing it. When we lose particular battles, we must keep repenting, keep renewing our mind in Scripture, and keep fighting to be like Jesus by the power of the Holy Spirit to live lives of self-control.

As a Christian you have been born again, or regenerated. You are now a new person with God the Holy Spirit living in you, and by his power you can put to death a worldly way of life and live as a Christian free from sin and connected to God.[24] To help you walk in this new life, Christian friends, a Christian pastor, and a Christian counselor may all be helpful to encourage your walk in holiness.

7) Live a celibate life, unless you are married.

Celibacy is living without sexual sin so long as one is single. If singles have sexual sin in their past, then they repent of that sin and live their current and future life in holiness. This also means that if they one day marry, they are no longer sexually chaste but rather are free to enjoy regular marital intimacy.

Celibacy was a lifestyle practiced by Jesus himself, along with other people in the Bible such as Jeremiah and Paul. All people are to practice celibacy at some point in their life, such as before they are married or after they are widowed.

For every Christian, in general, and celibate Christians, in particular, it is helpful to remember that Jesus is alive and that we can run to him in prayer. Hebrews 4:15–16 reminds us of this: "For we do not have a high priest who is unable to sympathize with our weaknesses, but one who in every respect has been tempted as we are, yet without sin. Let us then with confidence draw near to the throne of grace, that we

---

[23] Col. 3:5–8.
[24] Eph. 4:17–24.

may receive mercy and find grace to help in time of need." Our God became a human being and was tempted in every way as we are, which would include sexual temptation. However, Jesus responded to every temptation in a holy way and never succumbed to temptation and sin. Therefore, Jesus is able to sympathize with those who are tempted and gives grace to forgive us when we sin, but more importantly he gives us grace to empower us to say no to sin and yes to God and live holy lives patterned after his.

For those who are celibate, you have an opportunity to devote yourself wholeheartedly to the service of God, as Paul told the Corinthians. Just because people are celibate does not mean they are not allowed to enjoy emotionally healthy and appropriate friendships with Christian members of the opposite sex. In fact, the celibate Paul told the celibate Timothy, "Treat younger men as brothers, older women as mothers, and younger women as sisters, with absolute purity."[25] The church is a big family of sorts in which God is the Father, Jesus is the Big Brother, and men and women are brothers and sisters. In this way, the Bible allows a category of love and friendship among God's people that is not sexual and sinful but rather sacred and sane.

One point is worth mentioning here. In my church there are literally thousands of unmarried people. They often ask where to draw the line for sexual activity outside of marriage. What they are asking is how close they can get to sin while still being without sin. But there is already sin in their heart because they are seeking to get closer to sin and not closer to God. The Bible says, "But among you there must not be even a hint of sexual immorality."[26] Thus, the issue is not where the line is but when the time is. This is why the repeated refrain in the Song of Solomon is a warning not to "stir up or awaken love until it pleases."[27]

If you are a Christian wondering what to do in relationships with the opposite sex before marriage, it is wise to err on the side of caution and save yourself in every way for marriage. After more than a decade in ministry in a church with now hundreds of weddings each year, I've seen that nearly every young married couple regrets how far they went sexually while engaged, and I have yet to hear a couple say they regret-

---

[25]1 Tim. 5:1b–2, NIV.
[26]Eph. 5:3, NIV.
[27]Song 2:7; 3:5; 8:4.

ted doing nothing until marriage. So I tell the men to love their woman like a sister until she is their wife.

8) Pursue godly marriage, as you are able.

I was married at the age of twenty-one because I knew I was not made to be single. I was sexually active until after my conversion at the age of nineteen. As part of my repentance I stopped sleeping with my girl-friend until she became my wife. I know a lot of people like me. To be honest, I don't know how in the world I would make it if God called me to a life of singleness and celibacy. I'm sure his grace would get me through, but I'm not sure how. Simply, I need to be married, and so I am. I make no apologies for it, because God said to Adam, when he was single, that it is not good for us to be alone.

The Bible understands this God-given need for marriage and how it is a sexual safeguard against temptation. Paul makes this point in 1 Corinthians 7:1–2: "Now concerning the matters about which you wrote: 'It is good for a man not to have sexual relations with a woman.' But because of the temptation to sexual immorality, each man should have his own wife and each woman her own husband." Marriage is the holy outlet God has given us for our passions so that they do not lead us into sin.

9) Keep your spouse as your standard of beauty.

God made the earth and called it good, but even before sin entered the world, God said it was not good for the man to be alone. So God made Eve to be with the man as a lover, helper, and friend. Since they were the only two people who existed, they served as one another's standard of beauty.

In creation we see a wise pattern: an individual's standard of beauty should be his or her spouse. Elders, who are supposed to live as exam-ples for the entire church, are required to be one-woman men, which is how the Greek reads in the New Testament. Pornographic lust exists to elicit coveting and dissatisfaction that no spouse can satisfy, because one person cannot be like the harem laid out in pornography.

The book of wisdom gives some wise counsel to husbands on hav-ing their wife as their standard of beauty. Proverbs 5:18–19 says, "Let your fountain be blessed, and rejoice in the wife of your youth, a lovely deer, a graceful doe. Let her breasts fill you at all times with delight; be intoxicated always in her love." No man should break God's commandment and lust after another man's wife. Neither should a man seek to make his own wife so much like another woman that he is in effect seeking to commit adultery in an acceptable way by pretending to be with another woman. The same goes for the wife.

10) Pursue oneness.

In Genesis we see that the first account of married sexual intimacy, before sin entered the world, is described with the words "one" and "without shame." Therefore, these two considerations should guide every aspect of a Christian's marriage, including sexuality. Acceptable and unacceptable sexual practices between a husband and wife are to be determined by what the Bible gives as boundaries (e.g., no adultery, no lust of other people, no pornography), what increases oneness, and what does not include shame. If something causes the husband or wife to feel distanced, unloved, harmed, abused, forced upon, taken advantage of, demeaned, frightened, and the like, then it is not to be practiced because it is unloving, divisive, and shameful.

As a practical example, many Christian couples wonder whether they can use sex toys. The Bible does not speak of such things, even though there were forms of them during Bible times. Therefore, this is a matter of conscience that a husband and wife need to discuss lovingly and come to agreement on. If toys are used, they should be used together for building oneness and not alone or in lieu of natural and regular sexual intimacy, and they should not cause any shame.

Couples need to lovingly, graciously, and patiently discuss their sexual desires and fears. They must continually strive for oneness, both in and out of the bedroom, so that beyond just sex they can enjoy intimacy and oneness. Further, the foundation of all oneness is spiritual oneness. By worshiping God together, serving God together, praying to God together, repenting to God together, singing to God together, and reading God's Word together, a couple has intimacy and oneness at the deepest level that then enables and serves as the foundation for other aspects of intimacy and oneness—mental, physical, emotional, financial, and sexual. Any marriage built on a foundation of oneness other than a spiritual one is doomed to fail, which means that most problems in the bedroom are the result of problems outside the bedroom.

11) Have frequent and free married sex.

The Bible speaks of the frequency of married sex:

> The husband should give to his wife her conjugal rights, and likewise the wife to her husband. For the wife does not have authority over her own body, but the husband does. Likewise the husband does not have authority over his own body, but the wife does. Do not deprive one another, except perhaps by agreement for a limited time, that you may devote yourselves to prayer; but then come together again, so that Satan may not tempt you because of your lack of self-control.[28]

A married couple should be intimate to the satisfaction of both so that neither feels neglected and open to Satan's temptations for sin or bitterness. The average married couple, varying statistics say, has sex two to three times a week. However, those same statistics reveal that the average husband masturbates three to four times a week, usually in private without his wife's knowledge, which does not build oneness. So, while there is no *normal* frequency for marital sex mentioned in Scripture, it is fair to say that most Christian couples would be well served to discuss this openly and have more sex.

Additionally, not only is sex to be frequent, according to the Bible, but it is also supposed to be free. The Bible gives the following purposes for sex:

- pleasure[29]
- children[30]
- oneness[31]
- knowledge[32]
- protection[33]
- comfort[34]

---

[28]1 Cor. 7:3–5.
[29]Song of Solomon.
[30]Gen. 1:28.
[31]Gen. 2:24.
[32]Gen. 4:1.
[33]1 Cor. 7:2–5.
[34]2 Sam. 12:24.

Furthermore, the Song of Solomon gives great liberty for sexual freedom, including a variety of sexual activities and places for sex.[35]

To be honest, many of the Christian couples I have counseled over
the years do not have sex lives that are frequent or free enough. Often
either the husband or wife is dissatisfied because the sex is infrequent
and/or boringly predictable. What they need is more free and frequent
sexual pleasure within the bounds of their marriage.

A FINAL WORD ON MASTURBATION

In closing, I believe it is important to directly address the issue of masturbation. Many Christians ask, "Is masturbation a sin I need to repent
of?" So, in an effort to be helpful I will spend a bit of time addressing
this issue, both biblically and practically.

For the purposes of this book, I am defining masturbation as
genital self-pleasuring. What I am not counting as masturbation is
manual stimulation between married people. I am also not classifying
as masturbation self-stimulation done with the blessing of and in the
presence of one's spouse. What a married couple does together with a
clear conscience is for their pleasure and freedom. What I am referring
to by masturbation is self-pleasuring done in isolation, which is usually
accompanied by unbiblical lust.

Masturbation and Pornography

At the risk of pointing out the obvious, pornography exists primarily for the purpose of masturbation. The truth is that women watch
porn, and women masturbate. I have been in ministry long enough to
know that sin is not confined to any one gender. Still, masturbation
is more widely practiced among men. In fact, no survey seems to have
discovered any culture in which women masturbate more than men.
Nonetheless, any masturbation that is accompanied by pornography
and/or lust is sinful.

In any event, until recent years masturbation was widely regarded
as a deviancy. However, times have certainly changed, as it is now
championed as normal and natural. Comedian Jerry Seinfeld may have
summarized the modern opinion of masturbation best, saying, "We all
have to do it. It's part of our lifestyle, like shaving." The Janus Report

---

[35]Song 1:2; 2:3, 6; 4:5; 4:12–5:1; 6:13b–7:9; 7:11–13.

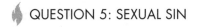

on Sexual Behavior and Sex in America indicates that masturbation is frequent, as the following results show:

- Single men who admit to masturbating once a week or more—48%
- Married men who admit to masturbating once a week or more—44%
- Divorced men who admit to masturbating once a week or more—68%

Many Christian pastors have tried in vain to find a mention of masturbation in the Scripture so they can condemn and forbid it. Unable to find any verses on the matter, some have used the story of Onan in Genesis 38:6–10 as their proof text. However, the story of Onan says nothing of masturbation. Instead, the story is about a man who died, leaving his wife a childless widow. The dead man's brother was then expected to marry his widowed sister-in-law, have normal sexual relations with her, and enable her to have children. Although Onan was happy to have sex with his sister-in-law, he would pull out of her just prior to his orgasm and ejaculate on the ground rather than obey God and become a father. To argue against masturbation with Genesis 38:6–10 is as exegetically accurate as arguing for masturbation, like one young guy did with me, by quoting Ecclesiastes 9:10, which says, "Whatever your hand finds to do, do it with your might."

Is Masturbation Permissible?

The question remains, is it permissible for God's people to masturbate? Yes and no. It must be noted that the Bible does not condemn masturbation outright. Though the practice is older than the Scriptures, the Bible's silence on the matter should cause us to avoid calling something a sin that God does not. So we must examine the issue principally with the following questions:

1) Can you masturbate without lusting?[36]
2) Can you masturbate in a way that builds oneness with your spouse, pulling you together more intimately through the act?[37]
3) Can you masturbate without experiencing shame?[38]

---

[36]Job 31:1.
[37]Gen. 2:24.
[38]Gen. 2:25.

4) Can you masturbate with a clear conscience?[39]
5) Can you masturbate without capitulating to the cravings of your sinful desires and thoughts?[40]

It is most certainly possible that someone could masturbate without violating the biblical principles revealed by these questions, but it is unlikely. There are some additional practical reasons why it may not be wise to do so.

First, masturbation can be a form of homosexuality because it is a sexual act that does not involve a spouse of the opposite gender. Conversely, if people were to masturbate themselves while engaged in sexual intimacy with their spouse, then they would not be doing so in a homosexual way.

Second, masturbation is a form of monosexuality because it does not include another person. Since sex is given for such purposes as oneness,[41] intimate knowledge,[42] and comfort,[43] having sex with oneself seems to miss some of the significant biblical reasons for sexual intimacy, though that does not make it inherently sinful.

Third, masturbation is often done in haste because of the mortifying embarrassment of possibly getting caught in the act. Subsequently, masturbation encourages a man to become unskilled in the self-control necessary to satisfy a wife. Also, a wife can become so accustomed to pleasing herself that she is incapable of being satisfied with her husband.

Fourth, masturbation can establish a pattern of laziness. I'll use men for an illustration here. If a single man wants to have an orgasm, he first needs to become a man and undergo the hard work of courting and marrying a woman. If a married man wants to have an orgasm, he first needs to undergo the hard work of loving, leading, and romancing his wife. But lazy men are prone to masturbate rather than undergo the labors usually associated with responsible masculine married life.

Fifth, though masturbation is biblically permissible, the question remains whether it is beneficial for you.[44] God's people are quite divided on this matter. Many find it to be very beneficial before they are married

---

[39]Titus 1:15.
[40]Eph. 2:3.
[41]Gen. 2:24.
[42]Gen. 4:1.
[43]2 Sam. 12:24.
[44]1 Cor. 10:23.

or during seasons of marriage when they are away from their spouse. Conversely, others claim that masturbating is not beneficial because they become mastered by it and are unable to keep it under control.[45] The latter is biologically caused by the fact that masturbating does temporarily relieve sexual urges and frustrations, but it also causes greater and more frequent biological urges for more. So, while masturbation may be permissible, people need to really examine if it is beneficial for them. In addition, since we are usually not the best evaluators of our hearts and lives, counsel from a mature, godly friend would be helpful on this point.

---

[45]1 Cor. 6:12.

QUESTION 4: **FAITH AND WORKS**

If salvation is by faith alone, then why are there so many verses that say or imply the opposite—that salvation is by works?

People are religious, which means they think they can justify themselves in one of three ways.

1) Loosely religious people *assume they are living a good enough life* so that no spiritual devotion or extra effort is required on their behalf for God to be pleased with them when they stand before him at the end of this life. Loosely religious people generally think they are pretty good people living decent lives and doing more good than harm in the world.

2) Secular religious people *work very hard at some social cause* because they think that they are good people and need to overcome the evil of bad people who are ruining the world. Such people tend to pursue their causes very passionately. These causes range from environmental issues, such as recycling and driving a hybrid vehicle, to animal rights causes, such as giving pets more legal rights. Others rally around moral issues, such as access to abortion and support of gay marriage. Others are concerned with basic lifestyle choices, such as eating organic food and supporting a political candidate. People can get passionate about virtually any conceivable cause. Important to note is that secular religious people do not often consider their efforts as justifying themselves in the sight of God so much as showing forth their goodness in support of what they deem to be good causes.

3) Devoutly religious people *work very hard at keeping the rules* of a particular religion in an effort to justify themselves as good and obedi-

ent people in the sight of God. Devout religion comes in various forms (e.g., works-based Christianity, Mormonism, Jehovah's Witness, Islam), but what they all share in common is a belief that God loves them more than the average person because their performance is superior.

In God's providence, as I was preparing the material on which this chapter is based, two events happened in my life. First, my friend and writing partner on other book projects, Gerry Breshears, spent some time explaining to me the doctrine of regeneration. To be honest, his explanation shed light on the experience that God the Holy Spirit has wrought in my life and gave me biblical language by which to differentiate between being religious (which I was) and regenerated (which I am).

Second, thanks to the arrangement of my friends at Crossway, I had the great pleasure of spending a good deal of time over the course of a few days with J. I. Packer, whose writings have been enormously influential in my life. At nearly eighty-two years of age, he was incredibly mentally sharp, and he graciously answered many questions for me. One of my questions concerned which theological issues he would commend young Christian leaders to study in order to be prepared for the next fifty years. His list was quite insightful, and the number-one doctrine he recommended was the doctrine of regeneration. He said that the doctrine of regeneration has not been fully appreciated by many who do not understand that to be born again with a new heart and new nature means that we have, at our deepest level, a new identity and new passionate desires for God's Word and ways. Because of this, he recommends that all young Christian leaders do a thorough study on the doctrine of regeneration.

Now, to answer the question on which this chapter is based we need to start with an explanation of the doctrine of regeneration, which begins with Jesus' work on our behalf. The doctrine of regeneration explains the changes that occur in a person's life by the Holy Spirit.

JESUS' JUSTIFYING WORK FOR US

God is a holy and just king who sits upon a throne ruling over creation and judging good and evil.[1] God deals with humanity through the rule of law to ensure justice and righteousness. These words are used

---

[1]Gen. 18:25; Pss. 50:6; 96:13; 2 Tim. 4:8.

to describe God and his works some 227 times in the New Testament alone. This law of God is written both on our hearts[2] and in Scripture.[3] God's justice and righteousness distinguish him from false gods who are unjust and capricious and therefore unloving and unpredictable. The great Old Testament word for law is *torah*, which is mentioned in reference to God some 203 times, in addition to 423 occurrences of other words referring to God's law scattered throughout the Old Testament. God even speaks of our relationship to him in the legal term *covenant*.

However, everyone is an unjust, sinful lawbreaker—both in their external actions and internal motives[4]—who stands condemned before God.[5] Our condition is so bad, the Bible teaches, that we are sinful in our nature,[6] totally depraved,[7] hostile to God,[8] children of Satan,[9] alienated from Christ,[10] and spiritually dead.[11]

This question then begs to be answered: how could God possibly justify us and make us just without himself becoming unjust by overlooking sin?[12] Since all unrighteous people deserve judgment and wrath in hell, God could simply have declared that no one would be saved; because all are unrighteous sinners, God would have remained perfectly just in damning everyone who ever lived. Although God does indeed condemn some people justly, in his loving mercy, he has also chosen to save some people justly through Jesus Christ.[13]

The Bible teaches that unjust sinners can be declared just or righteous in God's sight by being justified, or obtaining *justification*.[14] This legal term appears some 222 times in various forms throughout the New Testament. *Justification* refers to a double transaction whereby God takes away our sinful unrighteousness through Jesus' substitutionary death in our place and imputes to us the righteousness of Jesus Christ, thereby giving us positive righteousness.[15]

---

[2]Rom. 2:14–15.
[3]Acts 7:53; Rom. 2:12.
[4]Luke 16:15.
[5]Ps. 51:4; Rom. 3:8; 5:16, 18; James 2:10; 1 John 3:4.
[6]Rom. 8:4–5; Gal. 5:13, 16–24.
[7]Rom. 1:26–29; 2 Tim. 3:8; 2 Pet. 2:19.
[8]Rom. 5:10; 8:7; Col. 1:21.
[9]John 8:44.
[10]Eph. 2:12–13, 19.
[11]Eph. 2:1–2.
[12]Ex. 23:7; Prov. 17:15.
[13]Matt. 25:31–33, 46; Rom. 5:18; 8:33–34.
[14]Rom. 2:13; 3:20.
[15]Rom. 3:21–22; 4:4–6; 5:12–21; 10:4; 1 Cor. 1:30; 2 Cor. 5:21; Phil. 3:8–9; 1 Pet. 2:24; 3:18.

Second Corinthians 5:21 describes how a sinner obtains righteousness: "For our sake he made him to be sin who knew no sin, so that in him we might become the righteousness of God." Martin Luther rightly called this "the great exchange." On the cross Jesus took our sinful unrighteousness and gave us his sinless righteousness.

Justification is so vital that Christianity split into Catholicism and Protestantism over this very issue. The Reformers were faithful to Scripture, which clearly states that we are justified by grace alone,[16] through faith alone,[17] because of Jesus Christ alone,[18] who justifies us by his death[19] and resurrection.[20] In some instances Paul even packs these great truths of justification by grace through faith in Christ alone into one compressed section of Scripture.[21]

JUSTIFICATION IS ABOUT JESUS

To make this as simple as possible, let me say it this way: justification is about Jesus. Jesus saves us; we do not save ourselves. Jesus' life is our hope; our own life is not. Jesus' death is our payment; our religious works are not. Jesus alone forgives sin, so we are to repent of our sin to Jesus. Jesus alone gives righteousness, so we trust in Jesus for our justification.

Conversely, our justification is not accomplished in any way by any of our works, such as morality or religious devotion. One common error of religion in various forms is that it wrongly believes sinners can participate in their justification, in whole or in part, by good works. However, the Bible is emphatically clear that our good works are not accepted by God for our justification.

Isaiah 64:6 says, "We have all become like one who is unclean, and all our righteous deeds are like a polluted garment." Here we discover in graphic language that our religious efforts to justify ourselves in the sight of God are as appreciated by him as a bloody menstrual rag being offered as a birthday present.

Galatians 2:16 says, "A person is not justified by works of the law but through faith in Jesus Christ, so we also have believed in Christ Jesus, in order to be justified by faith in Christ and not by works of the law,

---

[16]Titus 3:7; Rom. 4:2–5; 5:10–21.
[17]Hab. 2:4; Acts 13:39; Rom. 3:23–28; 5:1, 10:10; Hebrews 11.
[18]Isa. 53:11; Rom. 3:21–25; 4:25; 5:9, 16; Gal. 2:16–17.
[19]Rom. 5:9.
[20]Rom. 4:25.
[21]E.g., Romans 3–4.

because by works of the law no one will be justified." The context of Paul's emphatic statement to the church at Galatia was that false teachers had infiltrated the church to wrongly teach that justification necessitates Jesus plus circumcision. Paul is clear that our justification is accomplished by Jesus plus nothing, because Jesus plus anything ruins everything. In our day, this kind of religious error is common among those who falsely teach that to be justified we must belong to Jesus and be baptized, speak in tongues, hold a particular narrow system of theology, join a particular kind of Christian church, and more.

In Philippians 3:2–9, Paul says:

> Look out for the dogs, look out for the evildoers, look out for those who mutilate the flesh. For we are the circumcision, who worship by the Spirit of God and glory in Christ Jesus and put no confidence in the flesh—though I myself have reason for confidence in the flesh also. If anyone else thinks he has reason for confidence in the flesh, I have more: circumcised on the eighth day, of the people of Israel, of the tribe of Benjamin, a Hebrew of Hebrews; as to the law, a Pharisee; as to zeal, a persecutor of the church; as to righteousness under the law, blameless. But whatever gain I had, I counted as loss for the sake of Christ. Indeed, I count everything as loss because of the surpassing worth of knowing Christ Jesus my Lord. For his sake I have suffered the loss of all things and count them as rubbish, in order that I may gain Christ and be found in him, not having a righteousness of my own that comes from the law, but that which comes through faith in Christ, the righteousness from God that depends on faith.

Reflecting on his former life of religion, Paul says that he was as moral, zealous, and religious as anyone could be—basically the Michael Jordan of religion. Yet, being justified by Jesus and receiving righteousness as a gift because of Jesus, in whom Paul trusted, and not because of something he merited or earned by his effort, taught him that religion is, at its best, a pile.

Finally, perhaps the entirety of this vital difference between false religious beliefs about how one is justified and the teaching of the Bible is illustrated most simply by Jesus' parable in Luke 18:9–14:

> He also told this parable to some who trusted in themselves that they were righteous, and treated others with contempt: "Two men went

up into the temple to pray, one a Pharisee and the other a tax collector. The Pharisee, standing by himself, prayed thus: 'God, I thank you that I am not like other men, extortioners, unjust, adulterers, or even like this tax collector. I fast twice a week; I give tithes of all that I get.' But the tax collector, standing far off, would not even lift up his eyes to heaven, but beat his breast, saying, 'God, be merciful to me, a sinner!' I tell you, this man went down to his house justified, rather than the other. For everyone who exalts himself will be humbled, but the one who humbles himself will be exalted."

In Jesus' parable, the religious man was proud of his religious devotion and failed to understand that pride is the worst sin of all, the very sin that got Satan kicked out of heaven and caused angels to become demons. Furthermore, by trusting in himself the religious man became very unkind and smug toward sinners who needed the grace of the gospel. To this day, religious people (regardless of their brand of religion) fall into the same trap as the man in Jesus' parable and trust in themselves for justification. Subsequently, they are prone to pride if they believe they are religiously succeeding and to despair if they believe they are religiously failing. Religious people become proud when they compare themselves to fellow sinners, as the man in the parable did, or despairing if they compare themselves to God, in general, and Jesus, in particular.

In contrast, the tax collector, who was a great and despised sinner in that culture, simply repented of his sin to God and cried out for undeserved mercy. Jesus said that the second man was justified, and we can see that it was by grace alone through faith alone in God alone.

Teaching from this parable, Jesus said that God will cut down in humiliation those who exalt themselves in religious pride. In contrast, God will lift up in exaltation those who humble themselves in gospel repentance. Therefore, in Jesus' amazing parable we see that the doctrine of justification preserves the grace of God from the errors of religion. It does so by calling sinners to repent of their sin and religious people to repent of their religion.

Because the innumerable benefits God bestows on us through his gift of justification include forgiveness of all sins,[22] peace with God,[23]

---

[22]Acts 13:38–39.
[23]Rom. 5:1.

escape from God's wrath and condemnation,[24] freedom from God's law,[25] ongoing sanctification,[26] Spirit-empowered enablement to do good works,[27] and a final glorification,[28] it is difficult to overstate the importance of defining and defending the doctrine of justification.

John Calvin regarded justification as "the principle of the whole doctrine of salvation and the foundation of all religion."[1] Martin Luther rightly declared that the doctrine of justification is the issue on which the church stands or falls, and that any church denying justification by grace alone through faith alone because of Christ alone can no longer be called Christian. How we walk in the good works of our justification is explained by the corresponding doctrine of regeneration.

THE HOLY SPIRIT'S REGENERATING WORK IN US

Regeneration is the biblical teaching that salvation includes God's work both for us at the cross of Jesus and in us by the Holy Spirit. Or to say it another way, regeneration is not a separate work of the Holy Spirit added to the saving work of Jesus; rather, it is the subjective actualization of Jesus' work.

While the word *regeneration* appears only twice in the Bible,[29] it is described in both the Old and New Testaments by a constellation of images. Before we examine them, it is important to note that each signifies a permanent, unalterable change in someone at his or her deepest level.

Old Testament Regeneration and the New Heart

In Scripture our individual lives and corresponding collective lives that we call "culture" are simply the showing forth of the condition of our heart. The *heart* is the seat and center of our identity, the essence of our total inner selves, which expresses itself outwardly in word and deed. This concept is central to the teachings of Scripture, and *heart* in its various forms (e.g., "hearts," "hearted") occurs over nine hundred times.

In Proverbs alone the heart is the seat of understanding,[30]

---

[24]Rom. 5:9, 18; 8:1, 33–34.
[25]Gal. 3:11, 24.
[26]1 Thess. 5:23; 2 Thess. 2:13.
[27]James 2:24.
[28]Rom. 8:30.
[29]Matt. 19:28; Titus 3:5.
[30]Prov. 2:2.

learning,[31] memory,[32] faith,[33] obedience,[34] rebellion,[35] planning,[36] imagination,[37] lust,[38] will,[39] perversity,[40] deceit,[41] folly,[42] anxiety,[43] hope,[44] joy,[45] hurt,[46] grief,[47] peace,[48] wisdom,[49] happiness,[50] discernment,[51] cheerfulness,[52] contemplation,[53] pride,[54] speech,[55] rage,[56] motives,[57] purity,[58] folly,[59] friendship,[60] gladness,[61] envy,[62] violence,[63] reasoning,[64] sadness,[65] evil,[66] sins,[67] and hardness toward God.[68]

Additionally, when Jesus taught from the Old Testament he said that our words come out of our hearts,[69] our lusts come out of our hearts,[70] and how we spend our money is determined by our hearts.[71] He taught that out of our hearts come evil thoughts, sexual immorality, theft, murder, adultery, greed, malice, deceit, lewdness, envy,

---

[31]Prov. 2:10.
[32]Prov. 3:1–3.
[33]Prov. 3:5.
[34]Prov. 4:4; 10:8.
[35]Prov. 5:12.
[36]Prov. 6:14; 16:1.
[37]Prov. 6:18.
[38]Prov. 6:25.
[39]Prov. 7:25.
[40]Prov. 11:20; 17:20.
[41]Prov. 12:20; 26:24.
[42]Prov. 12:23.
[43]Prov. 12:25.
[44]Prov. 13:12.
[45]Prov. 13:25; 15:30; 27:9.
[46]Prov. 14:10.
[47]Prov. 14:13.
[48]Prov. 14:30.
[49]Prov. 14:33; 23:15.
[50]Prov. 15:13.
[51]Prov. 15:14; 16:21; 18:15.
[52]Prov. 15:15; 17:22.
[53]Prov. 15:28.
[54]Prov. 16:5; 18:12; 21:4.
[55]Prov. 16:23.
[56]Prov. 19:3.
[57]Prov. 21:2.
[58]Prov. 22:11.
[59]Prov. 22:15.
[60]Prov. 23:7.
[61]Prov. 23:15.
[62]Prov. 23:17.
[63]Prov. 24:2.
[64]Prov. 24:32.
[65]Prov. 25:20.
[66]Prov. 26:23.
[67]Prov. 26:25.
[68]Prov. 28:14.
[69]Matt. 12:34.
[70]Matt. 5:28.
[71]Matt. 6:21.

slander, arrogance, and folly.[72] He said that good and evil proceed from the heart,[73] and sinful grief, anxiety, and drunkenness come out of our hearts.[74]

The Old Testament speaks frequently of regeneration in terms of deep work in the heart, as the following examples illustrate:

> The LORD your God will circumcise your heart and the heart of your offspring, so that you will love the LORD your God with all your heart and with all your soul, that you may live.[75]

> I will give them a heart to know that I am the LORD, and they shall be my people and I will be their God, for they shall return to me with their whole heart.[76]

> Behold, the days are coming, declares the LORD, when I will make a new covenant. . . . I will put my law within them, and I will write it on their hearts. And I will be their God, and they shall be my people.[77]

> I will give them one heart and one way, that they may fear me forever, for their own good and the good of their children after them. I will make with them an everlasting covenant, that I will not turn away from doing good to them. And I will put the fear of me in their hearts, that they may not turn from me.[78]

> And I will give them one heart, and a new spirit I will put within them. I will remove the heart of stone from their flesh and give them a heart of flesh, that they may walk in my statutes and keep my rules and obey them. And they shall be my people, and I will be their God.[79]

> I will give you a new heart, and a new spirit I will put within you. And I will remove the heart of stone from your flesh and give you a heart of flesh. And I will put my Spirit within you, and cause you to walk in my statutes and be careful to obey my rules.[80]

---

[72]Mark 7:21–23.
[73]Luke 6:45.
[74]Luke 21:34.
[75]Deut. 30:6.
[76]Jer. 24:7.
[77]Jer. 31:31–33.
[78]Jer. 32:39–40.
[79]Ezek. 11:19–20.
[80]Ezek. 36:26–27.

New Testament Regeneration and the New Birth

Like the Old Testament, the New Testament speaks of regeneration on many occasions and in many ways. Perhaps the most well-known example is Jesus' discussion with Nicodemus, the Old Testament scholar in John 3, in which he explains that a person must be born again to enter the kingdom of God. Nicodemus is understandably confused about Jesus' image of being born again. What Jesus meant is that we are all sinners, meaning we are born physically alive but spiritually dead.[81] Therefore, to be spiritually alive to God we must experience a second birth of our spirit, in other words, we must be born again. Jesus tells Nicodemus that this new birth, or regeneration, occurs by the work of God the Holy Spirit.

This depiction of being born again is repeated elsewhere in the New Testament, as the following examples illustrate:

> ... born, not of blood nor of the will of the flesh nor of the will of man, but of God.[82]

> Blessed be the God and Father of our Lord Jesus Christ! According to his great mercy, he has caused us to be born again to a living hope through the resurrection of Jesus Christ from the dead.[83]

> Since you have been born again, not of perishable seed but of imperishable, through the living and abiding word of God ... [84]

> Everyone who believes that Jesus is the Christ has been born of God, and everyone who loves the Father loves whoever has been born of him.[85]

Elsewhere in the New Testament many other images are used to explain regeneration. These include "partakers of the divine nature,"[86] "new creation,"[87] "new man,"[88] "alive together with Christ,"[89] and "created in Christ Jesus."[90]

---

[81]Eph. 2:1, 5; Col. 2:13.
[82]John 1:13.
[83]1 Pet. 1:3.
[84]1 Pet. 1:23.
[85]1 John 5:1.
[86]2 Pet. 1:4.
[87]2 Cor. 5:17.
[88]Eph. 2:15; 4:24.
[89]Eph. 2:5; Col. 2:13.
[90]Eph. 2:10.

Three very important truths help to illuminate regeneration in the New Testament. (1) It is vital to understand that regeneration is done to ill-deserving, not just undeserving, sinners.[91] Therefore, regeneration is a gift of grace, as Titus 3:5 says: "He saved us, not because of works done by us in righteousness, but according to his own mercy, by the washing of regeneration and renewal of the Holy Spirit." (2) Regeneration is something God the Holy Spirit does for us.[92] Therefore, unless God accomplishes regeneration in people, it is impossible for them to live the Christian life. (3) Without regeneration there is no possibility of eternal life in God's kingdom.[93] Therefore, regeneration is required for someone to be a true Christian.

TEN ASPECTS OF REGENERATION

Presented here are ten aspects of God's regenerating work in the new heart of those who are born again as Christians to a thoroughly new life.

1) New Lord

Regenerated people are no longer dominated by Satan and sin. Instead, they are born again to a new life with God as their new Lord, who ultimately rules over them. This rule of God as our new Lord, who liberates us from Satan and sin to live in freedom and joy, is the first benefit of regeneration, and it establishes the grounds upon which all the other benefits are possible. First John 5:18 says, "We know that everyone who has been born of God does not keep on sinning, but he who was born of God protects him, and the evil one does not touch him."

Practically, this means that regenerated people, at their deepest level, know and celebrate the fact that they belong to God. They desire to live in such a way that honors God. I recently spoke with a new Christian who had made some major changes in her life, such as moving out of her boyfriend's apartment, stopping her drug use, and joining a Bible study, and when I asked why, she said, "I belong to God now, so I'm living for him."

Among the wondrous benefits of having Jesus as a new Lord is that

---

[91]Eph. 2:1–5.
[92]John 3:5–8.
[93]John 3:3, 5; cf. 1 Cor. 2:6–16.

other previous and competing lords are dethroned. False lords such as self, Satan, sin, or the approval and rule of someone else (e.g., an abusive boyfriend, ungrateful spouse, discouraging parent) do not love, serve, and liberate as Jesus does.

2) New Creation

Regenerated people are new creations, changed from the deepest part of their being to the degree that the Scriptures refer to each as a "new creation." Second Corinthians 5:17 says, "Therefore, if anyone is in Christ, he is a new creation. The old has passed away; behold, the new has come."

What this means practically is that change in our behavior must be preceded by a change in our nature if there is to be any true holiness. Sadly, few people understand this wonderful benefit of regeneration; instead, they try to change their outward behavior without realizing that change begins on the inside at our deepest levels and then works its way out into the daily affairs of our lives. On this point, Galatians 6:15 says, "For neither circumcision counts for anything, nor uncircumcision [both outward acts], but a new creation [an inward act]."

Paul's big idea is that God desires us to be born again in him and live a new life as a new person in relationship with him rather than to seek to transform ourselves by our outward and religious efforts. Such religious efforts can help us exchange one sin for another, such as stopping gluttony and becoming proud of our successful weight loss, but are incapable of causing us to live a new life as a totally new person. To illustrate this, the Bible often renames people once they are regenerated so that, for example, Cephas becomes Peter, and Saul becomes Paul; they are transformed at the deepest levels.

3) New Identity

With a new Lord and as a new creation, regenerated people have a new identity that the Bible speaks of frequently as something that can be put on through faith. Ephesians 4:22–24 welcomes regenerated people "to put off your old self, which belongs to your former manner of life and is corrupt through deceitful desires, and to be renewed in the spirit of your minds, and to put on the new self, created after the likeness of God in true righteousness and holiness."

Whereas the sinful nature does not submit to God, the regenerated nature can, by God's enabling grace, put off the identity of the old life, like stained and worn clothing, and put on the identity of a new life, like the white robes of righteousness mentioned throughout Scripture, to live a life that increasingly reflects the character of God our creator.

I was recently speaking with a woman who has been a Christian for many years. She has recently come to understand that how she lives her life is, in many ways, not in accordance with her theological convictions. So she has decided to put off many aspects of her life, such as breaking up with her non-Christian boyfriend, stopping her frequent trips to the local bar to drink and flirt after work, and refusing to be pushed around by her friends who are skilled at persuading her toward various kinds of trouble. She has decided to put on such things as participating in a weekly women's Bible study, pursuing a godly older woman for a mentoring friendship, and exercising so as to be a good steward of her health. Her motivation for all this is that she sees herself as a Christian and wants to live all of her life as an act of worship to God. Simply put, as a new creation we have a new identity.

4) New Mind

Regenerated people have a new ability to think God's thoughts after him because God has given them a new mind. This does not mean that Christians are smarter than non-Christians, or that non-Christians are unable to come to great insights through general revelation in areas such as medicine or engineering. However, it does mean that apart from a new mind, the things of God are not perceived and embraced. First Corinthians 2:14–16 juxtaposes the unregenerate mind with the regenerated mind: "The natural person does not accept the things of the Spirit of God, for they are folly to him, and he is not able to understand them because they are spiritually discerned. . . . But we have the mind of Christ."

In particular, the new mind of a spiritually born-again person craves the nourishment of Scripture akin to how newborn babies crave milk. First Peter 2:2 encourages born-again people: "Like newborn infants, long for the pure spiritual milk, that by it you may grow up into salvation." Also, Romans 7:22 speaks of the regenerated person having a trust and interest in and submission to Scripture: "For I delight in the law of God, in my inner being."

As a nineteen-year-old college freshman and new Christian, I started reading the Bible for hours nearly every day, attending Bible studies, attending a Bible-preaching church, and buying Christian reference books to help me study the Bible without any pressure, guilt, coercion, legalism, or religion. I had a deep desire to learn the Bible and think God's thoughts after him. The way I thought about most of the world and my role in it changed and continues to change as my appetite for Scripture and the renewing of my mind only grows. Since being regenerated by God, I have never struggled to study Scripture, and I think much of that is because I have never seen Bible study as something I have to do but, rather, as something I get to do, because in my regenerated heart it is something I want to do.

5) New Emotions

The emotional mark of born-again people is that they love as Jesus loved with the love that God gives them to share. First John 4:7 says, "Beloved, let us love one another, for love is from God, and whoever loves has been born of God and knows God." Because God is love, regenerated people are connected to the source of all true love. Subsequently, they have the capacity, if they choose to walk in obedience, to love God, their spouse, their children, their friends, their neighbors, and even their enemies. In my pastoral work, I have seen even acrimonious, adulterous couples, in the process of filing for divorce, become Christians. They have gone on to live regenerated lives of hatred for their sin out of love for God. They became able to love their spouse with a love that they confessed flowed through them from God. They have not only remained married, but have also built happy, holy, and healthy marriages on the foundation of regenerating love.

6) New Desires

Regenerated people have new desires akin to new appetites for the things of God. Paul speaks of this in Galatians 5:16–17, saying, "But I say, walk by the Spirit, and you will not gratify the desires of the flesh. For the desires of the flesh are against the Spirit, and the desires of the Spirit are against the flesh, for these are opposed to each other, to keep you from doing the things you *want to do.*" That last phrase is incredibly important—regenerated Christians desire the will of God at their deepest level because of the indwelling, transforming presence and power of God the Holy Spirit.

Paul echoes this theme of regenerated deepest desires in Romans 7:4–6, saying,

> Likewise, my brothers, you also have died to the law through the body of Christ, so that you may belong to another, to him who has been raised from the dead, in order that we may bear fruit for God. For while we were living in the flesh, our sinful passions, aroused by the law, were at work in our members to bear fruit for death. But now we are released from the law, having died to that which held us captive, so that we serve in the new way of the Spirit and not in the old way of the written code.

Yet, so long as we live on this side of glorified perfection, we still wrestle with desires that tempt us to sin. When we do give in to sinful desires, our deepest desires remain unmet, and we are miserable until we repent and live in obedience to God and the deepest desires he gives us. Paul describes his own experience with this: "For I do not understand my own actions. For I do not do what I want, but I do the very thing I hate."[94]

Practically, this means that the Christian life is to be one of passion in which we pursue the deepest desires of our regenerated heart without settling for lesser, sinful desires. This is what Psalm 37:4 means when it says to "delight yourself in the LORD, and he will give you the desires of your heart."

Only a regenerated heart can be delighted with who God is and what he does. As the regenerated heart delights in God, he places deep desires in the heart. Because those desires are his desires, then the delighting Christian and God share the same desires. Thus, regenerated Christians pursue with great passion their deepest God-given desires; in doing so, they worship God not just by obeying what he commands in duty but by obeying in delight, as their will and God's will are one and the same.

This biblical understanding of regenerated new desires completely

---

[94]Rom. 7:15.

undermines a common error of religion. Religion in its various forms does not understand regenerated new, deep desires and wrongly assumes that Christians, at their deepest level, primarily have an appetite for sin. As a result, religion seeks to deaden a person's desires with guilt and man-made legalistic rules, assuming that passion will lead to sin.

However, the biblical understanding of regenerated desires is not that we overcome sin by religion and rules or by diminished passion. Rather, we overcome sin by not settling for lesser, weaker, sinful desires and by becoming more passionate and by pressing onward for the satisfaction of our deepest new desires, which are God's desires implanted on our heart by the Holy Spirit.

7) New Community

Regenerated people have their sins forgiven and are reconciled both to God as Christians and to fellow Christians as the church.[95] Subsequently, a regenerated person desires and pursues fellowship, which is loving relationship in community with fellow regenerated Christians as the church. This community of regenerated people is given multiple names in the New Testament, including citizens of God's kingdom,[96] members of God's family,[97] temple for God's presence,[98] and parts of one body.[99] By living in community with fellow Christians as the church, the regenerated person learns how to live a life that glorifies God and helps others do the same.

For me, personally, I can still vividly remember the new desires coming from my regenerated heart to be in community with God's people. As a new Christian and college freshman, I had a longing I had never experienced before, a longing to be involved in a Bible-based church. God, in his kindness, directed me to a wonderful church where Jesus was clearly taught from the Bible and loved by the people. I can still remember the joy of attending my first Bible study group, learning to pray with fellow Christians, and being invited into the homes of older godly families for meals to learn from them about such things as marriage and parenting.

---

[95] 1 John 1:3.
[96] Eph. 2:19–20.
[97] Eph. 2:19–20.
[98] Eph. 2:22.
[99] Rom. 12:5.

I also moved into a Christian guys' house, where together we prayed, studied Scripture, did ministry service projects in the community, went camping and played sports, opened our home for meals and parties, and stayed up late to debate theology. To be honest, I learned more in church than in classes while in college, and, because of my new community, I made it through college without ever drinking, doing drugs, or getting into any sort of trouble. I was having lots of sanctified fun and learning with my Christian friends and mentors. As a result, college was a wonderfully enjoyable season of my life.

8) New Power

Not only does God make our identity, desires, thoughts, feelings, and relationships new, but he also gives us a new supernatural power to live a new life by his enablement. This new power is the indwelling power of God the Holy Spirit in the regenerated Christian.

This is why Jesus called the Holy Spirit "the Helper"[100] and our teacher.[101] Through his teaching and by his power, God the Holy Spirit empowers us so that

> the righteous requirement of the law might be fulfilled in us, who walk not according to the flesh but according to the Spirit. For those who live according to the flesh set their minds on the things of the flesh, but those who live according to the Spirit set their minds on the things of the Spirit. . . . Those who are in the flesh cannot please God. You, however, are not in the flesh but in the Spirit, if in fact the Spirit of God dwells in you. Anyone who does not have the Spirit of Christ does not belong to him. . . . So then, brothers, we are debtors, not to the flesh, to live according to the flesh. For if you live according to the flesh you will die, but if by the Spirit you put to death the deeds of the body, you will live.[102]

This new power of God the Holy Spirit means that a regenerated person continually repents of sin in order to be filled with the Holy Spirit.[103] To be filled with the Holy Spirit is a word picture in the New Testament taken from the world of sailing. Just as a ship opens its sail

---

[100]John 14:26; 16:7.
[101]John 16:13.
[102]Rom. 8:4–13.
[103]Eph. 5:18.

so that it might be filled with the wind and powerfully driven toward a destination, Spirit-filled, regenerated Christians have their mind, heart, and will open to the things of God and welcome God's powerful direction of their life toward his purposes.

Lastly, this new power of the Holy Spirit, which accompanies regeneration, means that God helps us to live holy lives and, in fact, desires to enable us to obey him. In this way, regeneration is the opposite of religion. Tragically, religion teaches that if we obey God, he will love us. However, regeneration reveals that because God loves us, we can obey him by the power he gives us to do so.

9) New Freedom

Accompanying the new life and new power of regeneration is a new freedom. This new freedom is the ability to say no to sin and yes to God. The truth is that we either have our face toward sin and our back toward God, or we have our face toward God and our back toward sin. One of the freedoms of regeneration is the freedom to repent and literally turn our back on sin and our face toward God to live new lives of holiness.

This new freedom is incredibly liberating and one of the great gifts of regeneration. Paul speaks of this wonderful experience in Romans 6:6, saying, "We know that our old self was crucified with him in order that the body of sin might be brought to nothing, so that we would no longer be enslaved to sin." In Romans 7:6, he likewise says, "But now we are released from the law, having died to that which held us captive, so that we serve in the new way of the Spirit and not in the old way of the written code."

As a pastor, I must say that seeing new Christians experience this new freedom is among the most encouraging parts of my job. When people realize that they need not tolerate or manage their sin but can walk away from it and toward Jesus because he has broken its reign over them, their lives change forever. Seeing this is one of the main reasons I remain motivated to continue in ministry—I know that gospel ministry is not in vain.

10) New Life

The culmination of the effects of regeneration is a new life markedly different from how life would otherwise be. The New Testament is fond of contrasting the life of the sinful flesh with its Spirit-regenerated alternative to clearly distinguish for Christians what their life is and is not.[104] One example is found in Galatians 5:19–23, which was part of the original question on which this chapter is based. It says:

> Now the works of the flesh are evident: sexual immorality, impurity, sensuality, idolatry, sorcery, enmity, strife, jealousy, fits of anger, rivalries, dissensions, divisions, envy, drunkenness, orgies, and things like these. I warn you, as I warned you before, that those who do such things will not inherit the kingdom of God. But the fruit of the Spirit is love, joy, peace, patience, kindness, goodness, faithfulness, gentleness, self-control; against such things there is no law.

For the regenerated Christian, this new life is like a bud that flowers. Bit by bit, as we are sanctified and grow in holiness through faith and repentance, we blossom to become who God intends us to be.

One thing that has helped me to appreciate this fact is to occasionally ask myself some questions about what my life would be like had God not regenerated me. These questions include:

- Who would I be today?
- What would be different in my life?
- What would my marriage be like?
- What kind of spouse would I be?
- What kind of parent would I be?
- What kind of sin would ensnare me?
- What would my emotional state be?
- What would my future look like in this life?
- What would my eternity look like?

If I am honest, I find myself incredibly thankful and worshipful for the new life to which God has regenerated me. I can think of nothing in my life that I would exchange for the unregenerated alternative.

Having now established Jesus' work for us in justification and the Holy Spirit's work in us through regeneration, we can now explore God's sanctifying works through us.

---

[104]Rom. 6:19–22; 1 Cor. 6:9–11; 1 John 2:15–29.

GOD'S SANCTIFYING WORKS THROUGH US

People who are justified by Jesus and regenerated by the Spirit have a life in which their faith manifests itself in good works. In this way, the faith is seen in the good works that are birthed from regeneration.

Jesus' word picture in Matthew 7:15–20 is wonderfully clear in explaining how regenerated people live:

> Beware of false prophets, who come to you in sheep's clothing but inwardly are ravenous wolves. You will recognize them by their fruits. Are grapes gathered from thornbushes, or figs from thistles? So, every healthy tree bears good fruit, but the diseased tree bears bad fruit. A healthy tree cannot bear bad fruit, nor can a diseased tree bear good fruit. Every tree that does not bear good fruit is cut down and thrown into the fire. Thus you will recognize them by their fruits.

Jesus' point is that a regenerated Christian is like a healthy tree that bears fruit in the form of good works done as acts of worship out of a new heart that loves God. He contrasts the regenerated person with a diseased tree, the unregenerated person who bears bad fruit because his life is simply the harvest of his heart. That is what Jesus meant when he said in Matthew 7:21, which was part of the original question on which this chapter is based, "Not everyone who says to me, 'Lord, Lord,' will enter the kingdom of heaven, but the one who does the will of my Father who is in heaven."

The theme of faith in God that births works with God is a theme that Jesus' half-brother James also emphasizes in his New Testament letter, saying in James 2:14–26, which was also part of the original question on which this chapter is based:

> What good is it, my brothers, if someone says he has faith but does not have works? Can that faith save him? If a brother or sister is poorly clothed and lacking in daily food, and one of you says to them, "Go in peace, be warmed and filled," without giving them the things needed for the body, what good is that? So also faith by itself, if it does not have works, is dead. But someone will say, "You have faith and I have works." Show me your faith apart from your works, and I will show you my faith by my works. You believe that God is one; you do well. Even the demons believe—and shudder! Do you want to

be shown, you foolish person, that faith apart from works is useless? Was not Abraham our father justified by works when he offered up his son Isaac on the altar? You see that faith was active along with his works, and faith was completed by his works; and the Scripture was fulfilled that says, "Abraham believed God, and it was counted to him as righteousness"—and he was called a friend of God. You see that a person is justified by works and not by faith alone. And in the same way was not also Rahab the prostitute justified by works when she received the messengers and sent them out by another way? For as the body apart from the spirit is dead, so also faith apart from works is dead.

SUMMARY

In summary, we are not saved *by* but *to* our good works. Ephesians 2:8–10 says it this way: "For by grace you have been saved through faith. And this is not your own doing; it is the gift of God, not a result of works, so that no one may boast. For we are his workmanship, created in Christ Jesus for good works, which God prepared beforehand, that we should walk in them." Therefore, you do not have to do good works so that God will save you; rather, if you are justified and regenerated, you get to do good works because Jesus already has saved you.

Perhaps a recent experience of mine will help to illustrate the theological point of this chapter. While writing this book over the course of a few weeks, my family hosted dinner and a house party for the mainly young guys who work in one of the departments at our church. At one point in the evening I found myself sitting in the living room having a discussion about a theological issue with maybe a dozen young men in their twenties. Each of the men was holding a baby. Most of the babies were held by their fathers, men who love their wives and children. A few of the single guys were also holding babies to give a break to the mothers, who were chatting in the other room. To give you a picture, most of these guys have more than a few tattoos and were regenerated in the past few years; most have played in punk or alternative bands, and all of them have skills in areas such as design, video, audio, and the like.

A few years prior, nearly all of them were single but living with and sleeping with women, looking at porn, drinking too much, and acting immaturely. The difference between their past and their present life is solely due to the fact that God has changed them through Jesus' cross and the Spirit's indwelling, and they will never be the same. The changes in their life are evidence that they are now connected to the living God of the Bible, and had I seen no change, I would have been hard-pressed to believe that they had become Christians. Why? Because you cannot meet Jesus without changing.

QUESTION 3: **DATING**

How does a Christian date righteously, and what are the physical, emotional, and mentally connecting boundaries a Christian must set while developing an intimate relationship prior to marriage?

The past one hundred years have seen an incredible upheaval in male-female dating relationships.[1] In 1896 the word *dating* was introduced as lower-class slang in reference to prostitution. "Going on a date" was a euphemism for paying for sex. By the early 1900s, "calling" was the primary means of marrying. Calling involved a young man, a potential suitor, scheduling a time to meet a young lady in the parlor of her parents' home in the presence of her parents. These meetings were carefully overseen by the parents. Expectations for everything from formality of dress to food served and length of the meeting were spelled out in various books that defined proper courting.

Such a process protected young people from danger (e.g., abuse, rape), ensured the involvement of the entire family in the courtship of a young woman, allowed her father to keep away the wrong kinds of young men, minimized opportunity for fornication, and kept marriage as the goal of such relationships rather than such things as cohabitation. The major downside of calling was the expense, which made it impossible for many people in the middle and lower classes. They simply could not afford a sitting room or parlor designated for calling, complete with a piano, along with formal attire to wear and specific food to eat.

In the early 1900s young women were discouraged from going out alone with any male, even relatives, for fear of getting a bad reputation.

That kind of cultural conservatism began to wane as women's magazines hit the shelf (e.g., *Ladies' Home Journal* had over 1 million subscrib-
ers by 1900). These women's magazines began to inform women about
men, and an entire industry of beauty products, clothing styles, and
social norms was birthed, thereby weakening the influence of parents
over young women.

By the 1920s, urbanization provided social outlets for meeting
outside the home. Rather than calling at the woman's home, singles
were now able to go out together at places such as restaurants, movie
theaters, and dance halls. This began to create new social networks
for single people away from their homes and parents and opened up
greater opportunities for such things as casual dating and inappropriate sexual contact.

Everything changed dramatically in the 1930s. At that time the
automobile became widely available, thereby providing a new freedom
for younger people to gather away from their parents' home. This transition took the woman out of the home of her parents and into the world,
where she was driven around by the man to places where temptations to
sin from drunkenness to fornication were stronger than ever. Not surprisingly, by the 1930s dating overtook calling in prevalence, and money
became the means by which a man could pursue a woman, taking her
out on expensive dates. This altered the nature of male-female pursuit
so that the best men were those with the most money (symbolized by
which kind of car they drove) and therefore the most able to afford
the nicest dates, and the most prized women were the most outwardly
beautiful and sexual who could serve as the best trophy.

By the 1940s the prevalence of dating caused an economic view
of male and female dating relationships that was, in principle, akin
to prostitution in some ways. Since men were required to make good
money, purchase a car, and treat a woman for a date, men began expecting sexual favors in return for spending money on her. Men often pres-
sured women for sexual favors in exchange for an expensive date. Those
women who refused such requests were often no longer asked out on
dates, and looser women became more popular dates.

The 1960s saw one of the greatest social upheavals in the history of
singleness in the Western world. The feminist and sexual revolutions of
the day pushed for sexual anarchy of every kind (e.g., orgies, casual sex,

homosexuality, lesbianism, bisexuality) in conjunction with a widespread drug culture that only fueled recklessness, resulting in increased perversion and disease. In the 1960s *Playboy* was the first pornographic magazine widely published and was kept behind the counter at select stores. Also in the 1960s the birth control pill was made widely available, thereby encouraging even more sexual sin without the same levels of fear about out-of-wedlock pregnancy.

By the 1970s *Playboy* was taken from behind the counter at selected stores and displayed on the shelf alongside *Penthouse*, which was an even harder version of pornography. In 1973, abortion was legalized so that those not wanting to assume the responsibility that came with their sexual activity could legally murder their child. In 1974, no-fault divorce was legalized so that some of the legal difficulties and social stigmas associated with divorce were diminished.

The result? A cataclysmic alteration of sex, dating, marriage, and children. No longer were these seen as connected, or even related, issues.

COHABITATION

The sexual revolution of the 1960s and 1970s radically altered the sexual landscape of our nation:

> One of the most important consequences of this revolution in sexual behavior and beliefs is that the institution of marriage is much less likely to govern and guide the expression of sexual intimacy between adolescents and adults. More specifically, abstinence before marriage is now the exception to the behavioral and attitudinal norm when it comes to sex.[2]

For the first time in America's history, there are more single adults than married adults, and the number is expected only to rise. Still, more than nine out of ten people will eventually marry. In our culture of hook up, shack up, and break up, the expectation is that they will cohabit prior to marriage. From 1978 to 2008, the number of cohabitors in the U.S. rose from 1 million couples to 5 million couples. By simple definition, living together—or unmarried cohabitation—is the status of couples who are sexual partners, not married to each other, and sharing a household.[3] Others who are not cohabiting by definition because they have two residences still sleep over enough to qualify, even if the statistics do not count them.

It is estimated that about a quarter of unmarried women between the ages of 25 and 39 are currently living with a partner, and about half have lived at some time with an unmarried partner (the data are typically reported for women but not for men).[4] Over half of all first marriages are now preceded by cohabitation, compared to virtually none earlier in the century. The most likely to cohabit are people aged 20 to 24.[5]

However, the evidence actually challenges the popular idea that cohabiting ensures greater marital compatibility and thereby promotes stronger and more enduring marriages: "Cohabitation does not reduce the likelihood of eventual divorce; in fact, it is associated with a higher divorce risk."[6] Virtually all research on the topic has determined that the chances of divorce ending a marriage that was preceded by cohabitation are significantly greater than for a marriage that was not preceded by cohabitation.[7] Studies almost always find that cohabitation is associated with an increased divorce risk, with estimates ranging from as low as a 33 percent increased divorce risk to a 151 percent increased risk of dissolution.[8]

In addition to missing out on many of the benefits of marriage, cohabitors may face more serious difficulties.[9] Annual rates of depression among cohabiting couples are more than three times what they are among married couples.[10] Women in cohabiting relationships are twice as likely as married women to suffer physical abuse.[11] Two studies found that women in cohabiting relationships are about nine times more likely to be killed by their partner than are women in marital relationships.[12]

Furthermore, couples who have sex before marriage, especially couples who cohabit, are more likely to experience difficulties in their marriage.[13] For instance, a study of 2,034 married adults found that those who had cohabited prior to marriage reported less marital happiness and more marital conflict, compared to similar couples who did not cohabit.[14]

Conversely, abstinence before marriage is linked to greater marital stability.[15] Studies indicate that men and women who marry as virgins are significantly less likely to divorce.[16] For instance, men who marry as virgins are 37 percent less likely to divorce than other men, and women who marry as virgins are 24 percent less likely to divorce than other women.[17] Thus, adults who remain abstinent until marriage are more likely to enjoy a satisfying and stable marriage.[18]

Adults who waited to have sex until they married, and who have remained faithful to their spouses since they married, report higher levels of life satisfaction, compared to adults who engaged in premarital sex or adulterous sex.[19] Furthermore, "Those [adults] who have ever had sex outside their marriage also report notably low happiness scores."[20]

The reason why all of this is important is that people are prone to think their experience is normative. Singles today were born into a world that is unlike any other time in history, and it is peculiarly perverted. It seems normal to them because it is all they have ever known, but it must be evaluated in light of history and Scripture for perspective.

The bottom line? Satan is still a liar, and God's plan is still the best. That plan is chastity before marriage and fidelity in marriage.

I pastor a church where about half the people are single, and most of them are walking as Christians with Jesus for the first time in their lives. I am deeply sympathetic to the pressures and temptations that single Christians face. In a culture where people have "friends with benefits," where men are into scoring and not marrying, where the entire singles' scene from clubs to bars is built to oppose a life modeled after Jesus' singleness, and where Craig's List and other online portals in cities like mine have fifteen hundred people posting daily for a "casual encounter" (which is code for free sex), those wanting to honor Jesus in their singleness have nothing short of a war on their hands. Add to this the fact that both men and women are waiting later than ever to marry (men around twenty-six to twenty-seven and women around twenty-four to twenty-five), and the opportunities for sexual sin multiply.

When you consider that there are between eleven and thirteen million more women in church than men and acknowledge that the average man wants to attract the youngest and hottest wife he can afford, then Christian women—particularly older singles, divorcées, widows, and single moms—are at a distinct disadvantage and are tempted to settle and sin. My wife, Grace, has a particular heart for women in these situations and, as a result, a quiet aspect of our ministry is trying to help serve these women. I will spend the rest of this chapter sharing with you what my wife and I tell single men and women whom we love and minister to.

THE GIFT OF SINGLENESS?

First, there must be a biblical understanding of marriage. Biblically, singleness is not ideal,[1] marriage should be honored by all,[2] and it is demonic to teach against marriage.[3] Practically, however, there are seasons and reasons that provide exceptions to the rule of marriage for some people, as Paul explains in 1 Corinthians 7. This section of Scripture is widely misunderstood and has been throughout the history of the church. Indeed, singleness is not bad, as exemplified by Jeremiah, Jesus, and Paul.

Still, singleness is neither normative nor superior to marriage. The too-often popular misconception that singleness is ideal and superior to marriage is in fact rooted in worldly wisdom and not in Scripture. Ancient non-Christian Greek philosophers such as Plato and the Stoics taught that the physical part of existence is innately evil so our immaterial spirit is purer. The result was a disdain for the body and its pleasures, along with a bizarre asceticism, so that sex was seen as only for procreation, and celibacy was preferred.

The early church fathers and mothers were greatly steeped in this kind of thinking. Examples include Tertullian and Ambrose, who preferred extinction of the human race to ongoing sexual intercourse. Origen not only allegorized the Song of Solomon but also castrated himself. Chrysostom taught that Adam and Eve had no sexual relations until sin entered the world. Gregory of Nyssa taught that until sin entered the world, Adam and Eve did not have sex; rather, she was able to conceive through a special kind of vegetation that grew in Eden.

By the Middle Ages, the Catholic Church forbade priests to marry and regulated not only the sexual positions of married couples but also the days on which they could be intimate; eventually half of the year was forbidden for married sex. In the Victorian age, modesty became so extreme that long tablecloths were put over tables to hide the table

---

[1]Gen. 2:18; Matt. 19:4–6.
[2]Heb. 13:4.
[3]1 Tim. 4:1–3.

legs for fear that men would see them and think of women's legs and then lust.

My point? In our day of sinful sexuality, there are still many Christians overly influenced by pagan Greek thought who somehow think that only less holy Christians capitulate to marriage and sex rather than live a varsity life as a celibate single. To justify themselves and their viewpoint, such thinkers often take Paul's words in 1 Corinthians 7 out of context.

Be Holy

"To the unmarried and the widows I say that it is good for them to remain single as I am. But if they cannot exercise self-control, they should marry. For it is better to marry than to burn with passion."[4] Here Paul speaks to singles who were already in sexual sin. Besides, Paul urges them to marry rather than burn in their lust and burn in hell.

Today, the consequences of the sexual revolution can be seen in changes in sexual behavior and beliefs about sexual behavior among adults and teens. We have seen almost a complete reversal in sexual behavior and morals. Therefore, Paul's words are as true and timely as ever. For those called to singleness for a season, or for a lifetime (desires can and do change), their calling will be accompanied by a diminished sexual appetite so that remaining pure and chaste is not as difficult for them as for the person not called to singleness. Further, since most people are failing to remain chaste and holy in their singleness, most people should put their energies toward the goal of one day being married. I was one of these people, which explains why I married at the age of twenty-one, between my junior and senior years of college.

Be Wise

Now concerning the betrothed [virgins], I have no command from the Lord, but I give my judgment as one who by the Lord's mercy is trustworthy. I think that in view of the present distress it is good for a person to remain as he is. Are you bound to a wife? Do not seek to be free. Are you free from a wife? Do not seek a wife. But if you do marry, you have not sinned, and if a betrothed woman marries, she has not sinned. Yet those who marry will have worldly troubles, and I would

---

[4]1 Cor. 7:8–9.

spare you that. This is what I mean, brothers: the appointed time has grown very short. From now on, let those who have wives live as though they had none, and those who mourn as though they were not mourning, and those who rejoice as though they were not rejoicing, and those who buy as though they had no goods, and those who deal with the world as though they had no dealings with it. For the present form of this world is passing away.[5]

Chaste, single virgins were encouraged to remain single because of the "present distress," which may have included the coming bloody persecution at the hands of Nero and/or a deadly famine that had been prophesied in Acts 11:28. Singleness is often preferable in some seasons (e.g., persecution, famine, grave illness, war). Those who are able to refrain from marriage until a crisis has ended will save themselves and any children they might have birthed many heartaches and hardships. But if someone is married, Paul says, such a crisis is no excuse for a divorce, and if someone is married, he or she has not sinned. It is important to remember that Paul is not elevating singleness as generally preferable, but preferable only for some people and some circumstances. In this way, some people are called to remain single to serve Jesus in ministry; still others are called to be married, and their marriage is their ministry for Jesus. Anyone who is married will tell you that while it does restrict some ministry opportunities, it is in itself among the most difficult and important ministries.

Good reasons for remaining single in our day include living in a season of life when pursuing a potential spouse is unwise, such as experiencing personal illness, unemployment or underemployment, suffering through a traumatic life event such as the death of a parent, or undertaking education, work, or ministry in which the demands upon one's time are so severe that a relationship is not practically possible.

Be Devoted

I want you to be free from anxieties. The unmarried man is anxious about the things of the Lord, how to please the Lord. But the married man is anxious about worldly things, how to please his wife, and his interests are divided. And the unmarried or betrothed woman is anxious about the things of the Lord, how to be holy in body and

---

[5] 1 Cor. 7:25–31.

spirit. But the married woman is anxious about worldly things, how to please her husband. I say this for your own benefit, not to lay any restraint upon you, but to promote good order and to secure your undivided devotion to the Lord.[6]

In typical times, when there is not a major crisis, many of the issues in a church are best dealt with by married leaders.[7] This is because many of people's issues are related to marriage and parenting, and people with experience in those areas are generally best suited to serve as models and mentors. But in times of crisis or when ministry results in danger, single people are able to do more ministry work because their time and possessions are more easily freed up. Ministry is, in comparison, more complicating for, say, a pregnant woman or a man who is the sole provider for a large family. Therefore, in the circumstances Paul is addressing, singles are being called upon for vital ministry, though this call is not a restriction.

Obviously, Jesus Christ is the perfect example of someone who remained single for the purposes of living in poverty and suffering for the cause of ministry in a way that he could not have if he were a husband and father. In this way, those gifted with singleness, like Paul and Jesus, also often have a particular ministry calling that requires poverty or danger. A friend of mine who is working as a quiet evangelist in a closed Muslim country believes he will die for his faith and has not married as a result. Those who are simply selfish or irresponsible and therefore choose not to marry are not whom Paul is speaking of in the context of his words and life's example.

Be Considerate

If anyone thinks that he is not behaving properly toward his betrothed, if his passions are strong, and it has to be, let him do as he wishes: let them marry—it is no sin. But whoever is firmly established in his heart, being under no necessity but having his desire under control, and has determined this in his heart, to keep her as his betrothed, he will do well. So then he who marries his betrothed does well, and he who refrains from marriage will do even better.[8]

---

[6] 1 Cor. 7:32–35.
[7] 1 Tim. 3:4–5; Titus 1:6; 2:3–5.
[8] 1 Cor. 7:36–38.

With the "distress" of that day, men who were engaged to older virgins were considering backing out of their wedding. Paul counseled that men are free to do as they wish but must consider all the theological and practical variables surrounding their potential marriage.

IDOLS IN SINGLENESS

Having now cleared up some of the confusion around Paul's words, we can establish a biblical foundation for marriage.

The first thing God called "not good," even before sin entered the world, was Adam's solitary state.[9] God's answer was to create Eve as his wife, lover, fellow worshiper, helper, and friend. In so doing, God established that a marriage is one man and one woman[10] in a covenant[11] that is sexually consummated[12] and is intended to last a lifetime.[13]

There are two opposite errors about marriage into which a Christian single can fall. Idols that serve as functional saviors underlie these errors. The first idol is independence. When the idol of independence is worshiped, committed relationships, in general, and marriage, in particular, are dismissed or even disdained. Underlying this idol can be fear from a past hurt, the unhealed trauma of suffering through a parental divorce, or simply good old-fashioned selfishness, whereby someone does not want to make any life adjustments to accommodate another person. When heaven is conceived of as independence, and hell is conceived of as interdependence, then singleness is worshiped as a functional savior.

The second idol is dependence. When the idol of dependence is worshiped, then having someone to date is essential, being single is a crisis to be averted, and marriage is worshiped as the central guiding principle of life in which the longings for identity, joy, and relationship are to be satisfied. Underlying this idol can be a fear of being alone, a codependence that needs someone to lean on to an unhealthy degree, or a weak relationship with God so that it is not the primary defining and satisfying relationship in one's life. When heaven is conceived of as a couple, and hell is conceived of as being single, then a dating partner

---

[9]Gen. 2:18.
[10]Matt. 19:4–6.
[11]Prov. 2:17.
[12]Gen. 2:24–25; 1 Cor. 7:3–4.
[13]Mal. 2:16a.

or spouse invariably becomes the functional savior that is worshiped to get us out of our hell and into our heaven.

A FEW THINGS TO PONDER

Before we discuss the various ways in which a Christian can date, it is important for us first to repent of any sins and idols that are guiding our desires. In this way we can then be open to what God has for us, which is always best. Therefore, a few questions are worthy of pondering here.

First, how is your relationship with Jesus? Is that relationship strong, maturing, and growing, and is it your first priority above all other relationships? Do you need to wait to date someone until a time when your relationship with Jesus is stronger? Is your goal to meet someone with whom you can grow in your relationship with Jesus?

Second, are you believing cultural lies? Are you taking your cues not from Scripture, the Holy Spirit, and godly friends but from magazines, talk shows, the media, pornography, and godless acquaintances? Are you feeding sinful thoughts and desires that need to be repented of fully before you are fit for any serious Christian relationship?

Third, do you accept that marriage is for holiness before happiness? People who believe that marriage is meant to complete them or make them happy are invariably depressed in marriage. Why? Because when two sinners marry there will be struggles and pain. Those who rightly understand that marriage does have happiness but is first for our sanctification and holiness are in a much better theological frame of mind to marry and be able to lovingly serve their spouse and think more about *we* than *me*.

Once our relationship with Jesus is healthy and our view of marriage is biblical, we are ready to consider principles that are intended to guide Christian dating relationships.

SIXTEEN CHRISTIAN DATING PRINCIPLES FOR BOTH MEN AND WOMEN

1) Maximize your singleness for God.

While you are single, accept that you are in a season of life that affords some freedoms and benefits you will not have if and when you marry. It is a good season to finish your education, increase your theological knowledge, travel to serve in missions, give time to your church, work long hours to establish your career, and pay off any debt you may have accrued. In short, invest your single years in a way that they later pay a great return. Do not waste them.

2) Do not pursue a serious relationship until you are ready to marry.

There are many reasons why people should, for a season, devote their energies to something other than finding a spouse. Getting biblical counseling to overcome a habitual sin such as pornography or substance abuse, maturing as a Christian if they are a new or immature convert, or simply moving out of their parents' home and taking on adult responsibilities are all good reasons to delay a serious relationship until a better season of life. Basically, until people are mature enough to marry, they should not be in a serious romantic relationship but should use their energies to mature.

3) Be reasonable.

Do not set your expectations too high or too low. If you set your expectations too low, you may marry and be miserable, having made the biggest mistake of your life. If you set your expectations too high, you may never marry, or you may marry the person you think you want but who may not be the one God would consider best for you. As a practical matter, I discourage Christian singles from having too long a list of what they are looking for in a spouse. The truth is that most of these lists are simply idolatrous because they are comprised of the seekers' resume and what they like and do, as if the goal of marriage is to find someone just like them rather than someone different from them so that together they can learn to love and serve one another.

Few men are looking for a widowed, broke, and homeless gal from a family noted for incest who is a recent convert with a bitter mother-in-law in tow. But her name is Ruth, and Boaz was blessed to marry her, and through her came Jesus.

4) Do not be legalistic about dating.

There is a difference between a date and dating. A date can be two people spending time together, going out for a meal or coffee after church to get to know one another in a non-sexual manner. Dating as is practiced by non-Christians is not acceptable for Christians. Still, the word *dating* is not worth quibbling over, as Paul tells us not to quarrel over words.[14] Whether we call it "a date" or something else, time together does not need to be considered a dating relationship. In 1 Timothy 5:1–2, Paul tells Christian single men to treat Christian single women like sisters. Thus, since adult brothers and sisters talk to one another, enjoy one another's company, and occasionally enjoy a meal together, it is not a sin for two single Christians to enjoy time together, getting to know one another, so that they can see if there is the possibility of a more serious relationship that leads to courtship and marriage.

5) Do not have any romantic relationship with someone who is a non-Christian.[15]

The reasons here are almost limitless. Since you cannot marry a non-Christian, getting emotionally involved is pointless and only leads to sin and/or heartache. Since Jesus is at the center of your life, a non-Christian will not even understand who you are. Because you submit to Scripture and unbelievers do not, your relationship with one has no court of arbitration in which to resolve your differences. An unbeliever is not in covenant with Jesus, so he or she has no covenantal framework for any relationship with you. If he or she is not a Christian, you have no means of dealing with sin that will come between the two of you, because you do not both believe in the gospel of Jesus' death for sin. Indeed, you can have non-romantic evangelistic relationships with non-Christians, but if the parties involved are single, the odds of attraction are high, and it is usually best to introduce the non-Christians to your Christian friends of the opposite gender so that an evangelistic relationship can form.

6) You should be in a romantic relationship with only one person at a time.

Ultimately, the goal of a Christian not called to singleness is not to have a boyfriend or girlfriend but to have a spouse. It is cruel to date multiple people at one time, having them compete for your affections.

---

[14]1 Tim. 6:4.
[15]2 Cor. 6:14.

Furthermore, it is better preparation for adultery than it is for covenant marriage.

7) He should initiate and she should respond.

Because the Bible repeatedly states that the husband is to be the loving and leading head of the family,[16] any romantic relationship should begin with the man taking initiative to kindly and respectfully request an opportunity to get to know the woman better. Too many Christian men are too timid and need to have more courage to risk rejection in their pursuit of a wife. Any woman who is not interested in, say, a group outing or a cup of coffee need simply say no, and the man should respect that answer.

8) You need to look at who God puts in front of you.

Too many singles are looking over people in their church and life who do love God in pursuit of a mythical person, who does not exist. Yet, in God's providence, good potential spouses are right in front of them. Furthermore, while a woman should not chase a man, she can wisely put herself in front of him. This is precisely what happened in the story of Ruth and Boaz. Although God providentially put Ruth at work gleaning for food in the field of Boaz, Boaz did not consider her a potential wife until Ruth took the counsel of the older woman Naomi and got dressed up and went to the same big party as Boaz, where she did not chase him but did get in his way. The result? One of the greatest love stories in the Bible.

9) Feel free to use technology wisely.

While a Christian single should be careful not to troll Web sites and chat rooms where sexual sin is encouraged, there is nothing wrong with using online dating services. In the world of social networking, it is simply a new way for God's providence to bring people together. Some Christians retain a stigma about compatibility surveys and Internet Christian-dating sites, but they should not. Many singles attend churches where there are few possible spouses, and with the confusion and perversion that persists in the greater culture, they should not feel

---

[16]Eph. 5:22–32; Col. 3:18–21; 1 Pet. 3:1–7.

bad for using technology to find someone who loves Jesus and with whom they are compatible. As a pastor, I could tell you of dozens and dozens of wonderful marriages that began online at a Christian dating Web site.

10) Invest in a romantic relationship only with someone you are entirely attracted to.

This means more than the usual goal of finding someone rich and hot; attraction must be to the whole person. Are you sufficiently physically attracted to envision marriage to that person? Are you mentally attracted to him and enjoy talking with and learning from him? Are you spiritually attracted to her and her love for Jesus? Are you financially attracted to him so that you both agree on what lifestyle you will have? Are you "integrity attracted" to her and can see the Holy Spirit at work through her character? Are you "ministry attracted" to him and appreciate how he serves God in his ministry?

11) Only date someone who agrees with you on primary theological issues.

It is not enough simply to marry a Christian; for the sake of peace and unity in your home, you need to have the same theological convictions on primary issues. For Grace and me, this means we agree on the Bible as God's Word and our highest authority; we agree that God is Trinity and that Jesus died as our sinless God in our place for our sins; we agree on a Reformed Protestant view of the gospel. Our agreement extends to gender and family roles, and without this we would have an acrimonious marriage. We both believe that the husband is called to lovingly and sacrificially lead the family, that children are a blessing, that the wife should stay home with the children when they are young, and that solely qualified male elders should govern a church. If we disagreed on these things, even though we are Christians, we would not be able to build a life together, because we would disagree on the blueprint and spend our time fighting over which one of us is right. As it is, there is great peace, unity, and cooperation in our home because we agree on primary and secondary theological issues, and as a result we are allies, not enemies.

12) Guard your heart.[17]

Getting to know someone takes time. If you give your heart away too quickly, you will find yourself either pushing to make the relationship work or being heartbroken when it falls apart. It is good to want to give your whole heart away. However, you must wait until you are in the covenant of marriage to do so, or you risk lots of heartache and trouble.

13) Be careful of legalism and libertinism.

Legalists love to make lots of rules in addition to what's found in Scripture to govern male-female relationships, but they are simply man-made and unnecessary. I know a dating legalist, a woman, who would date only in groups, and as a result no man ever got to speak with her one-on-one, which explains, in part, why she is still single. I know a man who considers the purpose of every conversation with every Christian woman to be courtship, so that he comes off way too strong way too early and likewise remains single.

Libertines love to make themselves the exception to God's rules that govern male-female relationships, and in so doing act like their own god. Examples of dating libertines include those who cross physical boundaries, those who will date anyone who believes in some nebulous "god," those who fail to care about finding evidences of spiritual maturity, such as regular church attendance and Bible study participation, in a potential mate, and those who have snuggle sleepovers that they swear include no sexual activity but are beyond the scriptural bounds of the Song of Solomon, which repeatedly tells us not to arouse or awaken love until the time of marriage.

14) Marry someone who will be a fit for every season of the life that awaits you together.

As I've mentioned before, Grace and I met in high school, married in college, and then graduated to start Mars Hill Church together a few years later. She then quit work to stay at home and be a mother to our now five children, and we recently celebrated our sixteenth wedding anniversary and a total of over twenty years together including dating. So far, together we have been through high school, college, ministry,

---

[17]Prov. 4:23.

and parenting. One day our five children will be grown, and we will grow old together.

Grace does not get to travel with me often, but when she does, we talk frequently about how great our current season of life is but also how fun it will be when the kids are grown and we can travel together for ministry and also enjoy our grandkids. Marriage is about getting old and serving one another in every season of life. So marry someone with every season in mind. Too often, Christians marry only with children in mind and do not consider that one day the kids will be gone, but the couple will be together all the time; as a result, when the kids leave home, crisis hits the marriage because the kids were the glue that held things together. We love our children, but we also love being together and growing old together.

15) Pursue only someone you love.

The Bible says that husbands should love their wives[18] and that wives should love their husbands.[19] It is grievous when people marry who are not truly in love or willing to work on safeguarding and growing their love. Proverbs 30:21–23 says that the world cannot hold up under the weight of despair that is wrought by a married woman who is unloved. If a man and woman do not love one another and are not radically devoted to that love lasting a lifetime, then they should not marry.

16) Do not have any sexual contact until marriage.

As noted earlier, single Christians are prone to ask where the line is. That question is sinful because it is asking how to get closer to sin rather than closer to Jesus. The Bible says, "Among you there must not be even a hint of sexual immorality."[20] Paul says elsewhere that a single man should not touch any woman in any sexual way.[21] The issue is not where the line is, but, as Song of Solomon often says, when the time is. That time is the covenant of marriage. Until then, the New Testament repeatedly says to avoid *porneia*, that junk-drawer term for all kinds of sexual sin. As my friend John Piper often says, by God's grace and the Spirit's power, "theology can conquer biology." A marriage must be built on the

---

[18] Eph. 5:25.
[19] Titus 2:3–4.
[20] Eph. 5:3 (NIV).
[21] 1 Cor. 7:1.

worship of God so that spiritual intimacy can enable all other intimacy, such as mental, emotional, physical, and sexual, without shame and without sin.

SEVEN CHRISTIAN DATING QUESTIONS FOR MEN

1) Are you overlooking good women?

Examples include single mothers, widows, shy women, and those divorced on biblical grounds. Sometimes a woman's character is so sanctified and shaped through hardship that she is, in fact, more prepared than the average woman to be a devoted, faithful, resilient, and thankful wife.

2) Do you enjoy her?

Ecclesiastes 9:9 says, "Enjoy life with the wife whom you love, all the days of your vain life that he has given you under the sun." Much of your life will be spent working your job, cutting your grass, paying your bills, and dealing with sin and the curse. But if you have a wife you enjoy, life is better. I praise God that I enjoy my wife. I enjoy being at home with her, I enjoy traveling with her, and more than anyone else she is the friend with whom I enjoy having fun. This one fact has made my life satisfying.

3) Is she modest? [22]

An immodest woman may be fun to look at, but do you really want a wife who dresses immodestly so that everyone else can lust after her? Do you really want your daughters to grow up and be immodest? Sometimes a single man is attracted to a woman because she is immodest; meanwhile, more godly and modest women do not catch his eye as readily. A wise man knows that there is a difference between a good time and a good life with a good wife and patiently waits for the latter.

4) Will she follow your leadership?

Since the Bible calls you to lovingly and sacrificially lead your family, you need to have a wife who follows your leadership. This means she agrees with your theology, trusts your decision-making, appreciates the

---

[22] 1 Tim. 2:9.

other men you surround yourself with for counsel, and also respects the way you seek her input and invite her counsel as you make decisions. If she does not naturally follow your leadership, you can be sure that if you marry, there will be frequent conflict.

5) Does she have noble character? [23]

Is she a woman whom you want your daughters to be like (because they will be)? Is she the kind of woman you want your sons to marry (because they will)? Would you consider yourself honored to be with her because of how she speaks, carries herself, prays, worships God, makes decisions, serves others, works, and interacts with other men?

6) Can you provide for the lifestyle she expects? [24]

If you meet a woman who will not be satisfied with the level of income and lifestyle that you can provide, then she is not the woman for you. Since it is your responsibility to provide for the material and financial needs of your family, you must have a woman who will not grudgingly live at the level of provision you can give. So long as you work hard, tithe well, invest smartly, and save prudently, you need not feel guilty for not making a great deal of money. You will want a wife who appreciates how you can provide rather than one who is continually dissatisfied and, therefore, discouraging.

7) As you stand back and objectively consider her, is she like any of the women that Proverbs warns against?

Is she a nagging woman, likened to a dripping faucet?[25] Is she a loud and overbearing woman who would be exhausting at home and embarrassing in public?[26] Is she the kind of temperamental and quarrelsome woman that makes it better for you to camp on the roof alone than share a home with her?[27] Is she a gossip?[28] Is she an unfaithful woman prone to flirt with other men and likely to be an adulteress?[29] Is she disgraceful?[30]

---

[23]Prov. 31:10–31.
[24]1 Tim. 5:8.
[25]Prov. 27:15.
[26]Prov. 7:11; 9:13.
[27]Prov. 21:9; 25:24.
[28]Prov. 11:13; 16:28.
[29]Prov. 2:16–19; 5; 7; 11:22.
[30]Prov. 12:4.

If so, quickly but graciously extricate yourself from any relationship with her.

SEVEN CHRISTIAN DATING QUESTIONS FOR WOMEN

1) Do you want to help him and join his course of life? [31]

Since you are made to be the equal and complementing helper to your husband, you must share the direction in life he is going and be willing to join it if he is to be your husband. If he wants a career in sales or the military, where he is gone much or most of the time, and you are not okay with that, then he needs another career or you need another man to marry. Any woman who marries a man hoping to fix him, change him, or redirect his life course is with the wrong man. If she likes who he is and where he is going and wants to be a good life partner helping him to be and do what God has for him, then she may have found a man she is suited for.

2) Is he tough enough to remain strong in tough times? [32]

I am talking about a man who is tender with you, but tough for you. If you marry him and have children, will he be the kind of steady rock the family needs when times are tough? If hard economic times come, will he, for example, work two jobs to care for his family? If you have a hard pregnancy and find yourself bedridden, will he step up to do what is needed to care for his family? Too many men wilt under pressure or cave under crisis, and if you marry a man and entrust yourself and your children to him, you need to be certain that he will be there to lovingly lead the family in God's purposes, no matter what.

3) Will he take responsibility for you and your children? [33]

As the head of the home, a man must take responsibility for his family. This is what Jesus does by involving himself to help us in our life and with our sin. Any man who does not want to take responsibility to ensure that his wife and children are well loved, encouraged, and served is not going to be a good husband and father. In particular, if you are

---

[31]Gen. 2:18; 1 Cor. 11:9.
[32]2 Tim. 2:3.
[33]1 Cor. 11:3.

dating a man and you have to push him to take responsibility for himself or look after him as if you were his mother, he is nowhere near ready for marriage, and you should move on from being serious with him.

4) Is he considerate and gentle with you? [34]

Any man who does not consult with you, make decisions with you, ask what you think, and inquire how you feel is a selfish and inconsiderate man. Furthermore, any man who is harsh or in any way abusive (verbally, emotionally, sexually, physically), will only get worse once you are married. Do not kid yourself—when you are dating a man, he is on his best behavior, and if he is inconsiderate or harsh with you then, any future with him will be very painful.

5) Will he be a good father? [35]

A man might look at you as more than just a baby machine, but does he love children? Does he consider children a blessing, as Scripture says? The only way a man can be a good father is by being unselfish. If he is into his buddies, his hobbies, his activities, and the like, he will be a terrible father. Why? Because once a man decides to walk with Jesus as a faithful church member, to love his wife as Christ loves the church, to raise his kids as pastor-dad, and to work his job wholeheartedly unto the Lord, he will have little time for much of anything else. Yet he will be happy if the deepest desires of his heart are the things that are taking his time and energy. If you want to be a mom who stays home with the children, then you must have a man who will be a great daddy and longs for that role. Further, since your daughters will marry men like their daddy, and your sons will grow up to be men like their daddy, make sure to marry a man whom you want imitated for generations.

6) Is he a one-woman man? [36]

Church elders are to set the pattern as one-woman men for all God's men. Therefore, he should not be the porn guy, the flirt guy, the has-lots-of-female-friends-he-calls-buddies guy, the cheats-on-you-when-

---

[34]1 Pet. 3:7.
[35]Ps. 127:3–5; Eph. 6:4.
[36]1 Tim. 3:2.

you-are-dating guy, the dates-multiple-women-at-a-time guy, or the compares-you-to-other-women guy. If he is to be your husband, his heart, hands, mind, eyes, wallet, and life need to be solely devoted to you. If you have to keep trying to make him faithful or if you question his loyalty, he is not fit for marriage.

7) How valuable are you to him?

As a pastor I often see men who want to marry called to overcome some obstacle that, in God's providence, separates them from union with the woman they love. I believe God does this to test the man's devotion and to reveal to the woman how devoted he is to her. Too many women make it too easy for a man to catch them and, while not playing hard-to-get, a woman should not go out of her way to make it easy for a man to have her; he needs to earn her hand.

I had to work two jobs from 5 PM to 9 AM nearly every day for the entire summer before I married Grace. I often slept in my truck just to make enough money so that we could finish college without her having to work and go to school at the same time. One friend of mine had to wait a few years for his wife to be able to move legally to the U.S., and he faithfully waited for her because he treasured her. In Genesis 29:20 we read that Jacob worked fourteen long years (seven for Leah and another seven for Rachel) for the cruel and crooked Laban for the right to marry Rachel, "and they seemed to him but a few days because of the love he had for her." A woman needs to know that she is valuable, cherished, and treasured, and if a man does not labor to marry her, it is doubtless he will labor to keep her.

DATING METHODS

In this final section, we will examine two dating methods that Scripture permits for Christians. Some people will find it curious that I speak of *methods* instead of *a* method. There is quite a conflict between various Christians on this issue, and I find that each position has biblical merit for certain people. There is simply no one correct way for people to work toward marriage, although, as I have tried to explain in this chapter, there are principles that guide all Christians in their romantic relationships prior to marriage.

1) Prearranged Marriage

Many of the marriages in the Old Testament were prearranged by the parents. It was not uncommon in Old Testament times for women to marry in their early to mid teens. This process is described but never prescribed in the Old Testament as the way all God's people for all time in all cultures should be married.

Today in the Western world this form of marriage is not likely to catch on for a multitude of reasons. However, in some parts of the world it remains a common means of marriage. To be honest, I was incredibly skeptical of this method until I developed a close friendship with a very godly pastor from India. He and his wife were in a prearranged marriage that had been established by their parents with their approval. Having spent time in their home in India and knowing them for over a decade, I can attest to the fact that they are one of the most loving and beautiful Christian couples I have ever known. When I asked my friend why his prearranged marriage worked, he said that in our culture we choose our love, but in his culture they love their choice.

Admittedly, I am not arguing for a movement of prearranged marriages. Still, with the devastating statistics in our own culture regarding adultery, abuse, and divorce, we certainly have no moral high ground to criticize parents in other cultures who know and love their children well and, as a result, help to direct their spousal choice.

2) Courtship

Courtship is similar to calling in that a man pursues a woman under the oversight of her family. Biblically, the repeated refrain is that a man takes a wife, and a woman is given in marriage.[37] This principle of a man pursuing a wife under the loving oversight of the woman's father and family is illustrated in the traditional marriage custom where a father walks his daughter down the aisle and gives her in marriage.

This is illustrated in the Old Testament. One example is given in Deuteronomy 22:13–21 where a father is held legally responsible for the chastity of his daughter until marriage. If she was found guilty of being sexually active prior to marriage and lying to her husband about it, she was to be put to death on the doorsteps of her father's home because he

---

[37]Num. 10:30; 13:25; Judg. 21:1, 2, 7; 1 Sam. 18:17, 20, 27; 25:44; 1 Chron. 2:34–35; Ezra 9:2, 12; Ps. 78:63; Prov. 18:22; Jer. 16:2; 29:6; Dan. 11:17; Matt. 24:38; Luke 20:34.

was held legally responsible for her virginity. While this was rarely practiced, it illustrates the importance of a daddy taking responsibility for the life of his single daughter in that culture. Another example is given in Numbers 30:3–5. There we see that if a young woman tells her suitor that she will marry him but her father does not approve, the father has the legal right to nullify the engagement and protect his daughter from a marriage he does not believe is good for her.

In addition to the oversight of the father and mother, the Old Testament also speaks of the role of other family members in overseeing the courtship of a young woman. In the Song of Solomon the woman's father is never mentioned, which might indicate that she was raised by a single mother.

In Song of Solomon 8:8–10 we discover that there are two kinds of young women. Some are "doors" that welcome boys in, and others are "walls" that keep them away. The woman in that book was a wall, and her brothers said that because she was a wall, they would help to preserve her chastity, but had she been a door they would have stepped in to be proverbial walls and keep the wrong guys away from her. The principle is that even brothers can be helpful in looking out for their sister(s) and should help ensure she is not romantically ensnared with the wrong guy. Similarly, there is an extreme example in Genesis 34 in which Dinah is raped by her boyfriend, and in response her brothers murder not only him but also the entire city of men of which he is a part and plunder everything.

Fathers and Daughters

I am the very happy father of two beautiful daughters and three sons. In our home there will be courtship. Any male wanting to spend time pursuing my daughters will do so only with my approval, under my oversight, by my rules, and most often in my home. I adore my daughters and, as the pastor of maybe a few thousand women who were sexually abused, I want to do all I can to ensure the safety and sanctity of my lovely daughters.

I began taking my daughters on daddy dates when they were little. I get lots of time one-on-one to love and cherish them. I snuggle with them. I read the Bible with them. I pray with them. I escort them to the car. I open doors for them. I treat them as priceless treasures because they are. Grace and I often talk with them about boys, men, marriage, and what we and Jesus want for their future.

As I write this chapter, God brings to mind two memorable experiences with my oldest daughter, Ashley. The first happened when she was perhaps three or four years old. We were at Disney World, and although it was her bedtime she wanted me to take her swimming in the Mickey Mouse pool. So we went swimming. When we returned to our hotel room, I stood her up on the bed to dry her hair with a white towel. She took the ends of the towel in her tiny hands and held it like a white veil, looked me in the eye, and asked me if I would marry her. I lost it and started tearing up at the thought of the day when I would officiate the wedding of my little girl. I vowed to her that day that one day she would marry a man who loves Jesus and her, and I prayed over her and her future husband.

The second memory concerns an event that occurred some years later when I was in another pool during a summer vacation having fun with my five children. A teenage girl showed up at the pool with two boys. She jumped in the pool and shared a passionate kiss with one of the boys, and then swam to the other end of the pool where she passionately kissed the other boy. Ashley was perhaps ten years old, and Alexie was perhaps three years old, and they both saw what happened, made eye contact with me, and swam over to discuss it with me. Ashley asked me, "Daddy, did you see that girl kiss two boys?" I said, "Yes. What do you think of that?" She said, "I think she has a very bad daddy."

Too many daddies take too little responsibility to lovingly remain connected to their daughters as they mature into women. Too many ill-intentioned young men have access to such young women because daddies, as well as mommies, are not doing all they can to lovingly walk with their children through the rough waters of hormones, dating, and marriage.

So at our home my daughters will be courted. My sons will court by respectfully pursuing their future wives in the context of honoring their families, particularly the women's fathers.

I have seen some families become extreme and legalistic in their application of this principle. I am not advocating that kind of abusive application, where a father rules over his daughter at a distance rather than lovingly leading her through a close relationship built over years in which she trusts him and speaks to him from her heart because he has won her affection by being what my girls call a "poppa-daddy."

Of course, this kind of arrangement works only when both the courting man and woman are from godly Christian homes that agree on how marriage should be pursued. In my church, where there are a few thousand singles, very few have Christian families with any wisdom to offer. Tragically, I have often seen women who desire godly oversight of their dating relationships be counseled by their so-called Christian father to just live with the guy and not be so worried about getting married.

There is hope for those couples in which one or both lack godly families. They can lean on biblical wisdom for counsel and support. First, in a practical way, the church is a sort of additional family by new birth in which older men are to be like fathers and older women like mothers. This means that a healthy and biblical church should have godly older Christians, including pastors and their wives, who can lovingly help younger couples wisely make the important decision of whether to marry. For example, we now have a thorough premarital process for the few hundred couples who marry each year at Mars Hill Church, and our goal is to help ensure people are marrying the right person in the right way at the right time for the right reasons and then help them keep their covenant vows after the marriage.

I need to stress that courtship becomes abusive and legalistic when it is imposed on people apart from loving relationship, such as when some system is put in place so that spiritual mothers and fathers are forcibly assigned over adult couples. Grace and I have served many young couples at their request simply by giving them ongoing, specific counsel regarding their courtship and have greatly enjoyed serving in this way. In the end, this is all I'm advocating.

Second, throughout the Song of Solomon the woman's friends repeatedly give their opinion of her relationship.[38] Likewise, in the book of Ruth it is Ruth's older godly friend, Naomi, who gives her counsel regarding her relationship with Boaz and also gives her approval of their love. Therefore, godly friends should be involved in the courtship process. Any time a dating relationship causes one of the two involved to disappear from godly fellowship, there is reason for concern. If a

---

[38]Song 1:4b, 8; 5:1a, 9; 6:1, 13; 8:5, 8–9.

dating person has godly friends, those friends have every right to get to know the person their friend is dating and give their opinion of him or her out of love for their friend. Too many Christians say too little until it's too late.

OLDER SINGLES

The first two methods of Christian dating are generally designed to serve younger women. What about a godly older woman, established in her career, who has lived on her own for many years and has family that lives far away or is not Christian or is deceased? Does she need to be courted in her father's home or in the home of some man assigned to her in a fatherly role? No.

Speaking of an older single woman, 1 Corinthians 7:39 says, "She is free to be married to whom she wishes, only in the Lord." The principle here is that the circumstances of some older women are exceptions to the guidelines given to younger women. The basic requirement is that if a man who loves Jesus also loves a woman and wants to marry her, she can marry him if she wants to; the decision is hers to make.

One of my wife's dear friends, a godly virgin woman in her forties, was successful in her career. She served others in ministry and deeply loved Jesus, and she had always wanted to be married but was never pursued by a godly man. Then she met a godly man through a Christian Internet dating service. Wisely, she had him meet her friends and family and sought counsel, but in the end she chose to marry him, and they are doing great, by God's grace.

Ultimately, it is the heart and the principles that matter. The methods are important, but without hearts that are devoted to Jesus above all and lives that follow the principles of Scripture, it does not matter which method is used for dating; things will not go as well as God would desire.

QUESTION 2: **THE EMERGING CHURCH**

What can traditional or established churches learn from "emerging" churches?[1]

In 1997, I was the struggling church planter of the newly launched Mars Hill Church in Seattle, Washington, when an evangelical networking ministry in Texas named Leadership Network invited me to speak at a conference for young pastors that was focused on reaching younger people. Having never even been to a pastors' conference, I was honored at the request. I spoke about the cultural transition from the modern to the postmodern world rather than about generational issues.

Much to my surprise, the topic hit a nerve, and requests for media interviews, consultations, and speaking opportunities began coming in from around the country. At that time Leadership Network hired Doug Pagitt to oversee its Young Leaders Network. The Network's initial team included Pagitt, Chris Seay, and me, and soon we added Brian McLaren, at Pagitt's invitation. Loosely affiliated with the team were men such as pastor and author Dan Kimball; youth pastor Tony Jones; pastor and TheOOZE.com founder Spencer Burke; and blogger and itinerant pastor Andrew Jones. We began speaking around the country together at various conferences and churches.

Before long, I resigned from this team. Because I was still in my mid-twenties, I felt the need to focus my energies on caring for my pregnant wife, to mature personally, and to improve the health of our struggling church plant, rather than to travel around the country telling others how to do ministry. To be completely honest, my mouth, attitude, and disposition were not exemplary on many occasions while speaking at conferences in the mid to late 1990s, and I needed to grow in repentance and humility personally while getting a handle on my anger.

Furthermore, I had serious theological differences with some men on the team and was concerned about their drift from biblical truth. The team eventually split from Leadership Network (with whom I continue to partner, as they are evangelicals and friends) and formed what is now known as the Emergent Village.

Over the years, I and others have attempted to explain the difference between the emerging church and the Emergent Village (or emergent church). Despite our best efforts, the terms are so similar that they understandably cause confusion for those unfamiliar with them. Because of this confusion and ambiguity, some have moved away from using the terms *emerging* or *emergent*. I prefer to use the term *missional* to describe those who want the church to be a missionary in culture. Some people use the term *emerging church* as synonymous with *missional church*, but for others, *emerging church* is synonymous with *emergent*. I believe that when the question on which this chapter is based refers to "emerging churches," it means "missional churches." The Emergent Village is a liberal subset of the missional church. So, for the purposes of this chapter, I will speak of the *missional church* instead of the *emerging church* so as to ensure it is distinguished from the emergent church.

The missional church conversation, which began among generally younger pastors regarding how the church could best position itself to reach people being shaped by our postmodern culture, has grown considerably. What once was the equivalent of a dirt path walked by only a few young pastors has become a four-lane highway, complete with a growing caravan of Christians merging onto their preferred lane behind their leaders in an effort to find a church for the postmodern world. In this chapter I will seek to delineate the lanes and their leaders, though I would like to preface my remarks in four ways.

FOUR-POINT PREFACE

First, the people mentioned in this chapter, with the exception of Rob Bell, range from acquaintances to friends. Although there are some theological disagreements among us to varying degrees, I do love each one and have found all of them to be gracious and kind toward me over the years. They care deeply for their families, churches, and friends.

Second, we all agree that in the past generation or two there has been a significant cultural shift in the prevailing worldview from modernism, which led to rationalism, skepticism, and atheism, to postmodernism, which has led to experientialism, pluralism, spiritism, and the New Atheism. The ministry methods that succeeded in evangelizing people during the modern age just don't work anymore because the average lost person is culturally different than he or she was a few generations ago.

The transition from modernism to postmodernism also included the transition from the traditional church to the contemporary church and the current missional church.[2]

The era of modernism was also the era of Christendom, dominated by the traditional church, a time when it was assumed that most people had some idea of basic Christian beliefs; when the church had a privileged place in culture; when churches grew through birth and keeping people committed to their family's religion; when the church looked and felt traditional (e.g., crosses, stained glass, robes, hymnals, organs, liturgy); and when missionaries were sent to foreign countries to reach people who were not part of modernistic Christendom culture.

As the era of Christendom neared an end in the major cities and held only a weakening foothold in more rural areas, it became obvious that the baby boom generation—which rode the first big waves of postmodernism, rebelling against authority, doing drugs, and having free sex—was not attracted to traditional Christendom churches and ministries. So the contemporary church rose to prominence in the transition from a culture that was marked by modernism and Christendom to a culture that was increasingly postmodern and post-Christian.

These churches sought to meet the needs of spiritual seekers and saw themselves as competing with other religions and spiritualities to attract consumers by offering the best goods and services possible. Pastors of these churches and ministries were encouraged to take their cues from business and consider spiritual seekers as a market. The result was an explosion of Christian products and services of every sort and kind, contemporary worship music, megachurches, and church marketing.

Churches no longer met in traditional church buildings but in

warehouses without crosses. They put less emphasis on major theological doctrines, such as sin and hell, in favor of motivational, therapeutic,
spiritual teaching about happiness, parenting, business, marriage,
and self-worth, delivered by someone who was more sharing than
preaching and dressed casually rather than in a suit or robe. In its most
extreme version, the contemporary church inverted the gospel—that
we exist to glorify God—into a false gospel—that God exists to glorify
us by helping us achieve our potential, experience our joy, enable our
health, and expand our wealth.

With Christendom now essentially on life support in the U.S. and
officially finished in Europe, the traditional and institutional church
is dying, as its market share dries up, and the contemporary church
is scrambling to adjust to emerging postmodern cultures and generations. As a result, a third incarnation of the church, the missional
church, is rising. Viewing itself as a missionary to local culture, this
church desires to help the poor and needy, assumes it has no privileged
place in a pluralistic society filled with innumerable religious and
spiritual beliefs, and is experimenting with new forms of church and
ministry that often seek to blend ancient practices—such as living in
intentional community and contemplative devotional practices (e.g.,
meditation, prayer labyrinths)—with modern technology such as blogging and video.

I agree with the assumption that it is wise for Christians to recon-
sider how their ministry methods can be most effective in light of
culture change, and the question we will consider is whether Christian
doctrine rooted in Scripture should also be reconsidered.

Third, I agree that churches and Christians need to assume a missionary outlook to ministry. Not only should we send missionaries
across the world to evangelize lost pagan[3] peoples, but also we should
send missionaries across the street, because the people there are lost
pagans too. The gospel alone is the power of God for salvation, and I am
not suggesting in any way that we can make the gospel more powerful.
Nonetheless, I am saying that not only should we have Paul's theology
of the gospel, but we also should follow his lifestyle for the gospel,
which included using different methods to bring the same gospel to
different cultures most effectively. Paul himself commands a timeless
gospel and timely evangelistic methods:

For though I am free from all, I have made myself a servant to all, that I might win more of them. To the Jews I became as a Jew, in order to win Jews. To those under the law I became as one under the law (though not being myself under the law) that I might win those under the law. To those outside the law I became as one outside the law (not being outside the law of God but under the law of Christ) that I might win those outside the law. To the weak I became weak, that I might win the weak. I have become all things to all people, that by all means I might save some. I do it all for the sake of the gospel, that I may share with them in its blessings.[1]

Fourth, the lines between the lanes of the missional church highway are not always clearly marked, because the friendships between leaders in each lane compel them to refrain from a critical spirit; leaders even occasionally change lanes, depending on the issue. The lines are further unclear because the missional church includes seemingly every form of church—house church, church-within-a-church, church plant, established church, liturgical high church, non-liturgical charismatic church—from every kind of Christian tradition—mainline Protestant, Orthodox, Catholic, evangelical, denominational, independent.

As a result, there is great confusion that is only increased by the fact that the entire movement, or conversation, depending upon whom you ask, is referred to as the emerging church (what I am calling the missional church), but there is also the lane called the Emergent Village, which is a separate nonprofit organization. If that were not enough, the various lanes of the missional church are now present throughout the world, and the theological conversations and explorations that are occurring via the Internet, on everything from blogs to discussion boards, are ever changing.

FOUR LANES ON THE MISSIONAL CHURCH HIGHWAY

Wading through the entire missional church milieu, admittedly, is incredibly complicated; therefore, I will seek to provide a simple but accurate introduction to the missional church by focusing on the four lanes and their leaders. For the purposes of this chapter I will define them as "missional evangelicals," "missional house church evangelicals," "missional Reformed evangelicals," and "emergent liberals."

---

[1] 1 Cor. 9:19–23.

The first three lanes, missional evangelicals, missional house church evangelicals, and missional Reformed evangelicals, hold theological orthodoxy in common. They are not interested in reconsidering major Christian doctrines such as those that view the Bible as God's Word, God as triune, Jesus as God and the only means of salvation, humanity as sinful, all sex outside of heterosexual marriage (including homosexuality) as sin, and heaven and hell as literal, conscious, and eternal. Tony Jones, national coordinator of Emergent Village, admits this distinction between the first three lanes and the fourth:

> What's really intriguing about emergent Christianity? The theology. For several years now, two camps have formed in the movement. Among some who are emerging, the methods of Christianity have become irrelevant, and they must change. But for this group, the message of the gospel is unchanging—it's been figured out, once and for all, never to be reconsidered. But to another group, the methods *and* the message of Christianity are bound to be reconceived over time. Indeed, if one changes the methods, one will inevitably change the message. Another way of saying this is that the Christian gospel is always enculturated, always articulated by a certain people in a certain time and place. To try to freeze one particular articulation of the gospel, to make it timeless and universally applicable, actually does an injustice to the gospel. This goes to the very heart of what emergent is and of how emergent Christians are attempting to chart a course for following Jesus in the postmodern, globalized, pluralized world of the twenty-first century.[4]

Therefore, I will briefly examine each of the three evangelical lanes of the missional church and then spend most of our time on the emergent liberals, who are not theologically evangelical and are the most controversial.

Missional Evangelicals

Missional evangelicals are interested in updating worship styles, preaching styles, and church leadership structures so as to be relevant to postmodern-minded people. They do not place as much emphasis as do the other lanes on actively engaging in their local culture or loving and serving people as the church. They are divided over such things as the role of women in ministry, the proper mode of baptism, and charismatic gifts. Missional evangelicals commonly conduct alternative worship services to keep generally younger Christians from leaving their churches. They also plant new churches to reach people who are not being reached by existing churches.

Leaders in this lane look to pastors and authors such as Chris Seay, Dan Kimball, Rick McKinley, John Burke, Erwin McManus, and Donald Miller, whose book *Blue Like Jazz*,[5] which deconstructed the evangelical subculture, has become a best-seller. The common critique of missional evangelicals is that they are doing little more than cool church for hip young Christians.

Missional House Church Evangelicals

Missional house church evangelicals are dissatisfied with the current forms of church (e.g., traditional, seeker-sensitive, purpose-driven, contemporary). They bolster their criticism of traditional church by noting that America is becoming less Christian, and Christians are not living lives that are markedly different from non-Christians, thereby proving that current church forms have failed to create life transformation. They subsequently propose more informal, incarnational, and organic church forms, such as that of house churches.

However, they are prone to overlook the fact that when certain variables, besides just claiming to be Christian, are considered (e.g., regular church attendance, participation in a weekly Bible study group, regular personal Bible reading and prayer), there is a clear difference in major moral areas between practicing evangelicals and the average non-Christian (e.g., adultery, divorce, alcoholism, drug abuse). This shows that, as Jesus said, not everyone who says they are Christian is in relationship with him.

Missional house church evangelicals look to house church movement leaders such as Neil Cole and Shane Claiborne, who made the cover of *Christianity Today* for his efforts to encourage simple churches,[6] along with Australian missional authors Michael Frost and Alan Hirsch. Perhaps the best-known missional house church evangelical leader is George Barna, who argues, in his books *Revolution*[7] and *Pagan Christianity?*[8] against such things as Sunday church services in a building with a pastor preaching a sermon. Missional house church evangelicals are commonly critiqued as those who collect disgruntled Christians overreacting to the megachurch trend and advocating a house church trend that works well in some cultures but has not proven effective in Western nations.

Missional Reformed Evangelicals

Missional Reformed evangelicals see the postmodern world as an opportunity for the church to practice the *semper reformanda* ("always reforming") cry of the Protestant Reformation. Missional Reformed evangelicals are charismatic in terms of spiritual gifts and worship and aggressive in church planting, particularly in major cities. Missional Reformed evangelicals, unlike all the other lanes of the missional church, hold more rigidly to such things as gender roles, e.g., only qualified men may serve as pastors and preachers. It is curious that the September 2006 cover story of *Christianity Today* declared that the two hottest theologies among younger pastors in America are the missional Reformed evangelical and emergent liberal lanes.[9]

In addition to evangelical beliefs, missional Reformed evangelicals have a commitment to the Reformed theological tradition as shaped by such historical figures as Augustine, Martin Luther, John Calvin, the Puritans, Jonathan Edwards, and Charles Spurgeon, along with early evangelical Reformers such as Billy Graham, J. I. Packer, Francis Schaeffer, and John Stott. Missional Reformed evangelicals look to contemporary men such as John Piper, D. A. Carson, and Wayne Grudem for theology and to Lesslie Newbigin, Tim Keller, and Ed Stetzer for missiology. They also look to church planting leaders such as C. J. Mahaney, Matt Chandler, and Darrin Patrick.

Missional Reformed evangelicals are commonly critiqued as those who merely repackage tired Reformed fundamentalism. Critics say that they are outdated in their understanding of gender roles and too narrow in their theological convictions, and they do not really fit into the category of the missional church at all.

Before we discuss emergent liberals, it should be noted that even stalwart evangelical pioneers, such as the wonderful John Stott, believe that the first three lanes of the missional church have positive elements. *Christianity Today* reports that Stott "sketched three core practices of emerging churches: the way of Jesus, breaking down the sacred-secular divide, and community living. He says that 'emerging [his language for *missional*] churches are rediscovering [these core practices] and giving them fresh emphasis."[10]

Yet, despite the biblical and helpful rediscoveries in parts of the missional church, there are unbiblical and unhelpful theological errors in its fourth lane, the emergent liberals.

Emergent Liberals

Emergent liberals range from those on the theological fringe of orthodoxy to those caught up in heresy that critiques key evangelical doctrines, such as the Bible as authoritative divine revelation; God as Trinity; the sinfulness of human nature; the deity of Jesus Christ; Jesus' death in our place to pay the penalty for our sins on the cross; the exclusivity of Jesus for salvation; the sinfulness of homosexuality and other sex outside of heterosexual marriage; and the conscious, eternal torments of hell. Some emerging house churches are also emergent liberal in their doctrine.

Emergent liberals are networked by organizations such as the Emergent Village, which is led by author and theologian Tony Jones (Jones is no longer a youth pastor but is involved at Doug Pagitt's church), along with other prominent emergent leaders such as Pagitt, Karen Ward, and Tim Keel. The most visible emergent liberal leaders are Brian McLaren and Rob Bell.

Emergent liberals are commonly critiqued as those who are merely recycling the liberal doctrinal debates of a previous generation without seeing significant conversion growth; they are merely gathering disgruntled Christians and people intrigued by false doctrine. Albert Mohler, president of the Southern Baptist Theological Seminary, offers this critique:

> When it comes to issues such as the exclusivity of the gospel, the identity of Jesus Christ as both fully human and fully divine, the authoritative character of Scripture as written revelation, and the clear teachings of Scripture concerning issues such as homosexuality, this [emergent liberal] movement simply refuses to answer the questions.[11]

Mohler further asserts that the "Emergent movement represents a significant challenge to biblical Christianity."[12]

LEADERS OF EMERGENT LIBERALS

We now turn to the three most prominent leaders of the emergent liberal lane, two of which are key leaders of the Emergent Village. Before proceeding, a working definition of emergent is helpful. Tony Jones offers three definitions:

> 1) *Emergent Christianity*: The new forms of Christian faith arising from the old; the Christianity believed and practiced by the emergents.
>
> 2) *The emergent church*: The specifically new forms of church life rising from the modern, American church of the twentieth century.
>
> 3) *The emergents*: The adherents of emergent Christianity.[13]

Brian McLaren

Brian McLaren has a master's degree in English from the University of Maryland. He was the pastor of Cedar Ridge Community Church in the Baltimore/Washington D.C. area before leaving to focus on speaking, writing, and helping to lead the Emergent Village. Being older than many pastors in the emerging church, McLaren serves as a well-spoken father figure of sorts. He is also a gifted writer. Having spent some time with Brian, I can attest to the fact that he is a personally gracious, whimsical, engaging, and enjoyable man. His influence is so great that *Time* magazine declared him one of the twenty-five most influential evangelicals.[14] In the foreword of McLaren's *Generous Orthodoxy* (2006 edition), gay marriage advocate[15] Phyllis Tickle declares him to be the Martin Luther for the twenty-first century.

McLaren is admittedly eclectic in his theology and nearly impossible to define on most major theological issues, which makes him a lightning rod for interpretation and criticism. In the subtitle to his most theological book, *A Generous Orthodoxy*, McLaren explains himself as "a missional, evangelical, post/protestant, liberal/conservative, mystical/poetic, biblical, charismatic/contemplative, fundamentalist/Calvinist, Anabaptist/Anglican, Methodist, Catholic, green, incarnational, depressed-yet-hopeful, emergent, unfinished Christian."[16] Regarding McLaren's continual theological ambiguity, D. A. Carson, research professor of New Testament at Trinity Evangelical Divinity School and the author of more than forty-five books, has said:

It's not because he [McLaren] doesn't want to give any answer at all, it's because he wants to give answers that are fuzzy. That is his intent. It's not because he is a clever diplomat who is trying to avoid the toughest questions by using ambiguous answers of a diplomatic cast, but everybody who understands the language knows what he really means. He really does want all of these edges taken away. He wants to avoid what he perceives to be the angularity of confessional truth. And he's very good at dancing around. . . . At the end of the day, [he seems to avoid] some of the angularities of the Bible itself. . . . Brian is so careful to dance around the edges that he's shrewd enough not to come into the position where he simply says, "I know that's what the Bible says, and I disbelieve it." At some point, when a person does that, then categories like "heresy" are appropriate categories.[17]

Carson goes on to say that by skirting and being careful not to admit his disbelief in such issues, McLaren gives "the impression that they're either not important or he wants to reinterpret them," which makes Carson understand why others tend to apply such categories. He continues, "Do I think he's saying some dangerous things—dangerous in the sense that he's diverting people from things that are central to the Gospel, that are nonnegotiable as part of the Gospel—he's diverting people away from those things? Yes, in that sense, I think he's dangerous."[18]

Perhaps one of the most frequent criticisms of McLaren is his unwillingness to agree that homosexual activity is sinful. When asked for his position on homosexuality by *Time* magazine, he said, "You know what, the thing that breaks my heart is that there's no way I can answer it without hurting someone on either side."[19] In a story for *Leadership Journal*, he wrote, "I hesitate in answering 'the homosexual question' not because I'm a cowardly flip-flopper who wants to tickle ears, but because I'm a pastor, and pastors have learned from Jesus that there is more to answering a question than being right or even honest: we must also be . . . pastoral."[20] McLaren goes on to say, "Frankly, many of us don't know what we should think about homosexuality. We've heard all sides but no position has yet won our confidence."[21]

What is particularly troubling about McLaren's ongoing unwillingness to answer the gay issue is that he disguises his ambiguity and uncertainty as Christlike, pastoral care. It seems implausible that, having pastored a church for twenty-four years, he would have no idea whether homosexual activity is acceptable or that over the course of those years he declined to answer questions from his congregation about whether they could have gay sex.

McLaren's Theological Influences

Speaking of his influences, McLaren said:

> I really like [Jesus Seminar fellows] Marcus Borg and John Dominic [Crossan; they] have a new book coming out called *The Last Week* [that] follows . . . what we call passion week, or holy week. It is really a great book. . . . Evangelicals tend to think that they're the only people who take the Bible seriously. I am so impressed with how seriously these guys take the Gospel of Mark, really the last week of Jesus. It's really stunning. [22]

Marcus Borg is an avowed panentheist[23] and John Dominic Crossan, cochair of the Jesus Seminar, told *Time* magazine that after the crucifixion, "Jesus' corpse went the way of all abandoned criminals' bodies: it was probably barely covered with dirt, vulnerable to the wild dogs that roamed the wasteland of the execution grounds."[24] The subsequent "tales" of Jesus' entombment and resurrection, he says, were merely the result of "wishful thinking."[25]

McLaren appears to be influenced by other questionable works as well, which is another issue of concern. The fact that he recommends and endorses books filled with false teaching is also very concerning.

McLaren repeatedly has endorsed the book *Recovering the Scandal of the Cross*,[26] which says that the biblical categories for the explanation of Jesus' death were taken from paganism. The authors of the book go on to reason that we likewise should take present-day paganism, such as feminism and Marxism, as the categories by which we interpret the death of Jesus. In this book, the idea that Jesus died as a substitute in our place to pay our penalty for our sins (*penal substitutionary atonement*) is explained in this horrid manner: "God takes on the role of the sadist inflicting punishment, while Jesus, in his role as masochist, readily embraces suffering."[27] The authors say that penal substitution "has been understood in ways that have proven detrimental to the witness of the church."[28] They conclude that "it will not do, therefore, to characterize the atonement as God's punishment falling on Christ."²⁹ Yet, this is exactly what Paul calls the gospel: "that Christ died for our sins in accordance with the Scriptures."²

McLaren also endorsed Steve Chalke's book *The Lost Message of Jesus*, saying:

> Steve Chalke's new book could help save Jesus from Christianity. That's a strange way of putting it, I know. Not that the real Jesus needs saving. But when one contrasts the vital portrait of Jesus painted by Steve with the tense caricature drawn so often by modern Christianity, one can't help but feeling the "Jesus" of modern Christianity is in trouble. The Jesus introduced by Steve in these pages sounds like someone who can truly save us from our trouble.³⁰

Chalke's book equates the doctrine of substitutionary atonement, which is the essence of the gospel as defined in 1 Corinthians 15:3, to "a form of cosmic child abuse."³¹ Chalke says:

> The fact is that the cross isn't a form of cosmic child abuse—a vengeful Father, punishing his Son for an offence he has not even committed [as the doctrine of penal substitution makes it out to be]. Understandably, both people inside and outside of the Church have found this twisted version of events morally dubious and a huge barrier to faith. Deeper than that, however, is that such a concept stands in total contradiction to the statement "God is love." If the cross is a personal act of violence perpetrated by God towards humankind but borne by his Son, then it makes a mockery of Jesus' own teaching to love your enemies and to refuse to repay evil with evil.³²

On this error, D. A. Carson said, "I have to say, kindly but as forcefully as I can, that . . . if words mean anything, both McLaren and Chalke have largely abandoned the gospel."³³

McLaren's endorsement of Alan Jones's book *Reimagining Christianity* says, "Alan Jones is a pioneer in reimagining a Christian faith that emerges from authentic spirituality. His work stimulates and encourages me deeply."³⁴ In that book, Jones argues that the cross of Jesus should be "reimagined" because it is a vile doctrine: "The Church's fixation on the death of Jesus as the universal saving act must end, and the

---

²1 Cor. 15:3.

place of the cross must be reimagined in Christian faith. Why? Because of the cult of suffering and the vindictive God behind it."[35] Jones goes on to say, "The other thread of just criticism addresses the suggestion implicit in the cross that Jesus' sacrifice was to appease an angry god. Penal substitution was the name of this vile doctrine."[36]

Also alarming is the fact that McLaren wrote the foreword to Spencer Burke's book *A Heretic's Guide to Eternity*. Spencer Burke hosts Soularize, which he touts as the first postmodern emergent annual conference. In the foreword, McLaren says, "It's easy for inquisition-launchers to go on fault-finding missions. . . . What's more challenging, and, regarding this book, much more worthwhile, is to instead go on a truth-finding mission. And, yes, even in a book with 'heretic' in the title, I believe any honest reader can find much truth worth seeking."[37]

In the book, Burke argues that hell simply does not exist: "The God I connect with does not assign humans to hell."[38] In the same vein, he says, "When I say I'm a universalist, what I really mean is that I don't believe you have to convert to any particular religion to find God."[39] He also rejects the death of Jesus on the cross for our sins: "Although the link between grace and sin has driven Christianity for centuries, it just doesn't resonate in our culture anymore. It repulses rather than attracts. People are becoming much less inclined to acknowledge themselves as 'sinners in need of a Savior.'"[40]

Rejecting the exclusivity of Jesus Christ, Burke says God is "for anyone and everyone—Jewish, Christian, Buddhist, whatever. . . . What counts is not a belief system but a holistic approach of following what you feel, experience, discover, and believe."[41] Finally, he admits, "What's more, I'm not sure I believe in God exclusively as a person anymore either. . . . I now incorporate a panentheist view."[42] Scot McKnight, professor of religious studies at North Park University and an avowed fan of the Emergent Village,[43] says, "Is Spencer a 'heretic'? He says he is, and I see no reason to think he believes in the Trinity from reading this book. That's what heresy means to me."[44]

McLaren may have endorsed Burke's book because he himself does not believe that people will experience the conscious, eternal torments of hell (which Jesus spoke of more often than anyone else in Scripture) if they are not saved by Jesus. McLaren says that he is "trying to find an alternative to both traditional Universalism and the narrow, exclusivist understanding of hell [that unless you explicitly accept and follow Jesus, you are excluded from eternal life with God and destined for hell].["]45 He goes on to say, "We should consider the possibility that many, and perhaps even all of Jesus' hell-fire or end-of-the-universe statements refer not to postmortem judgment but to the very historic consequences of rejecting his kingdom message of reconciliation and peacemaking."46

In an audio interview, McLaren speaks of "the huge problems with the traditional understanding of hell" in this way:

> Because if the cross is in line with Jesus' teaching, then . . . a primary meaning of the cross is that the kingdom of God doesn't come like the kingdoms of this world, by inflicting violence and coercing people, but that the kingdom of God comes through suffering and willing, voluntary sacrifice, right? But in an ironic way, the doctrine of hell basically says no, but that's not really true, that in the end God gets his way through coercion and violence and intimidation and domination, just like every other kingdom does. The cross isn't the center, then; the cross is almost a distraction and false advertisement for God. . . . And I heard one well-known Christian leader—I won't mention his name just to protect his reputation because some people would use this against him—I heard him say it like this: the traditional understanding says that God asks of us something God is incapable of himself. God asks us to forgive people, but God is incapable of forgiving. God can't forgive unless he punishes somebody in place of the person he's going to forgive. God doesn't say to you, forgive your wife, and then go kick the dog to vent your anger. God asks you to actually forgive. And there's a certain sense that a common understanding of the atonement presents a God who's incapable of forgiving, unless he kicks somebody else.47

Doug Pagitt

Doug Pagitt has worked closely with McLaren for many years. Pagitt graduated with a master of arts in theology from Bethel Seminary and now pastors Solomon's Porch in Minneapolis. In the book *Listening to the Beliefs of Emerging Churches*, to which we both contributed, Pagitt said that "what we [Christians] believe is not 'timeless,'"48 that theology will be "ever-changing,"49 and that "complex understandings meant for all people, in all places, for all times, are simply not possible."50 For Pagitt, theology is not timeless truth, a "faith that was once for all delivered," as Jude 3 says, but changing perspective. There is so much of Pagitt's beliefs to be critiqued, corrected, and cautioned that entire volumes could be written, but for the sake of not wasting my time or yours, I will focus on two primary issues—our sin and Jesus' cross.

Pagitt and Sin

Regarding human sinfulness, Pagitt asserts that in the historic conflict between Augustine, who defended the doctrine of original sin, and Pelagius, who denied original sin, Augustine's influence has had "too much sway."[51] He also states that Pelagius was excommunicated from Rome "on false pretenses for personal and political, not primarily doctrinal reasons."[52] Pagitt thus doctrinally defends Pelagius, who was denounced as a heretic at the Council of Carthage in AD 418 for denying human sinfulness. Pagitt actually sounds like Pelagius when he writes, "We have an instinctive belief that there is a goodness in all human beings that needs to be protected and preserved."[53] He also argues for denying that people are born with a sin nature: "When we believe that people are inherently godly rather than inherently depraved, it follows that all people have worth, that all people have God-inspired goodness to offer."[54]

Furthermore, Pagitt argues that the creation and fall narratives do not support the doctrine of imputed sin, whereby we inherit a sin nature from Adam (as Romans 5:12–21 says):

> This story never suggests that the sin of Adam and Eve sends them into a state of depravity. There is nothing in the story that tells us that God steps over to the other side of some great chasm once Eve bites down on that fruit. Certainly there is sin, but the result of sin is a change in our relationship with God and with others, not a change in the basic makeup of humanity. The creation story tells us that although we are capable of tragic missteps, God's hope and desire is for us to continue to join in to the good things God is doing in the world. We are still capable of living as the children of God. Once the story of Adam and Eve is freed from the confines of out-of-date theology, it points us to a more accurate view of humanity: we are created in the image of God to be God's partners in the world.[55]

Pagitt calls the Westminster Confession of Faith's articles on the fall of man and total depravity "extreme theology" and goes on to say, "It's pretty clear that it's a sorry fate to be human. And as much as we'd like to believe we have moved beyond such extreme theology, this explanation has held so firmly that many churches still use this catechism in their teaching."[56] He continues, "We can say we believe that humanity is evil and depraved and that we enter the world this way. But I don't think this fits the Christian story, nor do many of us truly hold to it. . . . New life just doesn't seem to fit with this notion of inherent depravity."[57] Pagitt also says, "The disconnect between what I was taught about the human condition and what I knew and believed to be true finally made sense when I realized that the theology of depravity was yet another hand-me-down from the fifth century and the church's efforts to create a clear Greek-Christian hybrid."[58]

He thus explains why the doctrine of sin is no longer worthwhile:

> Theologies are contextual explanations of various aspects of faith. They aren't meant to stand in for truth or our common story. Instead, they act like adapters that allow our presuppositions and experiences to fit with the story of God. They are not the story itself. They are, at best, an explanation of the story for a given place and time. By definition, theologies are always limited and biased. And it's a good thing they are. Good theology makes sense of things that don't seem to make sense. But the things that don't make sense change with each generation, with each location. The Greco-Roman world had a terrible time making their assumptions of human frailty and limitation gel with the story that humans are created in the image of God. So the theology of depravity made sense to people who held a view of humans as being something less than God had intended. It answered significant questions about the church's role in saving people, which had real benefit in a world where conversion to the faith was now an act of citizenship. However, the rationale for this view of humanity has expired, and so ought the theology that grew out of it.[59]

In summary, Pagitt is saying we are not sinful and overlooks his own depravity in doing so.

Pagitt and the Cross

Regarding the cross of Jesus, Pagitt argues against the notion of penal substitution and the propitiating work of Christ on the cross. According to Pagitt, this view of God as an angry judge makes him a "Greek blood god."[60] Pagitt writes:

> For centuries, Christians have used the language of the legal system to define sin and its consequences. God is the judge, God's commandments are the law, and breaking the law brings on God's judgment in the form of death and damnation. There is a debt to be paid, so Jesus comes along and pays it on our behalf. This blood atonement is the restitution laid out for our crimes. For many Christians, this is more than just a metaphorical way of understanding sin; it is a synopsis of the gospel.[61]

He goes on to say:

> But the even more troubling version that many have heard, the one that makes us shiver when we hear it, gives us God as the angry judge who will exact his payment at any cost. In this view, God is not a softy but rather a hard-nosed, immovable, infallible judge who cannot abide defiance of the law. And boy, did we defy it. When Adam and Eve broke God's law in the garden, they offended and angered God. So heinous was their crime that their punishment extended to all of humanity for all time. The antidote to this situation is the crucifixion of the Incarnate Son of God because only the suffering and death of an equally infinite and infallible being could ever satisfy the infinite offense of the infinitely dishonored God and assuage his wrath. Yikes![62]

Thus, in Pagitt's version of Christianity we are not sinners who stand guilty before a holy and righteous God. Moreover, Jesus did not die in our place for our sins to reconcile us to God because, as Pagitt says, "the story of the gospel is so much better than the legal model suggests. It tells us that we are created as God's partners, not God's enemies. Sin does a lot of damage to that partnership—it disables us, it discourages us, it disturbs us—but it never destroys the bond that exists between God and humanity."[63]

The question then begs to be answered, why did Jesus die on the cross? Pagitt's answer is astonishing: "Jesus was not sent as the selected one to appease the anger of the Greek blood god. Jesus was sent to fulfill the promise of the Hebrew love God by ending human hostility. It was not the anger of God that Jesus came to end but the anger of people."[64]

At this point we must question which religion Pagitt is promoting. The answer is paganism. Paganism is the belief that there is no essential distinction between Creator and creation. Pagitt encourages such paganism: "The idea that there is a necessary distinction of matter from spirit, or creation from creator, is being reconsidered."[65] Pagitt describes this belief in depth:

> This world God created is one of peace and harmony and integration. Through Jesus, all humanity is brought into that world. And that is the point of the resurrection. . . . The Christian faith finds its center in the story of Jesus not because this is where the problem of God's anger is solved. Jesus is the core of Christianity because it is through Jesus that we see the fullness of God's hopes for the world. Jesus is the redemption of the creation plan. He shows us what it means to live in partnership with our creator. He leads us into what it means to be *integrated with God.*[66]

Furthermore, Pagitt says,

> At the heart of Jesus' kingdom language is the idea that God is at work in the world and that we are invited to enter into that work. The kingdom-of-God gospel of Jesus calls us to partner with God, to be full participants in the life God is creating, to follow in the way of Jesus as we seek to live as people who are fully integrated with our Creator.[67]

Romans 1:25 defines paganism plainly: "They exchanged the truth about God for a lie and worshiped and served the creature rather than the Creator." Simply, paganism does not see the crucial distinction between God the Creator and the rest of his creation, including humanity. The result of pagan thinking, according to the rest of Romans 1, is the approval of sexual sins including homosexuality; in many ways, sinful sex is the worship and sacrament of paganism. This helps to explain why, during a conference called Emergence 2007 hosted by our church in Seattle and moderated by Krista Tippett from National Public Radio

(NPR), when I asked Pagitt, "Is homosexuality an acceptable practice for a Christian?" Pagitt answered plainly, "Yes."

Pagitt's Theological Influences

Pagitt says that Henry Churchill King's book *Reconstruction in Theology*[68] "encapsulated [his] sentiment about theology."[69] In his day, King was among the premier liberal theologians. He taught and later served as president of Oberlin College, succeeding Charles Finney in each of those roles. Finney denied original sin and believed in the essential neutrality, if not goodness, of human nature.

King was among the heroes of liberal Christianity for reconciling Christianity with scientific evolution and historical and literary criticism and for rejecting the doctrine of penal substitutionary atonement, whereby Jesus died in our place to pay our penalty for our sins. King embraced the social gospel movement and the political agenda of *The New Republic* magazine with which he was involved and disdained the thought of God punishing sin. Perhaps most curious is that King's writings are littered with many of the same phrases commonly used by emergent liberals, such as "emergent evolution," "theology as conversation," "progressive revelation," and "personal relation."[70]

Rob Bell

The third and arguably most popular leader in the emergent liberal lane of the emerging church is Rob Bell. Bell received a master of divinity degree from Fuller Theological Seminary. He is the founding pastor of Mars Hill Bible Church in Grand Rapids, Michigan (not affiliated with the Mars Hill Church I pastor in Seattle), and a best-selling author, and he was dubbed the "next Billy Graham" by the *Chicago Sun-Times*.[71]

The NOOMA Videos

Bell is perhaps best known for his wildly popular NOOMA videos. Each of the videos is roughly ten to fourteen minutes in length and shows Bell teaching a spiritual concept. To be fair, the production quality of the videos is phenomenal, the concept of packing big ideas into small videos that are visually appealing so as to reach young people is really smart, and Bell himself is a very gifted communicator. The problem concerns what is actually taught, or not taught, on the videos. Greg Gilbert, who serves as director of theological research for the president of The Southern Baptist Theological Seminary, has made some poignant points about this problem, points that well-known pastors such as Mark Dever and C. J. Mahaney have supported.[72] After watching nearly all of the NOOMA videos, Gilbert writes:

> The gospel as Bell communicates it in NOOMA runs something like this: All of us are broken, sinful, selfish, and prideful people. We carry around the baggage of our hurts, our resentments, and our jealousies. As a result we are just a shell of the kind of people God intends us to be. But our God is a loving God who accepts us and loves us just as we are. He can comfort us, heal us, and make us whole, real, authentic, living, laughing people. Not only that, but Jesus came to show us how to live revolutionary lives of love, compassion, and acceptance. By learning from his teachings and following him, we can live the full and complete lives that God intended.
>
> And that's about it. That's not just the introduction that leads to an explanation of the cross, atonement, the resurrection and salvation, either. So far, at least, that's what NOOMA holds out as "The Gospel." Full stop....
>
> I have a theory about why Emergent church types seem to be able to communicate so well with "our generation," why they're able to relate so well to people who have always been hostile to the gospel. You can chalk it up to some kind of "authentic" style if you want, but I'd contend that a big part of their ability to communicate the gospel without offense to people who have always been offended by it is that they leave out all the offensive parts![73]

I do not want to be overly critical, but in the name of discernment it is important to consider some things that Bell actually says in the NOOMA videos. It is also important to note that preachers (including me) do misspeak and make errors, and our hearers need to have a bit of grace. However, when the NOOMA videos are carefully scripted so that an entire manuscript is carefully followed, and any mistakes are subsequently edited out, major theological errors cannot simply be overlooked as mistakes.

First, Bell tells lost people that they are already connected to God and not separated from him by sin. In his NOOMA video *Rhythm*, Bell likens God to a song playing everywhere in the heart of everyone: "The song is playing all around us all the time. . . . May you come to see that the song is written on your heart, and as you live in tune with the song, in tune with the Creator of the universe, may you realize that you *are* in relationship with the living God."[74]

In another NOOMA video called *Luggage*, Bell says that everyone, Christians and non-Christians alike, has their sins forgiven:

> It's like right at the heart of [Jesus'] message is the simple claim that God has forgiven us of all of our sins, doesn't hold any of our past against us—because none of us have clean hands, do we? . . . So when I forgive somebody, I'm giving them what God has given to me. . . . May you forgive as you've been forgiven. May you give to others what's been given to you.[75]

Second, Bell is incredibly unclear about the meaning, purpose, and accomplishments of Jesus on the cross. Gilbert explains why the emergent movement has so much trouble with the cross:

> They can't really find a place for it [Jesus' cross]. It doesn't fit neatly into the storyline. . . . Blood atonement just doesn't find a natural home in the Emergent story, so even though it can't be ignored entirely, the cross doesn't get mentioned very often. And when it does, it's never with any clear explanation of its meaning. . . .
>
> So what's going on here? My guess is that it's the same impulse that would lead Bell to ignore the fact that God judges sin. Wrath is uncomfortable, and it doesn't play well in the Emergent culture. People don't want to hear about a God who could be wrathful.[76]

Third, Bell turns Christianity into a moral way of life patterned after Jesus' example. For Bell, Christianity is not repenting of sin, believing in Jesus, and being filled by the power of the Holy Spirit for new life. Rather, we can live a good life like Jesus by believing in ourselves. In his NOOMA video *Dust*, Bell explains Peter's failure to walk on water in this way:

> He [Peter] sees his rabbi [Jesus] walking on water, and what's the first thing he wants to do? "I wanna walk on water, too. I wanna be like my rabbi." And so Peter gets out of the boat, and he starts walking on

water, and he yells out, "Jesus save me!" And the text reads that Jesus immediately caught him and said, "You of little faith, why did you doubt?" Now, I always assumed that Peter doubts Jesus. But Jesus isn't sinking. Who does Peter doubt? He doubts himself; he loses faith in himself, that he can actually be like his rabbi. . . . . I mean, all my life, I've heard people talk about believing in God. But God believes in us, in you, in me. I mean faith in Jesus is important. But what about Jesus' faith in us?[77]

Christianity is about us having faith in Jesus, but in Bell's gospel, Jesus has faith in us; salvation, or a new way of life, requires not just having faith in Jesus but also having faith in ourselves.

Fourth, Bell's Jesus is mainly just a really interesting teacher, kind of like Bell himself. Gilbert says: "[Bell] doesn't call him Savior, or Redeemer, or Son of God, and only very occasionally does he call him Lord. Instead, he very much seems to prefer calling Jesus 'teacher' or 'rabbi.' I'm sure part of that is that he wants to be fresh and edgy. But I think it also points to just how far these videos lower the meaning of Christianity."[78]

Bell's NOOMA videos are simply tired old moralisms where Jesus is a good person, and we are good people too who can live like him if we try hard enough and believe in ourselves. Sure, they're really uber-hip videos with trendy names and a title that even sounds like a Greek word, but that's simply a fresh coat of paint on a broken-down, rusty old car going nowhere.

Bell's Position Analyzed

I asked D. A. Carson to review an earlier version of what you are reading in this chapter. My work here originally appeared as a cover story for the *Christian Research Journal*[79] and culminated with my appearance on the *Bible Answer Man* radio show with Hank Hanegraaff.[80] In response, Carson sent me an e-mail in which he analyzed Bell's popularity, offering some perceptive insights (which I have included with his permission):

I think there is (ironically) a peculiar *cultural* reason that helps to explain Bell's remarkable "success": he is located in Grand Rapids. That city is populated by large numbers of Dutch Reformed believers who have been well catechized and indoctrinated, but who were brought up in churches that increasingly feel old-fashioned and culturally dated. When such Christians are exposed to Bell, not only do they feel and enjoy the pulse of something contemporary, they are inclined to read their strong *Christian* assumptions into what he is doing. They see his "Nooma" video on forgiveness, say, and read in a lot of Christian assumptions, making the video quite a powerful tool. But if a biblically-illiterate New Yorker were seeing the same clip, I doubt that he or she would find much in it that is distinctively Christian. In other words, as Bell has progressed, he has provided less and less material that is distinctively gospel-shaped, or even Christian. I suspect he would be neither popular nor effective in either Seattle or New York. The irony, then, is that in allegedly reaching out to a new generation of non-Christians, in the Grand Rapids environment a fair bit of his success can be credited to the fact that he is in reality reaching out to substantial numbers of disgruntled (former) conservatives who are (unknowingly) bringing a lot of their Christian baggage with them.

The relationship between Bell, McLaren, and Pagitt is in part based on the latter two having preached for Bell at his church. Rob Bell's wife, Kristen, spoke of McLaren's influence saying, "I grew up thinking that we've figured out the Bible . . . that we knew what it means. Now I have no idea what most of it means. And yet I feel like life is big again—like life used to be black and white, and now it's in color."[81] She goes on to say that during her and Rob's rethinking of the Bible and Christian doctrine, their "lifeboat was *A New Kind of Christian*," written by McLaren.[82]

Bell's teaching on hell is as vague and slippery as that of his friend McLaren. In his book *Velvet Elvis*, Bell says:

> The fact that we are loved and accepted and forgiven in spite of everything we have done is simply too good to be true. Our choice becomes this: We can trust his [God's] retelling of the story, or we can trust our telling of our story. It is a choice we make every day about the reality we are going to live in. And this reality extends beyond life. Heaven is full of forgiven people. Hell is full of forgiven people. Heaven is full of people God loves, whom Jesus died for. Hell is full of forgiven people God loves, whom Jesus died for. The difference is how we choose to

live, which story we choose to live in, which version of reality we trust. Ours or God's.[83]

This kind of peculiar universalism asserts that everyone has their sins forgiven by God, but some wind up in hell nonetheless. For lost people this kind of teaching is simply confusing because it teaches that their sins are already forgiven, and rather than repenting of their sin, which separates them from God[3], and trusting in Jesus' atoning death in their place for their sins, all they need to do to experience eternity in heaven is to live a good life.

Bell and the Virgin Birth

Regarding the virgin conception of Jesus, Rob Bell speculates that if "Jesus had a real, earthly, biological father named Larry, and archaeologists find Larry's tomb and do DNA samples and prove beyond a shadow of a doubt that the virgin birth was really just a bit of mythologizing the Gospel writers threw in to appeal to the followers of the Mithra and Dionysian religious cults that were hugely popular at the time," we would essentially not lose any significant part of our faith because it is more about how we live.[84]

To be fair, Bell does not deny the virgin conception of Jesus, but he does deny that it is of any notable theological importance. This, however, is a dangerous move for four reasons, as I have written in *Vintage Jesus*[85] and summarize as follows.

First, the only alternative to the virgin conception of Jesus is that Mary was a sexually sinful woman who conceived Jesus illegitimately.[4] Second, if the virgin conception were untrue, then the story of Jesus would change dramatically; we would have a sexually promiscuous young woman lying about God's miraculous hand in the birth of her son, raising that son to declare he is God, and then joining his religion.[5] Third, if we are willing to disbelieve the virgin conception, we are flatly and plainly stating that Scripture may contain mistakes, or even outright lies. In his book *The Virgin Birth of Christ*, J. Gresham Machen said, "Everyone admits that the Bible represents Jesus as having been conceived by the Holy Ghost and

---

[3]E.g., Isa. 59:2.
[4]Matt. 13:55; Mark 6:3; John 8:41.
[5]Acts 1:14.

born of the Virgin Mary. The only question is whether in making that representation the Bible is true or false."[86] Machen went on to argue that "if the Bible is regarded as being wrong in what it says about the birth of Christ, then obviously the authority of the Bible in any high sense, is gone."[87] Fourth, in the early days of the Christian church, there was, in fact, a group who rejected the virgin conception of Jesus, the heretical Ebionites, and it is both unwise and unfaithful for a prominent pastor to accept a doctrine that the church has condemned as false.

Can a true Christian deny the virgin conception of Christ? As Mohler has said:

> The answer to that question must be a decisive No.... Christians must face the fact that a denial of the virgin birth is a denial of Jesus as the Christ. The Savior who died for our sins was none other than the baby who was conceived of the Holy Spirit, and born of a virgin. The virgin birth does not stand alone as a biblical doctrine[;] it is an irreducible part of the biblical revelation about the person and work of Jesus Christ. With it, the Gospel stands or falls.[88]

Bell's Theological Influences

Bell has said, "For a mind-blowing introduction to emergence theory and divine creativity [which means we are cocreators with God], set aside three months and read Ken Wilber's *A Brief History of Everything*."[89] Curiously, McLaren similarly has said, "I am trying (with Ken Wilber's help) to make clear that I believe there is something above and beyond the current alternatives of modern fundamentalism/absolutism and pluralistic relativism."[90] McLaren enthusiastically recommends Wilber's *A Theory of Everything* and *The Marriage of Sense and Soul*: "The way of thinking Wilber promotes and exemplifies—which he calls 'integral' thinking and which I call 'emergent' thinking—is powerful and important, in my opinion."[91]

To learn more about Wilber I contacted author Peter Jones,[92] who is perhaps the leading Christian expert on paganism and the new spirituality. In a personal e-mail, he told me, "The arch pagan philosopher is Ken Wilber."[93] Jones said:

Wilber is a practicing Mahayana Buddhist who believes that reality is ultimately a non-dual union of emptiness and form. He speaks of "unitary non-dual (monistic) consciousness," what some call "the dharma of non-dual enlightenment," he is a promoter of the *Perennial Philosophy* (. . . a name for the religion of esoteric paganism) and the "great chain of being." Wilber promotes yoga, Zen, Kabbalah, [and] tantric Yoga (Hindu sex techniques). His think tank, *Integral Institute*, includes such luminaries as Deepak Chopra, Michael Murphy (of Esalen and a key figure in the Human Potential movement), Jon Kabat-Zin, Buddhist healer and professor of medicine at UMass, [and] Francisco Varela, a Chilean biologist and Tibetan Buddhist."[94]

Jones explained that according to Wilber (the author McLaren and Bell so enthusiastically recommend) in *A Theory of Everything*, Christianity is fourth among the nine levels of human evolutionary spiritual consciousness and will be outgrown and replaced with more enlightened understandings of God and the world, such as green egalitarianism, ultimately culminating in the integration of varying religions and ideologies into a global utopia of a sort—all without Jesus.[95]

THE END OF THE ROAD

The multilane highway of missional Christianity has continued its journey forward into the postmodern world with missional evangelicals, missional house church evangelicals, and missional Reformed evangelicals functioning as missionaries reaching out to postmodern people. The emergent liberals, however, have taken an off-ramp and now are not reaching out to postmoderns but are blazing a new path in search of a new land of postmodern Christianity.

As Rob Bell said, "This is not just the same old message with new methods. We're rediscovering Christianity."[96] Echoing this sentiment, despite a few millennia of Christianity since the days when Jesus last walked the earth, McLaren says, "I don't think we've got the gospel right yet. What does it mean to be 'saved'? . . . I don't think the liberals have it right. But I don't think we have it right either. None of us has arrived at orthodoxy."[97]

EMERGENT LIBERALS AND THE GOSPEL

So how do some emergent liberals define the gospel? In Tony Jones's definition, he does not mention our sin or Jesus as God and his sinless life, substitutionary death, and bodily resurrection. He defines the gospel as "the irreducible good news of God, ultimately delivered in the person of Jesus Christ. In other words, a reality that cannot be summed up in a call-out box."[98] He adds:

> Many Christians take great umbrage at the emergent assertion that the gospel is complex and irreducible. They argue that the gospel is simple and that emergents are making it too hard. They say the Bible has a "plain meaning," and that's the one meant by God. But emergents just don't see it. The more emergents read the Bible, the more complex it becomes. And in fact, that's a point in favor of the Christian Story, for that means it jibes with the complex realities of the globalized, pluralistic, often confusing world in which we live. In other words, emergents are drawn to a gospel that meshes with our own experience of the world.[99]

Regarding the overhaul project of Christianity that emergents are undertaking, Pagitt says:

> I am a Christian, but I don't believe in Christianity. At least I don't believe in the versions of Christianity that have prevailed for the last fifteen hundred years, the ones that were perfectly suitable in their time and place but have little connection with this time and place. The ones that answer questions we no longer ask and fail to consider questions we can no longer ignore. The ones that don't mesh with what we know about God and the world and our place in it. I want to be very clear: I am not conflicted because I struggle to believe. I am conflicted because I want to believe differently. I don't like feeling at odds with the faith I hold so deeply.[100]

The book jacket for his *A Christianity Worth Believing* describes the book:

> Pagitt points the way to a new kind of faith by asking the "off-limits" questions about God, Jesus, sin, the Bible, humanity, church, and the Kingdom of God. Rather than rehashing old debates, he offers

new insights, provocative possibilities, and hopeful alternatives. In *A Christianity Worth Believing* you may well discover questions you didn't think you could ask, ideas you didn't think you could pursue, beliefs you didn't think you could hold onto.[101]

EMERGENT LIBERALS: DIRECTION AND INFLUENCE

Emergent Liberal Drift

As the lane of the emergent liberals becomes its own highway that goes in a different doctrinal direction than historical orthodox Christianity, more and more evangelicals will turn around in order to drive in one of the other three lanes of the missional church. It seems inevitable, though I am no prophet, that the emergent liberal lane of the missional church will continue to drift away from a discussion about how to contextualize timeless Christian truth in timely cultural ways to an interfaith dialogue with less and less distinction between the religions of the world and the deity of Jesus Christ.

This is already encouraged by the teachings of McLaren, who said, "Jesus did *not* come to create another exclusive religion,"[102] and "I don't hope all Jews or Hindus will become members of the Christian religion. But I do hope all who feel so called will become Jewish or Hindu followers of Jesus."[103] He has also written:

> Many Hindus are willing to consider Jesus as a legitimate manifestation of the divine [not the divine] . . . many Buddhists see Jesus as one of humanity's most enlightened people [not God]. . . . A shared reappraisal of Jesus' message could provide a unique space or common ground for urgently needed religious dialogue—and it doesn't seem an exaggeration to say that the future of our planet may depend on such dialogue. This reappraisal of Jesus' message [as God] may be the only project capable of saving a number of religions.[104]

Since Jews do not believe Jesus is God and Hindus believe there are more than a million gods, but Jesus said he is the only God, it is inconceivable that one simultaneously could be a faithful follower of Jesus and a practicing devotee of any religion but Christianity.

To bring all religions together, emergent liberals will need to compromise the doctrinal truths of Christianity even further. McLaren essentially predicted this: "Christians in the emerging culture may look back on our doctrinal structures (statements of faith, systematic theologies) as we look back on medieval cathedrals: possessing a real beauty that should be preserved, but now largely vacant, not inhabited or used much anymore, more tourist attraction than holy place."[105]

Doug Pagitt has demonstrated this. Speaking on his video blog about his few days of interfaith dialogue with Muslims, Sikhs, Hindus, Buddhists, and others at the Seeds of Compassion event spearheaded by the Dalai Lama, he described it as a manifestation of God's kingdom, saying that he and his church have always sought to "join in the kingdom of God wherever we find it. That certainly was the case in these events the last couple of days."[106]

One is left to wonder what will replace that historic Christian orthodoxy, since the emergent liberals have a low view of the divine inspiration, perfection, authority, and timelessness of Scripture, which Rob Bell says does not consist of "first and foremost timeless truths,"[107] and McLaren says is "not a look-it-up encyclopedia of timeless moral truths,"[108] and Pagitt says, "I just don't think the Bible is always the best starting point for faith."[109]

Amid such great confusion, McLaren encourages us to look to Dorothy of *The Wizard of Oz* fame rather than to Jesus for insight: "At first glance, Dorothy is all wrong as a model of leadership. She is the wrong gender (female) and the wrong age (young). Rather than being a person with all the answers, who knows what's up and where to go and what's what, she is herself lost, a seeker, often bewildered, and vulnerable. These characteristics would disqualify her from modern leadership. But they serve as her best credentials for postmodern leadership."[110]

Two Myths

Incredibly, the great interest many Christians have shown in emergent leaders and their churches is fueled by two myths. The first myth is that emergents are converting lost postmodern people to Jesus. Yet that is simply not the case in most emergent communities, for two reasons. First, conversion is unlikely when the gospel of our sin and Jesus' death for our sin and resurrection for our salvation is not defined clearly. Second, emergents are not generally planting churches to convert lost people; rather, they are gathering disgruntled former evangelicals to do life and talk theology together. Emergent director Tony Jones admits exactly this:

> Both [Robert] Schuller and [Rick] Warren are progenitors of the "seeker-sensitive" church movement, which dominated American evangelicalism in the 1980s and 1990s. Massive church campuses in the suburbs were built to resemble shopping malls in an attempt to entice suburbanites.... This is an important backdrop for understanding emergents. Many of them were nurtured in these seeker-sensitive environments. Some even served on the staffs of these churches. But as the complexities of a globalized world have encroached on their psyches, the emergents have pursued a faith that spurns easy answers. If the seeker-sensitive church movement can be seen as a reaction to the failures of liberal theology or as a safe haven for people in a world awash with change, the emergent church movement is a counterreaction.[111]

Still, this counterreaction is not intended to convert lost people to Jesus. In fact, the emergent church plants are, according to Tony Jones, as selfish and inward-focused as the seeker megachurches they criticize. He flatly states, "Emergents start new churches to save their own faith, not necessarily as an outreach strategy."[112]

The second myth is that emergents are humble. The story is told by various emergent leaders in various ways that people of modernity arrogantly believed that all truth could be known, while those of postmodernism and its emergent offspring are humble.[113] Jones discusses this apparent humility:

> Humility about what human beings can know, about the limits of human knowledge and our ability to accurately articulate that knowledge—what philosophers call *epistemic* humility—is a common trait among emergents. . . . "I'm humble," an emergent might tell you, "because I don't know what I'm wrong about today. I'll speak with confidence, and I'll speak with passion, but I won't speak with certainty."[114]

Elsewhere Jones says, "Theology is *temporary*. Since our conceptions of God are shaped locally and in conversation, we must hold them humbly. We must carry our theologies with an open hand, as it were. To assume that our convictions about God are somehow timeless is the deepest arrogance."[115]

Thus, in the emergent world even heresy is fine because it is humble enough not to know anything. Yet again the reference point is erroneous, because the Bible reveals Jesus as the most humble man who ever lived who was ultimately killed because he kept speaking with certainty and was humble enough to stick to the truth even when it cost him his own life. Therefore, declaring that humility means not knowing anything with certainty except being certain that we cannot be certain is illogical, self-refuting, unbiblical, and not Christlike. Or, to say it another way, it is what philosophers call *epistemic arrogance* and what the Bible calls proud.

If you would like to see this pride, just log on to an emergent discussion board online, chat with an emergent pastor, or attend an emergent event and say you are a Calvinist who believes that only men should be pastors and that Jesus died in our place for our sins and that anyone who does not repent of sins like homosexuality and trust in Jesus will spend forever in the conscious eternal torments of hell. I bet you two *Left Behind* trading cards that you will learn that all the nice talk about not having any theological certainty and being humble is about as honest as a politician behind in the polls near election day. After all, one way you can know that people are not humble is when they write a book and say that they alone are humble enough to see their own humility, and when they call you arrogant if you disagree with them.

A GRIM PROGNOSIS

In closing, the cults of the modern world, such as Jehovah's Witnesses and Mormonism, sprang from the infecting of biblical truth by modern philosophy. Unless there is correction, similar cults will spring from the infecting of biblical truth by postmodern philosophy. With Rob Bell and Doug Pagitt recently participating in the Dalai Lama's Seeds of Compassion Tour by praying with members of other religions and sitting on the stage as panelists discussing the need for unity between all religions, I fear that they may have already passed the end of the road.[116]

That moment arguably came when Bell was on stage at the Seeds of Compassion event in front of an enormous crowd and the media cameras. He was supposed to speak from the Christian viewpoint along with panelists representing other religions. While he failed to mention the name of Jesus even once, he did manage to refer to the Dalai Lama as

"His Holiness." We can assume that our sinless God, Lord, Savior, Judge, and His Holiness—Jesus—was grieved, and we should be also. So where is all of this going? Sadly, it's going very south very quickly. One example is the subject of whether homosexuality is sinful. Analyzing Bell's teaching on homosexuality, theologian Ben Witherington explains that Bell's answers are "evasive in part, and disturbing in other parts, and clearly unbiblical in other parts and in this he sounds like some other leaders in the Emergent Church movement."[117] Tony Jones has also written, "I now believe that GLBTQ [gay, lesbian, transgender/transsexual, questioning and/or queer] can live lives in accord with biblical Christianity (at least as much as any of us can!) and that their monogamy can and should be sanctioned and blessed by church and state."[118]

I predict emergent leaders will not be correcting any of their doctrinal errors anytime soon, if ever. Friend of emergents and theologian Scot McKnight wrote in *Christianity Today*, "The emergents I know are numb to both the warnings and the lines; they have heard those warnings and they have crossed those lines. They are surprised by neither and are not likely to turn back."[119]

Similarly, Tony Jones has said, "Emergent Christians, too, are pushing over fences and roaming around at the margins of the church in America. Once domesticated in conventional churches and traditional seminaries, more and more Christians are moving into the wilderness. They occasionally wander back, feeding off the structures and theologies of traditional Christianity, but they never stick around long. Attempts to redomesticate them will fail. They've gone feral."[120]

This must have been what the apostle Paul was talking about when he said false teachers are "dogs."[6]

---

[6]Phil. 3:2.

QUESTION 1: **THE REGULATIVE PRINCIPLE**

Do you believe that the Scripture not only regulates our theology but also our methodology? In other words, do you believe in the regulative principle? If so, to what degree? If not, why not?

For the average Christian, the question addressed in this chapter is likely to sound completely foreign to all except a few Presbyterians and maybe seven hard-core young, single guys in a seminary somewhere, drunk on reading dead authors and in need of getting a wife, having a few kids, and learning to put the books down a bit more. Still, underlying the question is the very important matter of worship. To put the question another way, how should we worship the God of the Bible? That question is incredibly significant.

WHAT WORSHIP IS—AND ISN'T

To answer this question we must define what worship is and is not. Worship is not a style of music, a meeting in a church building, the corporate singing by God's people, something that starts and stops, or something that only some people participate in.

In his magnificent book *Unceasing Worship*, Harold Best states his thesis: "The burden of this book develops the concept of continuous outpouring as the rubric for our worship. As God eternally outpours within his triune self, and as we are created in his image, it follows that we too are continuous outpourers, incurably so."[1] Although there is one

God, the three persons of the Trinity continually exist with a ceaseless outpouring of love, communication, and joy. Human beings are made in the image and likeness of God. As such, we too are ceaseless worshipers pouring ourselves out for someone or something. However, because of sin, our worship is bent toward people and other created things rather than toward God our creator, which is, by definition, idolatry.[1] Subsequently, we need God to seek us and save us from sin through Jesus so that we can be free to worship as he commands in Scripture.

In many ways, this theme of worship is a major thread that weaves the entire storyline of the Bible together, because worship is the appropriate response of the creature to our Creator. Summarizing this thread, Best says:

> We begin with one fundamental fact about worship: at this very moment, and for as long as this world endures, everybody inhabiting it is bowing down and serving something or someone—an artifact, a person, an institution, an idea, a spirit, or God through Christ. Everyone is being shaped thereby and is growing up toward some measure of fullness, whether of righteousness or of evil. No one is exempt and no one can wish to be. We are, every one of us, unceasing worshipers and will remain so forever, for eternity is an infinite extrapolation of one of two conditions: a surrender to the sinfulness of sin unto infinite loss or the commitment of personal righteousness unto infinite gain. This is the central fact of our existence, and it drives every other fact. Within it lies the story of creation, fall, redemption, and new creation or final loss.[2]

Thus, the only difference between people is not whether they worship, but who or what they worship and how they worship. N. T. Wright speaks of this central truth, saying, "Christians are not defined by skin colour, by gender, by geographical location, or even, shockingly, by their good behaviour. Nor are they defined by the particular type of religious feelings they may have. They are defined in terms of *the god they worship.*"[3]

True Christians all agree that God must be worshiped biblically. That is, God must be worshiped as he wishes, not as we wish. The Bible is clear that God is to be worshiped in ways and forms that he deems

---

[1]Rom. 1:25.

acceptable. This explains why God judges those who seek to worship him with either external sinful forms[2] or internal sinful hearts.[3] This is incredibly important. Some churches care more about what is in people's hearts than about what they do in their life, whereas other churches are more concerned about doing things the "right" way and care little about the motivations behind those actions. When it comes to worship, which is all of life, the God of the Bible cares about both what we do and why we do it. We see this, for example, in Genesis 4, where Cain and Abel bring their worship offerings to God, and while what is in their hands is acceptable to God, Cain's offering is rejected because what is in his heart is unacceptable—he was jealous of his brother.[4]

Thus, we must look to Scripture for God's definition of biblical worship, because as 2 Timothy 3:16–17 teaches, "All Scripture is breathed out by God and profitable for teaching, for reproof, for correction, and for training in righteousness, that the man of God may be competent, equipped for every good work." Simply put, the Scripture is our highest authority and regulates all of life and worship. We are repeatedly warned to not add to or subtract anything from Scripture, because it is sufficient.[5]

This view of the Bible is often referred to as *sola scriptura*, whereby the Bible is our highest court of authority. This position is not *solo scriptura*, whereby Scripture is our only court of authority, because God does have lower courts of authority under his Word to help regulate our life and worship. Such lower courts include reason, conscience, tradition, the Holy Spirit, experience, government, parents, and pastors.

Worship Defined

A biblically informed Christian definition of worship is "glorifying God the Father through the mediatorship of God the Son by the indwelling power of God the Spirit." This definition of worship includes both adoration and action, according to Hebrews 13:15–16: "Through him then let us continually offer up a sacrifice of praise to God, that is, the fruit of lips that acknowledge his name. Do not neglect to do good and to

---

[2]Lev. 10:1–2; Isa. 1:11–17; Ezekiel 8–9; Jer. 7:9–10.
[3]Genesis 4; Isa. 1:11–17; Jer. 7:9–10; Mic. 6:6–8.
[4]1 John 3:12.
[5]Deut. 4:2; 12:32; Rev. 22:18–19.

share what you have, for such sacrifices are pleasing to God." Regarding worship as both adoration of God and action for God, John Frame says:

> In Scripture there are two groups of Hebrew and Greek terms that are translated "worship." The first group refers to "labor" or "service." . . . The second group of terms means literally "bowing" or "bending the knee," hence "paying homage, honoring the worth of someone else." The English term *worship*, from *worth*, has the same connotation. From the first group of terms we may conclude that worship is *active*. It is something we *do*, a *verb*. . . . From the second group of terms, we learn that worship is honoring someone superior to ourselves.[4]

Regarding worship as a life of action, Miroslav Volf rightly says:

> There is something profoundly hypocritical about praising God for God's mighty deeds of salvation and cooperating at the same time with the demons of destruction, whether by neglecting to do good or by actively doing evil. Only those who help the Jews may sing the Gregorian chant, Dietrich Bonhoeffer rightly said, in the context of Nazi Germany. . . . Without action in the world, the adoration of God is empty and hypocritical, and degenerates into irresponsible godless quietism.[5]

Our worship includes what we do as Christians when we scatter for witness[6] and gather for worship.[7] D. A. Carson has said, "We cannot imagine that the church gathers for worship on Sunday morning if by this we mean that we then engage in something that we have not been engaging in the rest of the week. New covenant worship terminology prescribes *constant* 'worship.'"[6] Likewise, Abraham Kuyper, in his legendary *Stone Lectures on Calvinism*, said that worship is "to praise God in the church and serve Him in the world."[7] Similarly, O. Noordman once said, "The real liturgy occurs on the street!"[8]

ASSEMBLY IN THREE PARTS

The New Testament is clear that God's people are to gather regularly for corporate worship. This is apparent by the frequent use of the Greek word *ekklesia*, which simply means a gathered assembly of God's

---

[6] 1 Cor. 10:31.
[7] Heb. 10:24–25.

people. Likewise, Hebrews 10:24–25 commands, "Let us consider how to stir up one another to love and good works, not neglecting to meet together, as is the habit of some, but encouraging one another." When God's people gather, it is incumbent upon the church leaders to do three things.

1) Forbid What God Forbids

First, church leaders must ensure that what God forbids is not done. This is incredibly important, because throughout the Old and New Testaments people who profess to worship the God of the Bible do so in ways that he forbids.

An Old Testament example is found in Deuteronomy 12:4, where God points to how other religions worship their demon-gods and commands, "You shall not worship the LORD your God in that way." Another Old Testament example is found in the second commandment,[8] which forbids idolatry—the worship of any created thing or seeking to reduce God to something that is made. The Puritans were particularly serious about this commandment, which explains why they rightly forbade the portrayal of God the Father in artwork in the form of anyone or anything created, such as an old man with a beard. From more recent history, much of the controversy surrounding the book *The Shack* involved a portrayal of God the Father as a woman, which is a violation of the second commandment.

A timely New Testament example is found in 1 Corinthians 10:14–22, where God, through Paul, forbids Christians from worshiping with members of other religions because doing so is to entertain demons. In our day this means that while Christians should have evangelistic friendships with members of other religions, we must never participate in the practices of other religions with its members because they worship different and false gods.

2) Employ Biblical Methods

Second, when God's people gather for worship, church leaders must ensure that the methods they employ align with the biblical principles for worship. Worship is to be:

---

[8]Ex. 20:4–6.

- God centered[9]
- intelligible[10]
- seeker sensible[11]
- unselfish[12]
- orderly[13]
- missional[14]

By *God centered*, I mean that worship is for God. While this may seem obvious, sadly it is not obvious to all people. Corporate worship is not about hearing a message that tells us what we can do to improve ourselves, singing songs about what we are going to do for God, and judging the quality of the meeting by how it feels to us. Rather, God-centered worship is about hearing a message that reveals, from the Bible, who God is and what he has done and is doing for and with us; singing songs about who God is and what he does; and judging the quality of worship based upon whether it accords with the Scriptures.

By *intelligible*, I mean that the words spoken are in the language of the hearers (unlike, for example, the old Catholic Latin Mass or the Protestant preacher who uses so many Greek words that the average person is altogether lost), and any technical words used are explained so that everyone knows what they mean. This includes words such as *propitiation* or even, at times, *God*. Defining theological terms is important because, in addition to being God-centered, worship is meant to build up God's people. The Bible itself is an example of this; the New Testament was not originally written in the academic version of ancient Greek but in the normal street-level vernacular of the average person so that it could be understood by as many as possible. Furthermore, this principle was a hallmark of the Protestant Reformation and a key distinctive of worship meetings influenced by men such as John Calvin, who argued strenuously that church meetings should be intelligible and accessible as an act of love.

By *seeker sensible*, I do not mean that the hard edges of doctrine are

---

[9]Matt. 4:8–10.
[10]1 Cor. 14:1–12.
[11]1 Cor. 14:20–25.
[12]1 Cor. 14:26.
[13]1 Cor. 14:40.
[14]1 Cor. 9:19–23.

sanded off and then given a few coats of varnish so that more consumers will buy Christianity. Instead, I mean we acknowledge that non-Christians do attend church services (which is a good thing), and that we need to help them understand who Jesus is and what he has done so that they can become Christians. I'm not saying that the entire church service should be ordered as an evangelistic rally week after week, but it should maintain a continual evangelistic undercurrent by offering hospitality to lost people.

By *unselfish*, I mean that if people want to express their personal response to God in a way that draws undue attention to themselves and distracts others from responding to God, then they should do that kind of thing at home, in private, because the meeting is for corporate, not just individual, response to God.

I was at a church where some guy brought huge flags and pranced around up front without anyone's permission throughout the entire worship service, making a fairy spectacle of himself. In worship, God gives to his people truth, love, hope, and the like, and those who distract others from receiving these things are being incredibly selfish and need to be rebuked so that they may mature and learn to consider others more highly than themselves, as Scripture says.

By *orderly*, I mean that the meeting flows in such a way that God's people are able to hear God's Word and respond without distraction. Distractions (apart from those of the selfish people we just considered) include constant feedback on the audio speakers; musicians who cannot keep time; singers who cannot keep pitch; long, awkward pauses because no one knows what is happening next; and people speaking in tongues or prophesying out of turn in a way that the Bible forbids.

By *missional*, I mean that the meeting fits the culture in which it takes place. This includes seating, the start and stop times for meetings, what kind of music is sung, and what technology is used. These things should reflect the culture in which God's people are gathering so that there is no cultural imperialism imposed on one culture from another. This does not mean that features from other cultures or eras cannot be used in the service, such as singing ancient hymns, but it does mean such things are used because they help God's people to worship, not just because they were mandated from headquarters.

3) Do What Scripture Commands

Third, when God's people gather, the church leaders are also required to ensure that what the Bible commands for worship is actually done. There are certain elements that Scripture prescribes for gathered corporate worship services. Many theologians refer to these as *the elements of corporate worship*, and they include the following:

- preaching[15]
- the sacraments of baptism and the Lord's Table[16]
- prayer[17]
- reading Scripture[18]
- financial giving[19]
- singing and music[20]

It is significant to stress that essentially all Bible-believing Christians agree on these basic biblical concepts. The point of debate arises over the fact that there is no clear prescription of an entire worship service in Scripture. According to Carson, "We have no detailed *first-century* evidence of an entire Christian service."[9] Furthermore, "the New Testament documents do not themselves provide a 'model service.'"[10] John Frame has also said that "we know very little of the church's liturgy in the first century."[11]

The question that subsequently arises is whether elements not mentioned in the Bible can be included in corporate worship. Such elements include creeds, special music, music style, service order, length, time, seating, technology, instruments, announcements, architecture, and clothing. The normative principle seeks to answer this question differently from the regulative principle.

THE NORMATIVE PRINCIPLE

The normative principle teaches that corporate church worship services must include all the elements that Scripture commands and may include others so long as Scripture does not prohibit them. To put it simply, this

---

[15]2 Tim. 4:2.
[16]Matt. 28:19; 1 Cor. 11:17–34.
[17]1 Tim. 2:1.
[18]1 Tim. 4:13.
[19]2 Corinthians 8–9.
[20]Col. 3:16.

is the green-light view of worship that says everything is permissible unless Scripture forbids it, and the forbidden things we must not do because God, in his Word, has given us a red light. Notable advocates of this position historically include Martin Luther, Archbishop Thomas Cranmer and the Book of Common Prayer, Anglican Richard Hooker, Catholics, Lutherans, Anglicans, and Methodists.

Strengths

The strengths of the normative principle are twofold. First, it sees the Bible as filled with principles for worship and gives freedom to church leaders to determine which methods in their culture are most faithful to the biblical principles. It allows cultural contextualization, so that as billions of people worship Jesus across millennia, scattered among the languages and nations of the earth, the Holy Spirit can lead church leaders to make informed decisions about how to worship God faithfully. Second, it treats gathered and scattered worship by the same principle.

Every day, Christians operate according to the normative principle; they go about their life freely, doing whatever they believe is right and good while seeking to avoid doing what God forbids in Scripture. This is because the Bible is not a daily checklist telling us what to do every minute of every day but rather a means by which we learn about staying connected to God and living in light of that relationship.

Weaknesses

The weaknesses of the normative principle are threefold. First, it can allow too much freedom and result in pagan syncretism. We see this in churches where icons are wrongly used to mediate God's presence or where the culture is elevated over Scripture, so that such things as preaching are done away with because our chat-room blogging culture does not like to have anyone teaching authoritatively. Second, it can make our enjoyment rather than God's approval the measure of "good worship" so that we, instead of God, subtly become the object of worship. This happens, for example, when people leave church saying that the worship was good because it made them feel a particular way, regardless of the theological content of the songs. Third, it can allow elements that are not mentioned in Scripture to be emphasized over those that are. We find this in churches that do not have much preaching or do not often partake of Communion but do make sure to include drama every week.

THE REGULATIVE PRINCIPLE

The regulative principle teaches that corporate church worship services must include all the elements that Scripture commands or that are a good and necessary implication of a biblical text, but nothing more. To put it simply, this is the red-light view of worship, which holds that we are essentially not permitted to do anything unless the Bible gives us a directly applicable green light. Notable advocates of this position historically include John Calvin, Puritans, the Westminster Confession, Presbyterians, and miscellaneous Reformed groups. Perhaps the most well-known statement of the regulative principle is found in the Westminster Confession of Faith 21.1, which says, "The acceptable way of worshiping the true God is instituted by himself, and so limited by his own revealed will, that he may not be worshiped according to the imaginations and devices of men, or the suggestions of Satan, under any visible representation, or any other way not prescribed in the Holy Scripture."

Strengths

The strengths of the regulative principle are threefold. First, it seeks to ensure that "good" worship is defined by God in his Word and not by the worshipers. In this way, the regulative principle earnestly seeks to retain God as the center of worship. Second, it seeks to retain the rightful place of Scripture as the highest authority governing the beliefs and actions of God's people. In this way, it helps to guard the church against pragmatism with biblicism. Third, it defends against syncretism by seeking to ensure that unbiblical practices taken from the culture and other religions and spiritualities that distract from or distort the worship of God are not included in corporate worship meetings.

In my city this is a very real issue, as we actually have interfaith worship services, and one woman who is both an Episcopalian priest and a Muslim is lauded for seeking to make Christianity and Islam into one religion. We also have a number of churches that use a labyrinth for prayer, even though it is an ancient pagan worship practice in which participants walk inward on themselves as the center of their lives rather than outward in repentance toward God.

Weaknesses

The weaknesses of the regulative principle are threefold. First, it bifurcates gathered and scattered worship by saying that we live our lives by the normative principle except for those times when we meet in a building together, where we are governed by the regulative principle. This error can cause people to view church meetings as more sacred than their own lives, which is where most of their worship to God is done.

Second, the principle is insufficient to deal with all aspects of corporate worship because the Bible does not say anything about how, for instance, to give announcements in church meetings. So, in the name of being biblical, unbiblical rules are brought into the church to help the Bible, as if it needs any help. Churches holding to the regulative principle will have such things as announcements and the reading of church creeds, despite the fact that they are not mentioned in Scripture. To defend themselves against this contradiction, they end up making silly arguments. They say such things are "implied" in Scripture, which is another way of saying, "It's not there, but we'd like it to be, so we'll pencil it in." In the end, the regulative principle is simply extrabiblical, so it leads to other extrabiblical inferences, assertions, and insertions.

Third, almost every worship meeting in which I have participated that is governed by the regulative principle has been marked by hypocrisy. That may sound harsh; what I mean is that while they claim to be biblical, they tend not to do all that Scripture commands, such as raise hands in song,[21] clap,[22] raise hands in prayer,[23] or shout "amen."[24] They claim that they don't do those things because they are not charismatic, but they fail to recognize that when it comes to such things, the charismatics are simply being biblical.

Analysis

At its core, the regulative principle holds to the belief that God's people should worship him only according to the precepts of Scripture. On this

---

[21] Pss. 63:4; 134:2.
[22] Pss. 47:1; 97:8.
[23] 1 Tim. 2:8.
[24] 1 Cor. 14:16.

point, Mars Hill Church, where I serve, agrees. However, we do reject the stricter and more extreme forms of the regulative principle. We are not alone. In many ways this issue is one of a handful of "state borders" between various kinds of old Reformed Christians and new missional Reformed Christians.

The resurgence of missional Reformed theology in our day, with mainly young leaders, is accompanied by a love for missiology, contextualization, creativity, innovation, technology, church planting, and evangelism—particularly in major cities where culture is created. Those of us in this "state" find ourselves getting shot at a lot by those holding a more fundamental, culturally separatistic, and oftentimes legalistic view of Reformed theology.

While acknowledging that churches practicing this principle are filled with many brothers and sisters in Christ, whom we love, Mars Hill Church does not endorse this restrictive theology, because of our biblical convictions. In philosophy there is an argumentative strategy called, in Latin, a *reductio ad absurdum*. This tactic assumes that the opponent's position is true and then reasons it out to its logical conclusion to demonstrate that it falls apart and is, therefore, fallacious. In this same spirit, I will explain the flaws in a strict regulative principle of worship.

First, since announcements, sound equipment, overheads, and PowerPoint projectors are never mentioned in Scripture, using them in a worship service contradicts the regulative principle. Second, those who say that we should sing only the Psalms would have to say that the Bible tells us to sin when it commands us to sing new songs.[25] Third, if we are allowed to sing only Psalms, then it follows that while it is not a sin to speak other parts of the Bible, it is a sin to sing them.

Fourth, churches that forbid the use of instruments in corporate worship must agree that the Bible sins when it mentions them[26] and that God will sin when he hands them out in heaven.[27] Fifth, if we can sing only the exact words that God inspired to be written in the Bible but no new songs, then, since the Psalms were written in Hebrew, they also should be sung in that language and accompanied by Hebrew musical forms. Sixth, to be consistent with the principle that we sing

---

[25]E.g., Pss. 33:3; 40:3; 144:9; 149:1; Isa. 42:10; Rev. 5:9; 14:3.
[26]E.g., Psalm 150.
[27]Rev. 15:2.

only songs from the Bible, we should also only teach lessons, preach sermons, and pray prayers that are found specifically in the Bible. Seventh, to be consistent we should apply the regulative principle to the general worship of God's people in their daily lives and not just to the narrow worship of a church service. We should likewise forbid them from doing anything unless the Scriptures command it, such as driving cars, using computers, talking on the phone, or playing sports. Eighth, since there are songs in the Bible that were in use before the Psalms,[28] the people who sang those songs were in sin because they were not singing only the Psalms. Ninth, since Jesus' name is never mentioned in the Psalms, it is a sin to sing the name of Jesus in his church.

While I personally love much of the writings of the Puritans, I believe it is obvious that the regulative principle (which they claimed was biblical) if applied too legalistically creates a home more akin to Egypt, where the freedom to worship was denied God's people, than to the desert, where they were liberated to dance and sing new songs to the Lord. Sadly, in an effort to be biblical, Christians holding this position have gravely taken to worshiping God by rules invented by men, which is condemned by God as wickedness.[29] Their concern for worshiping in truth is admirable, but what they have neglected is the spirit of worship and the Holy Spirit, who is better able to guide and lead God's people into worship than are manmade rules. This explains why Jesus commanded that we worship in both spirit and truth.[30]

Sadly, what can happen between loud advocates of the extreme versions of both the normative and regulative principles is that the moderates on both sides, who lean toward the sane center, are not well heard, as they should be. When they are, there is much more agreement than disagreement. On this point Carson has said, "Theologically rich and serious services from both camps often have more common *content* than either side usually acknowledges."[12]

So, in answer to the original questions on which this chapter is based—"In other words, do you believe in the regulative principle? If so, to what degree?"—my answer is yes and no. On one hand, I agree with Richard Pratt who says, "The regulative principle is quite biblical, if it is properly understood and applied. Unfortunately, today it is very

---

[28]Exodus 15; Num. 21:17; Deuteronomy 32; Judges 5.
[29]Isa. 29:13; Matt. 15:7–9.
[30]John 4:24.

often misunderstood and misapplied."[13] I also agree with John Frame who says, "The Westminster Confession is entirely right in its regulative principle—that true worship is limited to what God commands. But the methods used by the Puritans to discover and apply those commands need a theological overhaul. Much of what they said cannot be justified by Scripture."[14]

On the other hand, I believe that since the regulative principle has been so widely abused, misused, and misrepresented, it is not a very helpful term any longer. Still, the principle behind the principle is, in fact, both helpful and important. In theory, the elders of Mars Hill Church hold to the normative principle. However, in practice we generally go no further than a loose application of the regulative principle. Each week our corporate meetings include a congregational reading of Scripture, corporate singing, an hour-long sermon, an opportunity to give tithes and offerings, and observance of the Lord's Table. In many ways we simply follow the counsel of Pratt:

> To apply the regulative principle appropriately today, we cannot simply repeat the way it was applied in earlier centuries. Rather, we must identify the idols and attacks on liberty of conscience that are present among our churches today. This will differ from church to church and from time to time. One of the principles which the Reformation embraced was *ecclesia semper reformanda est*—the church is always reforming. This means that we cannot represent the Reformed tradition without re-presenting it. Simply to repeat it is not to represent it at all.[15]

THE MISSIONAL WORSHIP PRINCIPLE

As I prepared for this chapter, I created something that I call the *missional worship principle*, in which the mission is to faithfully worship God so as to encourage as many people as possible to faithfully worship God:

> All of Christian life is ceaseless worship of God the Father through the mediatorship of God the Son by the indwelling power of God the Spirit, doing what God commands in Scripture, not doing what God forbids in Scripture, in culturally contextualized ways for the furtherance of the gospel when both gathered for adoration and scattered for action in joyous response to God's glorious grace.

In principle, everything we do and do not do when we gather for worship at Mars Hill is rooted in deep biblical convictions. We do everything God commands. We do not do anything God forbids. Everything else we carefully and prayerfully and biblically consider.

Because the original question that resulted in this chapter was directed to me personally, I will try to explain myself. I am the pastor of a church filled with people I love in a city with more people I love who do not yet love Jesus. I want to do all we can within the bounds of Scripture to encourage and invite as many people as possible to be genuine worshipers of the God of the Bible.

Subsequently, in practice we are very creative. At the time I am writing this we have twenty services scattered across seven campuses each Sunday. I preach live at four services, and the rest are simulcast via television satellite technology. We have twenty worship bands of various styles that redo old hymns and write a lot of their own songs based on Scripture. We leave time at the end of each sermon so that I can answer questions received via text-message from the cell phones of people sitting in our meetings. We put the sermons on the Internet along with live recordings of our music and see upwards of ten million downloads a year.

Last week alone we saw our church grow by two thousand people, and many of those people are not yet Christians. They came to hear a more-than-one-hour sermon on how sex is now a god in our culture and how we offer our bodies in worship to that false god rather than the true God of the Bible. Many walked out because they wanted to keep fornicating, practicing homosexuality, committing adultery, and looking at pornography rather than to worship the God of the Bible. For us, every issue is a worship issue, and we are careful to paint all of life as an act of worship, both when we gather and when we scatter as God's people. Simply, we know that people become like whatever or whomever they worship. We want our people to worship God and in so doing to be continually conformed to the image of Christ in absolutely every area of their lives so that even when they wash their dishes, they do so to God's glory.

We want to be faithful to the Scriptures. We want to be fruitful in the culture. We see no reason to choose one or the other. We see no excuse for violating the Bible. And we see no excuse for not earnestly laboring so that as many people as possible participate in the worship of God the Father through the mediatorship of God the Son by the power of God the Spirit. Furthermore, we believe that every church worship meeting is culturally contextualized to some culture and some year. The only difference is which culture and which year.

Some churches are on the cutting edge of 1796, with hymns, pews, and a male preacher in a dress; they argue that being on the cutting edge of today is less holy. While neither style is sinful, the truth is that both are contextualized. We too contextualize our church meetings. In our case, we observe the Lord's Table and do most of our singing after the sermon to ensure that our repentance and singing is informed and inspired by Scripture in response to God's revelation and initiation, as the gospel teaches.

Occasionally, a tide of extreme Reformed malcontents rolls into our church, like litter on a beach. They usually want to argue about our worship style along with issues such as *padeocommunion* (communion for babies). Most of the time they are young guys with Internet connections and no wives, children, ministries, or careers to give them something better to do with their time than to pick the wrong hill to die on. They tend to argue a lot for being biblical while ignoring the Bible verses that say things about love and respecting your leaders or about being humble. Every time, it grieves me that they have such a little view of worship and such a big view of themselves.

It is my hope and prayer that these kinds of issues do not become battle lines over which the rising generation of missional Reformed Christian leaders declares war so that mission for the future is shot in the name of tradition from the past.

In closing, when something commanded by God is not done, that is sin. When something forbidden by God is done, that is sin. When Scripture is silent, it is not God's way of giving us a moment to speak for him but to be silent as an act of worship. To that end, this chapter will now close, remaining noticeably brief. That is because, while more could be said, I am unconvinced that more should be said.

BIBLE VERSES ON PREDESTINATION

The primary text on predestination is Romans 9–11. Less lengthy biblical treatises on the subject include the following passages.

In this city there were gathered together against your holy servant Jesus, whom you anointed, both Herod and Pontius Pilate, along with the Gentiles and the peoples of Israel, to do whatever your hand and your plan had predestined to take place. (Acts 4:27–28)

The God of this people Israel chose our fathers and made the people great during their stay in the land of Egypt, and with uplifted arm he led them out of it. (Acts 13:17)

And when the Gentiles heard this, they began rejoicing and glorifying the word of the Lord, and as many as were appointed to eternal life believed. (Acts 13:48)

For the wages of sin is death, but the free gift of God is eternal life in Christ Jesus our Lord. (Rom. 6:23)

For those whom he foreknew he also predestined to be conformed to the image of his Son, in order that he might be the firstborn among many brothers. And those whom he predestined he also called, and those whom he called he also justified, and those whom he justified he also glorified. (Rom. 8:29–30)

Who shall bring any charge against God's elect? It is God who justifies. (Rom. 8:33)

God chose what is foolish in the world to shame the wise; God chose what is weak in the world to shame the strong; God chose what is low and despised in the world, even things that are not, to bring to nothing things that are. (1 Cor. 1:27–28)

Blessed be the God and Father of our Lord Jesus Christ, who has blessed us in Christ with every spiritual blessing in the heavenly places, even as he chose us in him before the foundation of the world, that we should be holy and blameless before him. In love he predestined us for adoption as sons through Jesus Christ, according to the purpose of his will, to the praise of his glorious grace, with which he has blessed us in the Beloved. In him we have redemption through his blood, the forgiveness of our trespasses, according to the riches of his grace, which he lavished upon us, in all wisdom and insight making known to us the mystery of his will, according to his purpose, which he set forth in Christ as a plan for the fullness of time, to unite all things in him, things in heaven and things on earth. In him we have obtained an inheritance, having been predestined according to the purpose of him who works all things according to the counsel of his will, so that we who were the first to hope in Christ might be to the praise of his glory. (Eph. 1:3–12)

For it has been granted to you that for the sake of Christ you should not only believe in him but also suffer for his sake. (Phil. 1:29)

Put on then, as God's chosen ones, holy and beloved, compassionate hearts, kindness, humility, meekness, and patience. (Col. 3:12)

For we know, brothers loved by God, that he has chosen you, because our gospel came to you not only in word, but also in power and in the Holy Spirit and with full conviction. (1 Thess. 1:4–5)

But we ought always to give thanks to God for you, brothers beloved by the Lord, because God chose you as the firstfruits to be saved, through sanctification by the Spirit and belief in the truth. (2 Thess. 2:13)

Therefore I endure everything for the sake of the elect, that they also may obtain the salvation that is in Christ Jesus with eternal glory. (2 Tim. 2:10)

Paul, a servant of God and an apostle of Jesus Christ, for the sake of the faith of God's elect and their knowledge of the truth, which accords with godliness ... (Titus 1:1)

Peter, an apostle of Jesus Christ, To those who are elect exiles of the dispersion ... (1 Pet. 1:1)

As you come to him, a living stone rejected by men but in the sight of God chosen and precious . . . (1 Pet. 2:4)

But you are a chosen race, a royal priesthood, a holy nation, a people for his own possession, that you may proclaim the excellencies of him who called you out of darkness into his marvelous light. (1 Pet. 2:9)

Therefore, brothers, be all the more diligent to make your calling and election sure, for if you practice these qualities you will never fall. (2 Pet. 1:10)

JESUS' TEACHING ON PREDESTINATION

In agreement with the rest of Scripture, Jesus himself spoke on the topic with great regularity and clarity, as the following verses indicate.

For many are called, but few are chosen. (Matt. 22:14)

I am not speaking of all of you; I know whom I have chosen. But the Scripture will be fulfilled, "He who ate my bread has lifted his heel against me." (John 13:18)

For false christs and false prophets will arise and perform great signs and wonders, so as to lead astray, if possible, even the elect. (Matt. 24:24)

And he will send out his angels with a loud trumpet call, and they will gather his elect from the four winds, from one end of heaven to the other. (Matt. 24:31)

And will not God give justice to his elect, who cry to him day and night? Will he delay long over them? (Luke 18:7)

For as the Father raises the dead and gives them life, so also the Son gives life to whom he will. (John 5:21)

All that the Father gives me will come to me, and whoever comes to me I will never cast out. For I have come down from heaven, not to do my own will but the will of him who sent me. And this is the will of him who sent me, that I should lose nothing of all that he has given me, but raise it up on the last day. (John 6:37–39)

You did not choose me, but I chose you and appointed you that you should go and bear fruit and that your fruit should abide, so that whatever you ask the Father in my name, he may give it to you. (John 15:16)

If you were of the world, the world would love you as its own; but because you are not of the world, but I chose you out of the world, therefore the world hates you. (John 15:19)

NOTES

INTRODUCTION

1. The entire series is available for free in audio and video format at http://www.marshill-church.org/media/religionsaves.

QUESTION 9: BIRTH CONTROL

1. Ellen Liang, "Why Dogs Outnumber Children in Seattle," King5.com, April 20, 2005, http://www.king5.com/sharedcontent/northwest/specialreport/stories/NW_042005WABc hildrenEL.1f9295c3e.html.

2. Vanessa Ho, "Just 33% in State Attend Church, Yet Some Faiths Are Thriving," *Seattle Post-Intelligencer*, September 19, 2002, seattlepi.nwsource.com/local/87669_religion19.shtml? searchpagefrom=1&searchdiff=1014; Cathy Lynn Gossman, "Charting the Unchurched in America," *USA Today*, March 7, 2002, www.usatoday.com/life/ 2002/2002-03-07-no-religion. htm; Theron Zahn, "Washington State May Be Losing Its Faith," *KOMO News*, March 17, 2002, www.komotv.com/news/story_m.asp?ID=17365; Sara Clemence, "Most Overpriced Places in the U. S. 2005," *Forbes*, July 15, 2005, http://www.forbes.com/realestate/2005/07/14/ overpriced-cities-lifestyle-cx_sc_ 0715home_ls.html.

3. The following historical contraceptive methods are listed in William R. Cutrer and Sandra L. Glahn, *The Contraception Guidebook: Options, Risks, and Answers for Christian Couples* (Grand Rapids, MI: Zondervan, 2005), 26.

4. "Birth Control," Catholic Answers (San Diego: Catholic Answers, 2001), http://www.catholic.com/library/ Birth_Control.asp.

5. John Jefferson Davis, *Evangelical Ethics: Issues Facing the Church Today*, 3rd ed. (Phillipsburg, NJ: P&R, 2004), 28.

6. Ibid.

7. Ibid., 29.

8. Ibid.

9. Ibid., 30.

10. Ibid.

11. Ibid.

12. Cutrer and Glahn, *The Contraception Guidebook*, 27.

13. Most forms of birth control discussed in levels 2 through 5 are summarized from the definitions found at http://www.christiancontraception.com/contraceptives.php.

14. E.g., Rick and Jan Hess, *A Full Quiver: Family Planning and the Lordship of Christ* (Brentwood, TN: Wolgemuth & Hyatt, 1990); Charles D. Provan, *The Bible and Birth Control* (Monongahela, PA: Zimmer Printing, 1989).

15. Nancy Campbell, *Be Fruitful and Multiply* (San Antonio, TX: Vision Forum Ministries, 2003), 154.

16. Nancy Leigh DeMoss, *Lies Women Believe and the Truth That Sets Them Free* (Chicago: Moody, 2001), 169–70.

17. Mary Pride, *The Way Home: Beyond Feminism, Back to Reality* (Wheaton, IL: Crossway, 1985), 77, 75.

18. E.g., see "Age and Female Fertility," American Fertility Association, http://www.theafa. org/library/article/age_and_female_fertility/.

19. Candice Z. Watters, "The Cost of Postponing Childbirth," http://www.troubledwith. com/Transitions/A000000611.cfm?topic=transitions%253A%20having%20a%20baby.

20. American Society for Reproductive Medicine, "'Is In Vitro Fertilization Expensive?' Frequently Asked Questions About Infertility" (2008), http://www.asrm.org/Patients/faqs. html.

21. Watters, "The Cost of Postponing Childbirth."

22. Ibid.

23. To learn more about the history of Planned Parenthood, read George Grant, *Grand Illusions: The Legacy of Planned Parenthood* (Nashville, TN: Cumberland, 2000).

24. Ernst Rudin, "Eugenic Sterilization: An Urgent Need," *The Birth Control Review* (April 1933): 102.

25. Leon Whitney, "Selective Sterilization," *The Birth Control Review* (April 1933): 85.

26. H. Wayne House, "Should Christians Use Birth Control?" Christian Research Institute, http://www.equip.org/site/c.muI1LaMNJrE/b.2717865/k.B30F/DE194.htm.

27. David Goldstein, *Suicide Bent: Sangerizing America* (St. Paul: Radio Replies Press, 1945), 103.

28. Quoted in Campbell, *Be Fruitful and Multiply*, 156.

29. H. Wayne House, "Should Christians Use Birth Control?" Also see John T. Noonan Jr., *Contraception* (Cambridge, MA: Harvard University Press, 1966), 10–11.

30. "Does the Bible Permit Birth Control?" Desiring God Resource Library, January 23, 2006, http://www.desiringgod.org/ResourceLibrary/Articles/ByDate/2006/1440_Does_the_Bible_permit_birth_control/.

31. Pulling out is not an effective form of birth control for at least two reasons. (1) The timing is difficult since the average male ejaculation occurs at 28 miles per hour (Cutrer and Glahn, *The Contraception Guidebook*, 73). (2) There are roughly 250 to 500 million sperm in one male ejaculation, many are present in the seepage before the ejaculation, and it only takes one good swimmer to make a baby (Douglas E. Rosenau, *A Celebration of Sex: A Guide to Enjoying God's Gift of Married Sexual Pleasure* [Nashville, TN: Thomas Nelson, 1994], 62).

32. Augustine, *Adulterous Marriages*, 2.12.

33. Davis, *Evangelical Ethics*, 45.

34. *The Good of Marriage* 16.18, in Davis, *Evangelical Ethics*, 45.

35. *Against Faustus* 15.7, in Davis, *Evangelical Ethics*, 45.

36. Simon P. Wood, trans., "The Fathers of the Church," *Clement of Alexandria* (New York: Fathers of the Church, 1954), *xxxiii*, 175.

37. C. W. Scudder, ed., *Crises in Morality* (Nashville: Broadman, 1964), 47–48.

38. Pride, *The Way Home*, 27.

39. H. Wayne House, "Should Christians Use Birth Control?"

40. John T. Noonan Jr., *Contraception*, 46.

41. H. Wayne House, "Should Christians Use Birth Control?"; *Ocellus Lucanus*, text and commentary by Richard Harder (Berlin, 1926).

42. W. A. Strange, *Children in the Early Church: Children in the Ancient World, the New Testament and the Early Church* (Carlisle, UK: Paternoster, 1996), 1–37.

43. Ibid.

44. Timothy Roche, "The Yates Odyssey," *Time*, January 20, 2002, http://www.time.com/time/ printout/0,8816,195325,00.html.

45. Ibid.

46. Ibid.

47. http://www.yateskids.org/.

48. Cutrer and Glahn, *The Contraception Guidebook*, 31–32.

49. Ibid., 72.

50. Ibid., 78–79.

51. Ibid.

52. Ibid., 75.

53. Ibid.

54. Ibid.

55. Ibid., 26–27.

56. Ibid., 27.

57. Ibid., 74.

58. Ibid., 75.

59. Ibid., 77.

60. Davis, *Evangelical Ethics*, 35.

61. Cutrer and Glahn, *The Contraception Guidebook*, 82–83.

62. Davis, *Evangelical Ethics*, 35.

63. Ibid., 36.

64. Ibid., 37.

65. Ibid., 30.

66. Ibid.

67. "Your Sexual Health: Methods of Contraception," http://www.healthpromotion.ie/sexual_health/contraception/ (accessed August 28, 2008). See also Planned Parenthood, "Birth Control Pill—How Effective Are Birth Control Pills?" February 9, 2008, http://www.plannedparenthood.org/health-topics/birth-control/birth-control-pill-4228.htm.

68. L. S. Potter, "How Effective Are Contraceptives? The Determination and Measurement of Pregnancy Rates," *Obstetrics and Gynecology* 88 (September 1996): 135–235, in "Oral Contraceptives—An Update" *Population Reports* (Spring 2000), http://findarticles.com/p/articles/mi_mo856/is_1_28/ai_62723391/print?tag=artBody;col1.

69. One of his great works on the subject is his book *Does the Birth Control Pill Cause Abortions?* You can download the entire book or read condensations of the book for free here: http://www.epm.org/books/does_the_birth_control_ pill_cause_abortionsDetail.php. In addition, articles on abortion, birth control, and related issues can be found here: http://www.epm.org/resources-prolife_abortion.html.

70. H. I. Abdalla, A. A. Johnson, et al., "Endometrial Thickness: A Predictor of Implantation in Ovum Recipients?" *Human Reproduction* 9 (1994): 363–65.

71. J. M. Bartoli, G. Moulin, et al., "The Normal Uterus on Magnetic Resonance Imaging and Variations Associated with the Hormonal State," *Surgical and Radiologic Anatomy* 13 (1991): 213–20; B. E. Demas, H. Hricak, et al., "Uterine MR Imaging: Effects of Hormonal Stimulation," *Radiology* 159 (1986): 123–6; S. McCarthy, C. Tauber, et al., "Female Pelvic Anatomy: MR Assessment of Variations during the Menstrual Cycle and with Use of Oral Contraceptives," *Radiology* 160 (1986): 119–23; H. K. Brown, B. S. Stoll, et al., "Uterine Junctional Zone: Correlation between Histologic Findings and MR Imaging," *Radiology* 179 (1991): 409–13.

72. Focus on the Family, "Position Statement: Birth Control Pills and Other Hormonal Contraception," December 30, 2005, http://www.family.org/sharedassets/correspondence/pdfs/miscellaneous/Position_Statement-Birth_Control_Pills_and_Other_Hormonal_Contraception.pdf.

73. "Possible Post-Fertilization Effects of Hormonal Birth Control," Hormonal Birth Control, http://www.cmda.org/AM/Template.cfm?Section=Search&template=/CM/HTMLDisplay.cfm&ContentID=3045.

74. Randy Alcorn, *Prolife Answers to ProChoice Arguments* (Multnomah: Sisters, OR: 1994), 118.

75. Thomas W. Hilgers, "The Intrauterine Device: Contraceptive or Abortifacient?" *Minnesota Medicine* (June 1974): 493–501.

76. Davis, *Evangelical Ethics*, 32.

77. Focus on the Family, "Position Statement: Birth Control Pills and Other Hormonal Contraception."

78. "Who Has Abortions?" Heartlink.org, 2005, http://www.heartlink.org/directors/abortion/a000000073.cfm.

79. *Didache* 2.2.

80. Epistle of Barnabas, 19:5.

81. Charles H. H. Scobie, *Ways of Our God: An Approach to Biblical Theology* (Grand Rapids, MI: Eerdmans, 2003), 834.

82. A helpful source of external counsel on various biomedical ethics issues has been the Northwest Center for Bioethics in Portland, OR, http://www.ncbioethics.org.

QUESTION 8: HUMOR

1. Leland Ryken, James C. Wilhoit, et al., eds., *Dictionary of Biblical Imagery* (Downers Grove, IL: InterVarsity, 1998), s.v. "Humor," 407.

2. Ibid., s.v. "Comedy as Plot Motif," 160–61.

3. Ibid., s.v. "Satire," 762.

4. Herbert Lockyer, *All the Men of the Bible* (Grand Rapids, MI: Zondervan, 1958).

5. Ryken, et al., *Dictionary of Biblical Imagery*, s.v. "Humor," 408.

6. Wallace has extensive experience and expertise on this subject. He has taught Greek and New Testament courses at the graduate-school level since 1979. He has a PhD from Dallas Theological Seminary and is currently professor of New Testament Studies at his alma mater. His *Greek Grammar Beyond the Basics: An Exegetical Syntax of the New Testament* has become a standard textbook in colleges and seminaries. He is the senior New Testament editor of the NET Bible. Wallace is also the executive director for the Center for the Study of New Testament Manuscripts.

7. Daniel B. Wallace, "A Brief Word Study on Skuvbalon," Bible.org, http://www.bible.org/page.php?page_id=5318.

8. Ibid.

9. Douglas Wilson, *A Serrated Edge: A Brief Defense of Biblical Satire and Trinitarian Skylarking* (Moscow, ID: Canon Press, 2003), 62.

10. Ibid., 13

11. G. K. Chesterton, *Orthodoxy: The Romance of Faith* (New York: Doubleday, 1990), 160.

12. Stephen Prothero, *American Jesus: How the Son of God Became a National Icon* (New York: Farrar, Straus & Giroux, 2003), 11.

13. Philip Yancey, *The Jesus I Never Knew* (Grand Rapids, MI: Zondervan, 1995), 20.

14. Elton Trueblood, *The Humor of Christ* (New York: Harper & Row, 1964), 10.

15. Ibid., 15.

16. Ryken, et al., *Dictionary of Biblical Imagery*, s.v. "Humor—Jesus as Humorist," 410.

17. Trueblood, *The Humor of Christ*, 127.

18. Ryken, et al., *Dictionary of Biblical Imagery*, s.v. "Humor—Jesus as Humorist," 410.

19. John M. Frame, *Worship in Spirit and Truth: A Refreshing Study of the Principles and Practice of Biblical Worship* (Phillipsburg, NJ: P&R, 1996), 83.

20. Charles Haddon Spurgeon, "The Uses of Anecdotes and Illustrations," in *Lectures to My Students* (Grand Rapids, MI: Zondervan, 1954), 389.

21. Trueblood, *The Humor of Christ*, 15.

22. Mark Driscoll and Gerry Breshears, *Death by Love: Letters from the Cross* (Wheaton, IL: Crossway, 2008).

23. Charles Haddon Spurgeon, *Eccentric Preachers* (London: Passmore & Alabaster, 1879), iv–v, 13–14, 37, 104–5.

QUESTION 7: PREDESTINATION

1. Millard J. Erickson, *Christian Theology* (Grand Rapids, MI: Baker, 1985), 908.

2. Emanuel Stickelberger, *Calvin*, trans. David Georg Gelzer (London: James Clarke, 1959), 148.

3. See John Wesley, "On Working Out Our Own Salvation," in *The Works of John Wesley*, 3rd ed. (Kansas City, MO: Beacon Hill, 1979).

4. Henry C. Thiessen, *Introductory Lectures in Systematic Theology* (Grand Rapids, MI: Eerdmans, 1949), 344–45.

5. Sam Storms, *Chosen for Life: The Case for Divine Election* (Wheaton, IL: Crossway, 2007), 29.

6. Bruce Demarest, *The Cross and Salvation* (Wheaton, IL: Crossway, 1997), 208.

7. Erickson, *Christian Theology*, 925.

8. A list of Bible verses on predestination can be found in the appendix.

9. Augustine, *Against Two Letters of the Pelagians* 1.5; 3.24.

10. Augustine, *Predestination of the Saints* 17.34.

11. James Arminius, *The Writings of James Arminius*, trans. James Nichols, 3 vols. (Grand Rapids, MI: Baker, 1977), 1:248.

12. John Wesley, *The Works of John Wesley*, 14 vols., ed. T. Jackson (1831; repr., Grand Rapids, MI: Baker, 1979), 6:509.

13. Paul K. Jewett, *Election and Predestination* (Grand Rapids, MI: Eerdmans, 1985), 70.

14. Stickelberger, *Calvin*, quoted in Storms, *Chosen for Life*, 52.

15. John Stott, *Romans: God's Good News for the World* (Downers Grove, IL: InterVarsity, 1994), 269–70.

QUESTION 6: GRACE

1. Bruce Demarest, *The Cross and Salvation: The Doctrine of Salvation* (Wheaton, IL: Crossway, 1997), 70–72.

2. Ibid., 72–73.

3. John Calvin, *Institutes of the Christian Religion*, ed. John T. McNeill, vol. 1 (Philadelphia: Westminster Press, 1975), 3.14.2, p. 769.

4. Demarest, *The Cross and Salvation*, 77.

5. Ibid., 72.

QUESTION 5: SEXUAL SIN

1. Mary S. Calderone and Eric W. Johnson, *The Family Book about Sexuality* (New York: Harper & Row, 1981), 171.

2. Most of the statistics in this chapter were gathered by my Christian brother Justin Holcomb, who teaches on these issues at the University of Virginia. He also serves as a pastor at his church and teaches at Reformed Theological Seminary. His wife, Lindsey, has a master's degree in international public health and works at a sexual assault crisis center. They are both very informed and active regarding issues involving prostitution and the sex trade. Many of the facts throughout this chapter are the result of Justin's teaching on these issues and his wife's service to rape victims in her ministry, and I am deeply grateful for their service to victims of sexual sin and their assistance in my writing of this chapter.

3. Many of the statistics about premarital sex come from W. Bradford Wilcox's report "A Scientific Review of Abstinence and Abstinence Programs," February 2008. Wilcox is a top-notch sociologist of family and religion and wrote the book *Soft Patriarchs, New Men: How Christianity Shapes Fathers and Husbands* (Chicago: University of Chicago Press, 2004), which examines the ways in which the religious beliefs and practices of American Protestant men influence their approach to parenting, household labor, and marriage.

4. Hannah Bruckner and Peter Bearman, "After the Promise: The STD Consequences of Adolescent Virginity Pledges," *Journal of Adolescent Health* 36 (2005): 275; Jennifer Manlove, et al., "Patterns of Contraceptive Use within Teenagers' First Sexual Relationships," *Perspectives on Sexual and Reproductive Health* 35 (2003): 246–55.

5. Robert E. Rector, Kirk A. Johnson, et al., "Teens Who Make Virginity Pledges Have Substantially Improved Life Outcomes," *Center for Data Analysis Report* 04–07 (Washington, DC: Heritage Foundation, 2004).

6. Elizabeth Terry-Humen, et al., "Trends and Recent Estimates: Sexual Activity among U.S. Teens," *Child Trends Research Brief 2006–2008* (Washington, DC, 2006): 2.

7. Stephanie J. Ventura, et al., "Births: Final Data for 1998," *National Vital Statistics Reports* 48.3 (2000): 24.

8. B. E. Hamilton, et al., "Births: Preliminary data for 2005," Health E-Stats, Hyattsville, MD, National Center for Health Statistics. Released November 21, 2006. The study is posted on the Center for Disease Control Web site, http://www.cdc.gov/nchs/products/pubs/pubd/hestats/prelimbirths05/prelimbirths05.htm.

9. Ibid.

10. Catherine M. Grello, Deborah P. Welsh, et al., "No Strings Attached: The Nature of Casual Sex in College Students," *The Journal of Sex Research* 43 (2006): 255–67; Catherine M. Grello, et al., "Dating and Sexual Relationship Trajectories and Adolescent Functioning," *Adolescent and Family Health* 3 (2003): 103–12; Denise D. Hallfors, et al., "Adolescent Depression and Suicide Risk: Association with Sex and Drug Behavior," *American Journal of Preventative Medicine* 27 (2004): 224–30; Denise D. Hallfors, "Which Comes First in Adolescence—Sex and Drugs or Depression?" *American Journal of Preventative Medicine* 29 (2005): 163–70; Riittakerttu Kaltiala-Heino, et al., "Pubertal Timing, Sexual Behavior, and Self-reported Depression in Middle Adolescence," *Journal of Adolescence* 26 (2003): 531–45; Lori Kowalski-Jones and Frank L. Mott, "Sex, Contraception, and Childbearing among High-Risk Youth: Do Different Factors Influence Males and Females?" *Family Planning Perspectives* 30 (1998): 163–69; Donald P. Orr, Mary Beiter, et al., "Premature Sexual Activity as an Indicator of Psychosocial Risk" *Pediatrics* 87 (1991): 141–47; Sandhya Ramrakha, et al., "Psychiatric Disorders and Risky Sexual Behaviour in Young Adulthood: Cross Sectional Study in Birth Cohort," *British Medical Journal* 321 (2000): 263–66; Robert E. Rector, Kirk A. Johnson, et al., "Sexually Active Teenagers Are More Likely to Be Depressed and to Attempt Suicide," *Center for Data Analysis Report* 03–04 (Washington, DC: Heritage Foundation, 2003).

11. Nicole Else-Quest, et al., "Context Counts: Long-Term Sequelae of Premarital Intercourse or Abstinence," *The Journal of Sex Research* 42 (2005): 102–12; Jonathan G. Tubman, et al., "The Onset and Cross-Temporal Patterning of Sexual Intercourse in Middle Adolescence: Prospective Relations with Behavioral and Emotional Problems," *Child Development* 67 (1996): 327–43.

12. Orr, et al., "Premature Sexual Activity as an Indicator of Psychosocial Risk," 141–47.

13. Wilcox, "A Scientific Review of Abstinence and Abstinence Programs," 13.

14. Ellen Johnson Silver and Laurie J. Bauman, "The Association of Sexual Experience with Attitudes, Beliefs, and Risk Behaviors of Inner-City Adolescents," *Journal of Research on Adolescents* 16 (2006): 29–45.

15. Lydia A. Shrier, et al., "The Association of Sexual Risk Behaviors and Problem Drug Behaviors in High School Students," *Journal of Adolescent Health* 20 (1996): 381.

16. Wilcox, "A Scientific Review of Abstinence and Abstinence Programs," 13.

17. John O. G. Billy, et al., "Effects of Sexual Activity on Adolescent Social and Psychological Development," *Social Psychology Quarterly* 51 (1988): 190–212.

18. Linda A. Fairstein, *Sexual Violence: Our War Against Rape* (New York: William Morrow, 1993), 171–77.

19. Jerry Ropelato, "Internet Pornography Statistics," Top Ten Reviews, 2008, http://internet-filter-review.toptenreviews.com/internet-pornography-statistics.html.

20. "American Porn: Corporate America Is Profiting from Porn—Quietly," *ABC News*, May 27, 2004.

21. Jerry Ropelato, "Internet Pornography Statistics."

22. Ibid.

23. Jessica Williams, *Fifty Facts That Should Change the World* (New York: Disinformation Company, 2004), 250–51.

24. Jerry Ropelato, "Internet Pornography Statistics."

25. Ibid.

26. "Alexa Research Finds 'Sex' Popular on the Web," *Business Wire*, February 14, 2001.

27. Eric Retzlaff, "Pornography's Grip Tightens by Way of Internet," *National Catholic Register*, June 13–19, 2000.

28. Ropelato, "Internet Pornography Statistics."

29. Ibid.

30. Ibid.

31. Ibid.

32. Ibid.

33. Ibid.

34. Steve Kroft, "Porn in the U.S.A.," *60 Minutes*, September 5, 2004, http://www.cbsnews.com/stories/2003/11/21/60minutes/main585049.shtml (accessed September 29, 2008). Originally aired November 25, 2003.

35. *Des Moines Register*, April 1, 2003.

36. Robert Grove and Blaise Zerega, "The Lolita Problem," *Red Herring*, January 2, 2002, http://www.redherring.com/Home/5996.

37. Ropelato, "Internet Pornography Statistics."

38. Ibid.

39. Jane D. Brown, et al., "Sexy Media Matter: Exposure to Sexual Content in Music, Movies, Television, and Magazines Predicts Black and White Adolescents' Sexual Behavior," *Pediatrics* 117 (April 2006): 1018–27, http://pediatrics.aappublications.org/cgi/content/abstract/117/4/1018.

40. Robert Jensen, "Cruel to Be Hard: Men and Pornography," *Sexual Assault Report* (January/February 2004), 33–48.

41. *Adult Video News*, AVN director's roundtable (January 2003), 60, in Robert Jensen, *Pornography and Sexual Violence* (Harrisburg, PA: VAWnet, July 2004), a project of the National Resource Center on Domestic Violence/Pennsylvania Coalition Against Domestic Violence (accessed September 25, 2008), http://www.vawnet.org.

42. Ibid., 46.

43. Ropelato, "Internet Pornography Statistics."

44. Ibid.

45. John Schwartz, "Leisure Pursuits of Today's Young Man," *New York Times*, March 29, 2004, http://www.nytimes.com/2004/03/29/technology/29guy.html?ei=5007&en=fa719ado c712efd7&ex=1395982800&pagewanted=print&position=.

46. John C. LaRue Jr., "Churches and Pastors Rate Sexual Issues," *Your Church* (January/February 2005): 88, http://www.christianitytoday.com/yc/2005/001/13.88.html.

47. See Patrick Carnes, *Don't Call It Love* (Minnesota: Gentle Press, 1991), 38ff.

48. Eric Griffin-Shelley, *Sex and Love: Addiction, Treatment, and Recovery* (Westport, CT: Praeger, 1997), 52.

49. From "A Facilitator's Guide to Prostitution: A Matter of Violence against Women," Women Hurt in Systems of Prostitution Engaged in Revolt (WHISPER) (Minneapolis, MN: 1990), quoted in Melissa Farley, "Prostitution: Factsheet on Human Rights Violations,"

Prostitution Research and Education, April 2, 2000, http://www.prostitutionresearch.com/faq/000008.html.

50. The transcript of this interview, "Fatal Addiction: Ted Bundy's Final Interview," can be found online at http://www.pureintimacy.org/gr/intimacy/understanding/a0000082.cfm.

51. E.g., see Debra Boyer and Susan Breault, "Danger for Prostitutes Increasing, Most Starting Younger," *Beacon Journal* (September 21, 1997); Melissa Farley, Howard Barkan, et al., "Prostitution, Violence against Women, and Posttraumatic Stress Disorder," *Women & Health* (1988): 37–49; David Finkelhor and Angela Browne, "The Traumatic Impact of Child Sexual Abuse," *American Journal of Orthopsychiatry* 55, no. 4 (1985): 530–41. Mimi H. Silbert, "Compounding Factors in the Rape of Street Prostitutes," in *Rape and Sexual Assault*, vol. 2, ed. A. W. Burgess (New York: Garland, 1988), 77.

52. Rita Belton, "Prostitution as Traumatic Reenactment," International Society for Traumatic Stress Annual Meeting, 1992; M. H. Silbert and A. M. Pines, "Victimization of Street Prostitutes," *Victimology: An International Journal* 7 (1982): 122–33; C. Bagley and L. Young, "Juvenile Prostitution and Child Sexual Abuse: A Controlled Study," *Canadian Journal of Community Mental Health* 6 (1987): 5–26.

53. Ibid.

54. Ibid.

55. Andrea Dworkin, "Prostitution and Male Supremacy," in *Life and Death* (New York: Free Press, 1997), 143.

56. Silbert and Pines, "Victimization of Street Prostitutes," 122–33.

57. *Trafficking Victims Protection Reauthorization Act of 2005*, HR 972, 109th Cong., 1st sess. (January 4, 2005): 2.5.

58. Denise Gamache and Evelina Giobbe, *Prostitution: Oppression Disguised as Liberation*, National Coalition Against Domestic Violence, 1990.

59. Melissa Farley, Isin Baral, et al., "Prostitution in Five Countries: Violence and Posttraumatic Stress Disorder," *Feminism & Psychology* (1998): 405–26.

60. Phyllis Chesler, "A Woman's Right to Self-Defense: The Case of Aileen Carol Wuornos," in *Patriarchy: Notes of an Expert Witness* (Monroe, ME: Common Courage Press, 1994).

61. D. Kelly Weisberg, *Children of the Night: A Study of Adolescent Prostitution* (Lexington, MA: Lexington Books, 1985).

62. "How Sexual Experiences Become Addictions," http://www.new-life.net/sex2.htm.

63. Bruce Marshall, *The Word, the Flesh, and Father Smith* (Boston, MA: Houghton Mifflin, 1945), 108.

QUESTION 4: FAITH AND WORKS

1. John Calvin, *Institutes of the Christian Religion*, 3.2.7.

QUESTION 3: DATING

1. The data that follows, tracing the history of calling and dating, is summarized from Beth Bailey's "From Front Porch to Back Seat," in *Wing to Wing, Oar to Oar: Readings on Courting and Marrying*, ed. Amy A. Kass and Leon R. Kass (Notre Dame, IN: University of Notre Dame Press, 2000), 27–37.

2. Kristin Luker, *When Sex Goes to School* (New York: Norton, 2006); Arland Thornton and Linda Young-DeMarco, "Four Decades of Trends in Attitudes toward Family Issues in the United States: The 1960s through the 1990s," *Journal of Marriage and Family* 63 (2001): 1009–37.

3. David Popenoe and Barbara Dafoe Whitehead, "Should We Live Together? What Young Adults Need to Know about Cohabitation before Marriage," 2nd ed., The National Marriage Project (Piscataway, NJ: Rutgers, 2002), 3.

4. Ibid.

5. Larry Bumpass and Hsien-Hen Lu, "Trends in Cohabitation and Implications for Children's Family Contexts in the U.S.," *Population Studies* 54 (2000): 29–41.

6. Popenoe and Whitehead, "Should We Live Together?" 4.

7. Ibid.

8. Claire M. Kamp Dush, et al., "The Relationship between Cohabitation and Marital Quality and Stability: Change Across Cohorts?" *Journal of Marriage and Family* 65 (2003): 539–49; Edward O. Laumann, et al., *The Social Organization of Sexuality: Sexual Practices in the United States* (Chicago: University of Chicago Press, 1994); Andrew Cherlin, *Marriage, Divorce, Remarriage* (Cambridge, MA: Harvard University Press, 1992).

9. Popenoe and Whitehead, "Should We Live Together?" 7.

10. Lee Robins and Darrel Reiger, *Psychiatric Disorders in America* (New York: Free Press, 1990), 72; Susan L. Brown, "The Effect of Union Type on Psychological Well-Being: Depression among Cohabitors versus Marrieds," *Journal of Health and Social Behavior* (2000): 41–3.

11. Jan E. Stets, "Cohabiting and Marital Aggression: The Role of Social Isolation," *Journal of Marriage and the Family* 53 (1991): 669–80; Margo I. Wilson and Martin Daly, "Who Kills Whom in Spouse Killings? On the Exceptional Sex Ratio of Spousal Homicides in the United States," *Criminology* 30–32 (1992): 189–215. One study found that, of the violence toward women that is committed by intimates and relatives, 42% involves a close friend or partner whereas only 29% involves a current spouse. Ronet Bachman, "Violence Against Women" (Washington, DC: Bureau of Justice Statistics, 1994), 6. A New Zealand study compared violence in dating and cohabiting relationships, finding that cohabitors were twice as likely to be physically abusive toward their partners after controlling statistically for selection factors. Lynn Magdol, T. E. Moffitt, et al., "Hitting Without a License," *Journal of Marriage and Family* 60–61 (1998): 41–55.

12. Todd K. Shackelford, "Cohabitation, Marriage and Murder," *Aggressive Behavior* 27 (2001): 284–91; Margo Wilson, M. Daly, et al., "Uxoricide in Canada: Demographic Risk Patterns," *Canadian Journal of Criminology* 35 (1993): 263–91.

13. Dush, et al., "The Relationship Between Cohabitation and Marital Quality and Stability," 539–49; Stanley, Scott. et al., "Sliding versus Deciding: Inertia and the Premarital Cohabitation Effect," *Family Relations* 55 (2006): 499–509.

14. Dush, et al., "The Relationship Between Cohabitation and Marital Quality and Stability," 544.

15. W. Bradford Wilcox, "A Scientific Review of Abstinence and Abstinence Programs," February 2008, 6.

16. Laumann, et al., *The Social Organization of Sexuality*; Reginald Finger, et al., "Association of Virginity at Age 18 with Educational, Economics, Social, and Health Outcomes in Middle Adulthood," *Adolescent and Family Health* 4 (2004): 164–70; John R. Kahn and Kathryn A. London, "Premarital Sex and the Risk of Divorce," *Journal of Marriage and Family* 53 (1991): 845–55.

17. Laumann, et al., *The Social Organization of Sexuality*, 503.

18. Wilcox, "A Scientific Review of Abstinence and Abstinence Programs," 7.

19. David G. Blanchflower and Andrew J. Oswald, "Money, Sex and Happiness: An Empirical Study," *Scandinavian Journal of Economics* 106 (2004): 393–415; Nicole Else-Quest, et al., "Context Counts: Long-Term Sequelae of Premarital Intercourse or Abstinence," *The Journal of Sex Research* 42 (2005): 102–12; Laumann, et al., *The Social Organization of Sexuality*, 360.

20. Blanchflower and Oswald, "Money, Sex and Happiness," 405.

QUESTION 2: THE EMERGING CHURCH

1. This chapter originally appeared as an article I wrote titled, "Navigating the Emerging Church Highway," *Christian Research Journal* 13, no. 4 (2008).

2. I write about this transition in my book *Confessions of a Reformission Rev.: Hard Lessons from an Emerging Missional Church* (Grand Rapids, MI: Zondervan, 2006), 16–21, and the following summary is adopted from that book.

3. By *pagan* I mean the worship of created things other than the Creator God, as Romans 1:25 explains. Practically, paganism is living one's life in ultimate devotion to someone or something other than Jesus Christ. Examples include devotion to things created by God, such as the environment, the human body and sinful sexuality, and demons in the name of vague spirituality, along with things human beings create, such as philosophies, like postmodernism, and new spiritualities that accommodate all religions.

4. Tony Jones, *The New Christians: Dispatches From the Emergent Frontier* (San Francisco: Jossey-Bass, 2008), 96.

5. Donald Miller, *Blue Like Jazz: Nonreligious Thoughts on Christian Spirituality* (Nashville, TN: Thomas Nelson, 2003).

6. Rob Moll, "The New Monasticism," *Christianity Today*, September 2005, http://www.christianitytoday.com/ct/2005/september/16.38.html.

7. George Barna, *Revolution* (Carol Stream, IL: Tyndale, 2006).

8. Frank Viola and George Barna, *Pagan Christianity?* (Carol Stream, IL: Tyndale, 2008).

9. Collin Hansen, "Young, Restless, Reformed," *Christianity Today*, September 2006, http://www.christianitytoday.com/ct/2006/september/42.32.html.

10. Scot McKnight, "McLaren Emerging," *Christianity Today*, September 2008, 59.

11. Albert Mohler, "'A Generous Orthodoxy'—Is It Orthodox?" Crosswalk.com, February 16, 2005, http://www.crosswalk.com/root/1336217/page0/.

12. Ibid.

13. Jones, *The New Christians*, xix–xx.

14. David Van Biema, "The 25 Most Influential Evangelicals in America," *Time*, February 7, 2005, http://www.time.com/time/covers/1101050207/photoessay/.

15. E.g., Tickle wrote that the work *What God Has Joined Together? The Christian Case for Gay Marriage*, by David G. Meyers and Letha Dawson Scanzoni (San Francisco: HarperOne, 2005), left her "giddy with . . . hope and belief" (http://www.davidmyers.org/Brix?pageID=118).

16. Brian McLaren, *A Generous Orthodoxy* (Grand Rapids, MI: Zondervan, 2004), cover.

17. D. A. Carson, interview by Kim Lawton, *Religion and Ethics Newsweekly*, July 8, 2005, episode no. 845, http://www.pbs.org/wnet/religionandethics/week845/interview2.html.

18. Ibid.

19. Van Biema, "The 25 Most Influential Evangelicals in America."

20. Brian D. McLaren, "Brian McLaren on the Homosexual Question: Finding a Pastoral Response," Out of Ur, Leadership Journal Blog, January 23, 2006, http://blog.christianitytoday.com/outofur/archives/2006/01/ brian_mclaren_0.html.

21. Ibid.

22. Brian D. McLaren, interview by Leif Hansen, The Bleeding Purple Podcast, January 8 and 12, 2006, http://www.understandthetimes.org/ec/ecmclaren.shtml.

23. See Marcus Borg, interview by Liza Hetherington, "Meeting God Again," http://www.gracecathedral.org/enrichment/interviews/int_19970601.shtml. *Panentheism* is a form of paganism that does not see a distinction between God the creator and his creation but rather considers creation to be the body that houses God so that the two are not separate.

24. Richard N. Ostling, "Jesus Christ, Plain and Simple," *Time*, January 10, 1994, http://www.time.com/time/magazine/article/0,9171,979938,00.html.

25. Ibid.

26. E.g., see McLaren, *A Generous Orthodoxy*, 47 n. 17.

27. Joel B. Green and Mark D. Baker, *Recovering the Scandal of the Cross* (Downers Grove, IL: InterVarsity, 2000), 30.

28. Ibid., 32.

29. Ibid., 113.

30. Brian D. McLaren, "Praise for *The Lost Message of Jesus,*" in Steve Chalke and Alan Mann, *The Lost Message of Jesus* (Grand Rapids, MI: Zondervan, 2003).

31. Chalke and Mann, *The Lost Message of Jesus*, 182.

32. Ibid., 183–83.

33. D. A. Carson, *Becoming Conversant with the Emerging Church* (Grand Rapids, MI: Zondervan, 2005), 186.

34. Brian D. McLaren, "Advance Praise," in Alan Jones, *Reimagining Christianity: Reconnect Your Spirit without Disconnecting Your Mind* (Hoboken, NJ: John Wiley, 2005), back cover.

35. Jones, *Reimagining Christianity*, 132.

36. Ibid., 168.

37. Brian D. McLaren, foreword, in Spencer Burke and Barry Taylor, *A Heretic's Guide to Eternity* (San Francisco: Jossey-Bass, 2006), ix–x.

38. Burke, *A Heretic's Guide to Eternity*, 199.

39. Ibid., 197.

40. Ibid., 64.

41. Ibid., 130–31.

42. Ibid., 195.

43. McKnight is a member of the Emergent Village Coordinating Group. See http://www. emergentvillage.com/about-information/emergent-village-coordinating-group.

44. Scot McKnight, "Heretic's Guide to Eternity 4," blog entry, Jesus Creed, August 8, 2006, http://www.jesuscreed.org/?p=1319.

45. Brian D. McLaren, "Brian McLaren's Inferno 2: Are We Asking the Wrong Questions about Hell?" Out of Ur, Leadership Journal Blog, May 8, 2006, http://blog.christianitytoday. com/outofur/archives/2006/05/ brian_mclarens_1.html.

46. Brian D. McLaren, "Brian McLaren's Inferno 3: Five Proposals for Reexamining Our Doctrine of Hell" Out of Ur, Leadership Journal Blog, May 11, 2006, http://blog.christianityto-day.com/outofur/archives/2006/05/ brian_mclarens_2.html.

47. Quoted in Matt Kennedy, "Mark Driscoll Talks about Some Emergent Errors and Errant Teachers: Brian McLaren and Rob Bell," Stand Firm blog, September 10, 2008, http://www. standfirminfaith.com/index.php/site/article/ 16032/.

48. Doug Pagitt, "The Emerging Church and Embodied Theology," in *Listening to the Beliefs of Emerging Churches*, ed. Robert Webber (Grand Rapids, MI: Zondervan, 2007), 138.

49. Ibid., 121.

50. Ibid., 137.

51. Ibid., 128.

52. Ibid.

53. Doug Pagitt, *A Christianity Worth Believing: Hope-filled, Open-armed, Alive-and-Well Faith for the Left Out, Left Behind, and Let Down in Us All* (San Francisco: Jossey-Bass, 2008), 120.

54. Ibid., 137.

55. Ibid., 136–37.

56. Ibid., 123.

57. Ibid., 124.

58. Ibid., 125.

59. Ibid., 127–28.

60. Ibid., 194.

61. Ibid., 150.

62. Ibid., 154.

63. Ibid., 153.

64. Ibid., 194.

65. Pagitt, "The Emerging Church and Embodied Theology" in Webber, *Listening to the Beliefs of Emerging Churches*, 142.

66. Pagitt, *A Christianity Worth Believing*, 194–95, emphasis added.

67. Ibid., 226.

68. Henry Churchill King, *Reconstruction in Theology* (London: Macmillan, 1903).

69. Pagitt, "The Emerging Church and Embodied Theology" in Webber, *Listening to the Beliefs of Emerging Churches*, 122.

70. Gary Dorrien, *The Making of American Liberal Theology: Idealism, Realism, and Modernity 1900–1950* (Louisville: Westminster John Knox, 2003), 65.

71. Cathleen Falsani, "Maverick Minister Taps New Generation: Wheaton Grad Reaches Out in Films—Is He 21st Century Billy Graham?" *Chicago Sun-Times*, June 4, 2006.

72. Greg Gilbert, "The Scoop'a on NOOMA," 9Marks Ministries, March/April 2008, http://sites.silaspartners.com/partner/Article_Display_Page/0,,PTID314526|CHID598014|CIID2396222,00.html. This material is used by permission of 9Marks and can be found at http://www.9Marks.org.

73. Ibid., part 1.

74. Ibid., part 2.

75. Ibid.

76. Ibid.

77. Ibid.

78. Ibid.

79. Mark Driscoll, "Navigating the Emerging Church Highway," *Christian Research Journal*, vol. 31, no. 4 (2008).

80. "Interview with Mark Driscoll: Navigating the Emerging Church Highway," http://bam.edgeboss.net/ download/bam/mark_driscoll_interview_from_09-09-08_bam.mp3.

81. Andy Crouch, "The Emergent Mystique," *Christianity Today*, November 2004, 38, http://www.christianitytoday.com/ct/2004/november/12.36.html.

82. Ibid.

83. Rob Bell, *Velvet Elvis: Repainting the Christian Faith* (Grand Rapids, MI: Zondervan, 2005), 146.

84. Ibid., 26.

85. Mark Driscoll and Gerry Breshears, *Vintage Jesus: Timeless Answers to Timely Questions* (Wheaton, IL: Crossway, 2008).

86. J. Gresham Machen, *The Virgin Birth of Christ* (New York: Harper, 1930), 382.

87. Ibid., 383.

88. Albert Mohler, "Can a Christian Deny the Virgin Birth?" Commentary, http://www.albertmohler.com/commentary_read.php?cdate=2006-12-25.

89. Bell, *Velvet Elvis*, 192 n. 143.

90. McLaren, *A Generous Orthodoxy*, 287.

91. Brian D. McLaren, "Brian's Recommendations," http://www.brianmclaren.net/archives/books/brians-recommen/.

92. Jones holds a master's degree in theology and a PhD in theology from Princeton Theological Seminary. He is a scholar in residence at Westminster Seminary in California and the director of Christian Witness to a Pagan Planet, and he has written many books and articles on paganism.

93. Peter Jones, e-mail message to author, September 11, 2007.

94. Ibid.

95. Ibid.

96. Crouch, "The Emergent Mystique."

97. Ibid.

98. Jones, *The New Christians*, 110.

99. Ibid.

100. Pagitt, *A Christianity Worth Believing*, 2.

101. Ibid., front matter.

102. McLaren, *A Generous Orthodoxy*, 109.

103. Ibid., 264.

104. Brian D. McLaren, *The Secret Message of Jesus* (Nashville: Thomas Nelson, 2006), 7.

105. Brian D. McLaren, "Emerging Values," *Leadership Journal* (July 1, 2003): 35.

106. Doug Pagitt, "Seeds of Compassion Reflections" blog post, DougPagitt.com, April 17, 2008, http://dougpagitt.com/podcasts/seeds-of-compassion-reflections.

107. Bell, *Velvet Elvis*, 62.

108. McLaren, *A Generous Orthodoxy*, 171.

109. Pagitt, *A Christianity Worth Believing*, 64.

110. Brian D. McLaren, "Dorothy on Leadership," *Rev. Magazine* November/December 2000, http://www.brianmclaren.net/emc/archives/imported/dorothy-on-leadership.html.

111. Jones, *The New Christians*, 109.

112. Ibid., 197.

113. E.g., see Jones, *The New Christians*, and Pagitt, *A Christianity Worth Believing*.

114. Jones, *The New Christians*, 140.

115. Ibid., 114.

116. See Seeds of Compassion, "InterSpiritual Day," http://www.seedsofcompassion.org/involved/interreligious_ day.asp.

117. Ben Witherington, "Rob Bell hits Lexington and a Packed-Out House," Ben Witherington blog, February 15, 2007, http://benwitherington.blogspot.com/2007/02/rob-bell-hits-lexington-and-packed-out.html (accessed December 22, 2008).

118. Tony Jones, "How I Went from There to Here: Same Sex Marriage Blogalogue," Beliefnet, November 19, 2008, http://blog.beliefnet.com/tonyjones/2008/11/same-sex-marriage-blogalogue-h.html.

119. Scot McKnight, "The Ironic Faith of Emergents," *Christianity Today*, September 2008, 62.

120. Jones, *The New Christians*, 219–20.

QUESTION 1: THE REGULATIVE PRINCIPLE

1. Harold M. Best, *Unceasing Worship: Biblical Perspectives on Worship and the Arts* (Downers Grove, IL: InterVarsity, 2003), 10.

2. Ibid., 17–18.

3. N. T. Wright, *For All God's Worth: True Worship and the Calling* (Grand Rapids, MI: Eerdmans, 1997), 28, emphasis in original.

4. John M. Frame, *Worship in Spirit and Truth: A Refreshing Study of the Principles and Practice of Biblical Worship* (Phillipsburg, NJ: P&R, 1996), 1–2, emphasis in original.

5. Miroslav Volf, "Reflections on a Christian Way of Being in the World," in *Worship: Adoration and Action*, ed. D. A. Carson (Eugene, OR: Wipf and Stock, 1993), 203–11.

6. D. A. Carson, "Worship under the Word," in *Worship by the Book*, ed. D. A. Carson (Grand Rapids, MI: Zondervan, 2002), 24, emphasis in original.

7. Klass Runia, "Reformed Liturgy in the Dutch Tradition," in *Worship: Adoration and Action*, ed. D. A. Carson (Eugene, OR: Wipf and Stock, 1993), 96.

8. Ibid.

9. Carson, "Worship under the Word," 21, emphasis in original.

10. Ibid., 21–22.

11. Frame, *Worship in Spirit and Truth*, 67.

12. Carson, "Worship under the Word," 55, emphasis in original.

13. Richard L. Pratt Jr., "The Regulative Principle," 1, http://reformedperspectives.org/new-files/ric_ pratt/TH.Pratt.Reg.Princ.pdf.

14. Frame, *Worship in Spirit and Truth*, xiii.

15. Pratt, "The Regulative Principle," 2.

SUBJECT INDEX

SCRIPTURE INDEX

RE:LIT

Resurgence Literature (Re:Lit) is a ministry of the Resurgence. At www.theResurgence.com you will find free theological resources in blog, audio, video, and print forms, along with information on forthcoming conferences, to help Christians contend for and contextualize Jesus' gospel. At www.ReLit.org you will also find the full lineup of Resurgence books for sale. The elders of Mars Hill Church have generously agreed to support Resurgence and the Acts 29 Church Planting Network in an effort to serve the entire church.

FOR MORE RESOURCES

Re:Lit – www.relit.org
Resurgence – www.theResurgence.com
Re:Sound – www.resound.org
Mars Hill Church – www.marshillchurch.org
Acts 29 – www.acts29network.org